What Professionals and Parents Are Saying About Betsy Brown Braun

"*Just Tell Me What to Say* is a perfect parenting book filled with practical, easy-to-understand "tips and scripts" to help parents know how to talk with their children about the most difficult and challenging issues that every parent must face. Betsy Brown Braun is a master teacher and one of the wisest parenting experts I have ever known."

—Steven Carr Reuben, Ph.D., author of *Children of Character: Leading Your Children to Ethical Choices in Everyday Life*

"Parents of young children will find themselves reaching for this wonderful book by Betsy Brown Braun over and over again! . . . I certainly look forward to recommending it as a must-read to the parents I work with!"

—Reveta Bowers, Head of School, The Center for Early Education, West Hollywood, CA

"Raising a healthy child to become a self-sufficient, satisfied adult is the aim of this well-written book. Betsy Brown Braun is a fine observer of children and has the remarkable ability to offer practical solutions to the everyday task of child-rearing in a readable, informative, and careful text. This is a book I will recommend to all my parents."

—Robert M. Landaw, M.D., Pediatrician and Assistant Clinical Professor of Pediatrics, UCLA

"As a parent and as a kindergarten teacher, I constantly '911' Betsy when I need help with a specific behavior issue. She has been an ongoing source of practical support both in raising my three boys and in my classroom."

—Bruce Michael Green, Los Angeles, CA

"As a pediatrician who has referred countless patients to Betsy for nearly 10 years, I trust her unique and successful blend of wisdom, compassion, and insight. . . . Betsy knows *exactly* what needs to be said. Simply put, this book should be required reading for every parent."

—Alisa Bromberg, M.D., Palisades Pediatrics, Pacific Palisades, CA

"Betsy's vast experience combined with her extraordinary intuition has guided us and our children through some of the most challenging family experiences."
—Michele Ruiz, Beverly Hills, CA

"Betsy is a wise, humorous, and caring advisor whose words cut through the often saccharine and confusing mountain of information on the ways to be a parent in today's world. Due in large part to Betsy, we are smarter parents and our children are happier and healthier as a result."
—Steven Weber, Los Angeles, CA

"Betsy has been an invaluable source of wisdom and encouragement for my family and me, the mother of four children (including triplets)."
—Melinda Friedrich, Rye, NY

"Betsy has taught me to see the world through a six-year-old's eyes."
—Carol Wetsman, Los Angeles, CA

"Betsy helped me understand how to explain death to my 2- and 4-year-olds. At the same time, she taught me and my children about living."
—Lisa Wolf, Pacific Palisades, CA

"Through the years I have been to many parenting experts. Only with Betsy did I receive clear, concise advice."
—Eve Newhart, Los Angeles, CA

"In following Betsy's advice you will find that life starts getting more peaceful and you will enjoy your children so much more."
—Alisha Hayes, Los Angeles, CA

"Betsy's advice about the birds and the bees gave me a solid strategy for answering those normal questions that can turn intelligent adults into blathering idiots."
—Lori Furie, Beverly Hills, CA

"Without Betsy's help we never would have survived my daughter's tantrums"
—Ricki Booker, Boulder, CO

Just Tell Me What to Say

Sensible Tips and Scripts for Perplexed Parents

BETSY BROWN BRAUN

HARPER

NEW YORK · LONDON · TORONTO · SYDNEY

HARPER

HarperCollins books may be purchased for educational, business, or sales promotional use. For information please write: Special Markets Department, HarperCollins Publishers, 10 East 53rd Street, New York, NY 10022.

Designed by Ellen Cipriano

Library of Congress Cataloging-in-Publication Data

Braun, Betsy Brown.
Just tell me what to say : sensible tips and scripts for perplexed parents / Betsy Brown Braun. — 1st ed.
p. cm.
Includes bibliographical references and index.
ISBN 978-0-06-145297-0
1. Parenting.   2. Parent and child.   3. Communication in the family.   I. Title.
HQ755.8.B727 2008

649'.1—dc22   2007032023

11 12 13 WBC/RRD 10 9

For Jessie, Ben, and Lucas,
the inspiration for and source of my parenting education.
The proof is in the pudding.

Contents

• ❖ •

Acknowledgments

It is said that writing a book is not unlike giving birth; there's gestation, labor, and delivery. To that I say, *"Amen!"* Much as I had a full support team in the delivery room when my triplets were born, so I have had a village surrounding me as I gave birth to this book. There are many people to whom I owe thanks.

Toni Sciarra, my editor at Collins and a word craftswoman, guided me through this process with patience, humor, and responsiveness. Mindy Werner, editor, word surgeon, and new friend, skillfully and sensitively cut my manuscript in half when it was twice too long and held my hand as I entered the delivery room. Thank you to Bob Myman and Jennifer Grega, my attorneys, for sage advice delivered in their calm and confident manner.

For their generosity and expertise, I thank Phyllis Rothman and Kathy Wexler, both family therapists and dear friends; Dr. Ian Russ, family therapist; Rabbi Steven Carr Ruben; Pam Siegel, nutritionist and family therapist; and Diane Applebaum and Cherry O'Meara at Children's Book World.

Thank you to the ever-witty Rich Leonard for his efforts during my book title quest.

I am grateful beyond words to all my incredible friends, in particular Janie O., Nanci, Jill, and Lucie, who shared my excitement and tolerated my *"Sorry, I can't talk now, I'm writing,"* as well as all my whining during the editing months. There is no way to sufficiently thank Barb, my dearest friend for thirty-six years, who is my confidante and *bff*.

How proud my parents would be if they were still here—my mother, the children's book author; my father, the literary agent. It is my mother whom I credit for my resourcefulness, my willingness to take a risk, and my ability to write. I hope my parents can feel my deep appreciation.

I owe my husband, Ray, the greatest debt of gratitude. His patience, his ongoing enthusiasm and encouragement, his always available ear, and his unwavering support buoyed me throughout this book's creation.

Finally, I must acknowledge my clients. It is you who kept asking, *"Why don't you write a book?"* So I did. Thank you for allowing me to accompany you on your parenting pathway, for the privilege of sharing your journey, for enabling me to learn from your successes and failures, and for helping to give birth to my book, my fourth greatest creation.

Introduction

.   .   .   ❖   .   .   .

"Betsy, please, just tell me what to say."

Over the past thirty-seven years, I've heard this plea from parents count-less times. Whether during a parenting group, an individual consultation, or a desperate phone call, it's the bottom line. Parents want real, hands-on, just-give-it-to-me-straight, can't-you-see-I'm-floundering-here help. But it doesn't start out that way.

When children are but a twinkle in your eye, your dreams of parenting are visions of snuggles, hugs and kisses, a toddler's first step, pony rides, learning to ride a two-wheeler, and lively family discussions around the kitchen table. And life with real, live children brings all of that and more: what an incredible jour-ney raising children is. Before you know it, you look back on your children's growth years and wonder where the time went. But when you're in the middle of it, especially when your children are two to six years old, the age range that is the subject of this book, it's a whole different story.

When my husband and I were raising our triplets (two boys and a girl, now adults), I needed help. Yes, I had been a teacher, the director of a preschool, and a child development specialist, and I thought I was supposed to know how to do it all. But knowing the theory is much different from actually raising your *own* children, the ones who don't go home at 3:00 P.M. I needed someone who could answer my questions and help me navigate this territory. I wanted some-one who would *just tell me what to say . . . and do.*

Being a parent is physically exhausting, especially at first; it is also *psychi-cally* demanding, especially for the first eighteen years! It's not as if your baby arrives with a little direction booklet dangling from his big toe. Keeping up (or even one step ahead) and knowing how to respond are daunting, to say the least. As much as my husband loves our children, he used to welcome Monday mornings because his work at the office was so much less perplexing (and tiring!) than parenting his young triplets.

Parenting is a journey, a fascinating, thrilling, tremendously challenging and gratifying journey. It is an experience that enriches your life and makes you a better *you*, but it's really, really hard. However, the surest way to raise a child who is healthy and on track for becoming a self-sufficient, satisfied adult human being is to get your own house in order. Emotionally healthy and "together" adults will head their children in the direction of becoming the same. And you can't be the parent your child needs you to be unless your own needs are being met. So take care of *yourself.* Whether that means taking time for a walk, practicing your favorite sport, lunching with a friend, reading a book, or getting the emotional support you need from a mental health professional—just do it! Your children will be the better because of it.

Not infrequently a parent shares with me his concern that his child isn't *normal.* There are those children who will be diagnosed with a specific problem, such as ADHD, Asperger's, or sensory integration dysfunction. (See the box in chapter 1, page 10, for an explanation of sensory integration.) Such a diagnosis is not a reflection on the quality of the child's parenting. Rather, issues like these are part and parcel of that child and will need to be addressed. But the vast majority of children do fall within the range of *normal.* I would even venture to say that there are so many variations on the theme of *normal* that, really, there is no such thing as *normal.* Child development experts look at the way in which most children *typically* develop and behave. How can you, the parent, know about *most* children when you have only seen one or two, and they are both yours? The stories your friends tell seldom include the problems and challenges they are having with their children. Not many people air their dirty linen, as the saying goes. The reality is that *normal* includes a whole lot of perplexing situations and behaviors. This book discusses how to deal with many of these issues, from whining and back talk to your child wondering about death or where babies come from.

Nowhere in this book will you see the word *easy.* The easiest part of parenting is loving your child, and you don't need a book to tell you how to do that. In fact, it is that love that fuels you when you hit the bumps on the parenting pathway.

This book and my practice as a child development specialist are about dealing with the bumps. Sometimes they are related to a child's behavior, and sometimes they arise from a serious event or issue. It's hard to talk about things that are difficult, such as a major illness in the family. In fact, it's harder for you than for your child, because you can appreciate what's at stake. Not so for your child. For him, every experience is one to be discussed and learned about.

There's not much on the planet that's new about raising children. Kids still need to be nurtured, fed, and educated about life. They need an emotionally steady and safe home environment that is patient and accepting. They need limits, boundaries, guidance, and lessons. And your children need *you*, lots of you, in the form of your loving and sometimes undivided attention. They need roots and wings, as the saying goes.

Giving your child all that he needs all of the time is draining, to say the least. Actually, it's not even possible—and that's a good thing. One of the two most important lessons all children need to be taught begins here. Every child must *learn to delay gratification*. During the first two years of his life, your child was the center of the universe, with his every need being met almost immediately. But a new day dawns the moment those two birthday candles are blown out. It's time for your child to take his place on the sidelines along with everyone else. Cultivating patience is one hard lesson to learn. It comes with lots of crying and whining and is a companion to the second lesson, *learning to tolerate frustration and disappointment*. This is the raw stuff that tantrums are made of. It is a real parent-killer. No one enjoys seeing her child feeling sad or mad, to say nothing of *hearing* it. Your child's ability to learn these crucial lessons depends not only on her age and development but also on you, dear parent.

In my practice, I try to be the person I needed to turn to for parenting advice when my children were young. And there is no doubt in my mind that raising children is really about raising parents. I am reminded of a parent who comes to me about her child's sleep issue. The ten-month-old still doesn't sleep through the night. I listen; I sympathize; I hear how she has tried everything . . . everything except tolerating the protest. And I tell her, major problems and complications aside, *"Your child will sleep through the night when* you *are ready."*

What *is* new about parenting are certain matters that must be added to the list of bumps, including terrorism and divorce, which are now much more prevalent. What's also changed is how we respond to our children. While our parents "left well enough alone" or swept children's questions under the rug, we know the importance of talking with our children.

There are going to be many experiences that your *normal* child needs to slog through in order to learn and grow, and his reactions will be excruciating for you. That's where this book comes in. In these pages you'll find information about your child's development as well as specific tips and scripts to help you handle a multitude of situations. From food and manners to talking with your child about serious illness, divorce, and terrorism, each chapter covers a specific topic of great concern to parents of young children. Depending upon your child and his development and needs, you can use a part or the whole script that is presented. Whether you choose to read the book from cover to cover or to dip into a particular chapter, I suggest you begin with chapter 1, which is on communication, as it lays the groundwork for the rest of the book.

Although this book is directed at parents of children two to six years old, there is information that will be helpful for parents of children both older and younger. All of this advice is tried and true, having been put to the test by the hundreds of clients I've worked with over the years. I hope you'll find it as helpful as they have. Keep this book on your reference shelf or nightstand; chances are you will reach for it over and over again. I am happy to be the voice you need to hear just when you need it.

CHAPTER I

❖

Small Talk Is Big Talk:

Communicating with Your Children

Remember the television cartoon specials based on Charles Schulz's *Peanuts*? The parents, offscreen, were represented by the sound *"Waaaaaaohh, waaaohh, waaaohhh."* You couldn't see them, but you knew they were making that droning noise. Everyone remembers that because it struck a chord. It was a powerful representation of one kind of parent-child communication.

In reality, there are probably times when that *"waaaohh"* is exactly how your child is hearing you too. *"It's time for dinner,"* you say. *"Waaaoh waaaooh,"* she hears, and does nothing. *"Let's clean up your toys,"* you suggest. *"Waaaooh,"* she hears, and doesn't move.

This day-to-day communication helps to mold the adults your children will become. In order for communication to be more than *"waaaoooh,"* to make a difference, it needs to be purposeful and deliberate. As the parent, you are the mirror reflecting to your child who she is. Your communication with her directly affects her growth, development, self-image, and her behavior. Knowing that should make you want to pay attention to how you are communicating.

The Talk about Talk

Along with love, food, and physical contact, talk is one of the ways that you nourish your children. The brain requires certain kinds of stimulation in order to develop fully. Talk is one of those kinds of stimulation. There is plenty of research evidence to support the finding that children who grow up in environments without a lot of verbal interaction are disadvantaged in their development. Young children who are encouraged to share their comments, ideas, and opinions do better in school, in their social relationships, and in life.

Talking with children not only helps them to learn and grow but also gives you a window into their souls, who they are, and what they are thinking and feeling. It is through talk *with* and not *at* the child that the parent-child bond is enriched and strengthened.

But *talk* is just one of the four ways with which we communicate with children.

The Four Types of Communication

First and obviously, there is **verbal communication**. Included in this is everything that comes out of your mouth: the *vocabulary* you use, the *tone of your voice*, and the *decibel level* with which you are expressing yourself.

Next is your **nonverbal language**, which includes your physical proximity to the person with whom you are communicating, your body posture, your facial expression, your touch and its intensity, and the environment in which you are communicating.

An often-overlooked aspect of communication is **listening**. There are at least two players in any communication, and only one is the talker. The other is the listener, and the kind of listener you are sends a strong message in any communication with your child.

Finally, there is **modeling**, which is quite possibly the most powerful communication of all.

Modeling

You are communicating and giving your children messages through everything that you do. Your children are always watching you, noticing what you do, absorbing what you say, and taking in how you behave. Actually, you may even be communicating more to your child when you are *not* talking directly to her than when you are. It is in those unselfconscious moments that you give powerful cues to your child about how to *be* in the world.

Cell phones offer a perfect example. You've just been lecturing your child about the evils of gossip. Suddenly, your cell phone rings. It's your best friend, who absolutely must tell you the latest dirt about your neighbor who has finally decided to leave her husband. Your child hears, *"Oh my gosh, you've got to be kidding! . . . She what . . . ? When? . . . Oh no! I can't believe she would do that. . . . Who told you that? . . . I have to call Susan. . . . I'll call you back."* Why do parents think that their children have suddenly been struck deaf when they talk on the phone? That phone conversation just sent a pretty clear message, and your actions superseded your previous admonitions about gossip.

The old adage *"Do as I say, not as I do"* might be a parent's dream, but it sure isn't reality. Your children are likely to do just as you do, sooner or later. You are your child's first and most powerful model. Believe it or not, many years from now, YOU are how your children will be. Or they might be the opposite, if they look back on what you did with disdain and disrespect.

> *"We don't read books at the breakfast table,"* is not liable to work if Daddy is reading the newspaper at the table.

> *"We treat our brother kindly,"* isn't going to happen when you are overheard screaming on the phone at Uncle Steve.

> *"We treat all people respectfully,"* will not be learned if you berate the service person who has kept you waiting for two hours.

Remember, your child is watching. You need to *be* the person you want your child to become. That takes awareness and focus.

Setting up Verbal Communication

Unlike your other relationships, the one you have with your child doesn't really have to be built. Mother Nature took care of that. From the moment of birth the foundation for that relationship is laid. Your infant cries, you hurry to pick her up; she's hungry, you run to feed her. You are there to meet all of her needs. As you do so, the trust between parent and infant grows. That is the beginning of communication.

Building on that early connection to your child, formed in part by your verbal communication, is one of the ways you affect your child's emotions and behavior. When your communication is meaningful and powerful, it feeds your child's trusting relationship with you and deepens your connection.

Research has shown that teens who seem to stay on the straight and narrow, who have a healthy social life and achieve well in school, usually also describe their relationship with their parents as being closer than the relationship their peers have with their parents. There must be a lot of conversations going on in those homes.

Tips and Scripts for Setting up a Communication

You can increase the effectiveness of your verbal communication and improve your connection to your child by consciously setting up your communication. Of course, no one follows these tips all of the time, but implementing even one or two will make a big difference.

- **Pay attention to the physical distance between you and your child.** This will be determined, in part, by the child's age. Young children want to be close to their parents. A good distance for personal conversation is from two to four feet apart. Any closer than that invades what is known as "personal space." Though being physically close is needed for intimacy and snuggling, invading personal space is not so good for verbal communication. So, no more calling out to your child from the kitchen sink or computer.

- **Be aware of barriers between you.** Ever notice that when you are about to be reprimanded, whether by the boss or the school principal, there is always a desk between you? That barrier serves a purpose: it is a buffer zone that limits closeness and communication. When you communicate with your child, nothing should be between you. Barriers can be a coffee table, the kitchen island, the shower door, or anything that is physically drawing you away from your child: a cell phone conversation, the dinner dishes being washed, the laundry you are folding. It can also be a noise distraction such as the television droning in the background. Clearing the path between you and your child sends a very clear message and opens a direct route for your communication: *"I want to talk to you, and I want you to hear me. Nothing is going to get between us."*

  I have often started teacher trainings by having one teacher stand on a chair and the other one sit on the floor. Then I ask them to converse.

That's when they begin to understand how a young child feels in the great big adult world, always straining her chin upward to make contact with the face of the teacher or parent way overhead. Not much of a connection there.

Your position, too, gives a clear message. If you are sitting at the computer, typing as you talk, body facing away from the child, that conveys a message. *"I want to talk to you, but I am not willing to make the effort to reach you."* These parents may later wonder why their teenager barely looks up from the keyboard or TV to listen or respond to them.

Likewise, if you want to have a conversation with your child (and not just deliver a command), it would serve you well to suggest that you sit together and chat: *"Why don't we sit and face each other while we have a talk?"*

- **Do not demand eye contact.** Believe it or not, your child really can hear you even when she is not looking into your eyes. I have a strong visual image of a parent grabbing a child's face by the jaws, pulling it forward so they are eye to eye, and demanding, *"Look into my eyes when I speak to you."* This demand can actually impede your child's hearing what you have to say and sabotage your communication. In order for many a child to keep looking into your eyes, she has to concentrate on doing so. It's really hard to do that and listen to what you are saying at the same time. In normal conversation, eye contact isn't constant. People look away when they are gathering a thought, because looking directly at the person is distracting. Children are no different. While they do need to learn to look a person in the eye, when a child is in a relaxed state it is much easier to do. When the *"look into my eyes"* demand is part of a "lesson," the focus it requires just may detract from the message you are trying to impart.

- **Create a multisensory connection.** All children choose to ignore their parents at some time or other. To ensure that your child has heard what you are saying, create a multisensory connection with her. Rather than yelling from the den, approach your child, get down on her level, and gently put one hand on her—on her leg, arm, or back. When you do this, you are engaging three senses: your child hears you, she feels you, and (even if just with her peripheral vision) she sees you. There is no question that the connection for communication has been made. Now, if she doesn't do as you ask, it won't be because she didn't hear you, as she may claim. The message you are communicating here is not only *"I mean what I say"* but also *"I care enough about you and about this communication that I will make sure you have heard it."*

- **Encourage your child to talk, but recognize that some venues and times of the day are better than others.** Great chats can be had in unselfconscious moments, such as while in the car ("car talks"), when taking a walk, or during tuck-in time before bed.

Tips and Scripts for Talking with Your Child

- **Forgo the baby voice and baby talk.** All of Mother Nature's infant creatures respond to high tones or "the baby voice," but very quickly the need for that voice ends. Your toddler notices when you use one voice for adults and a different one for her. Using that baby voice says to her that she doesn't have to listen; she is not big enough to merit your regular voice; she is a baby. Using a normal voice with your toddler communicates your expectations. Treat her like a baby and she'll act like one.

  For the same reasons, eliminate the baby talk once your child is a toddler. Somewhere along the line, it was decided that young children best understand words that are *cutified*, or are made to end in *y* or *ie*. If you give the child the real words that she needs for communicating, she will use them. As tempting as it is to refer to spaghetti as *pisghetti* or a bottle as a *baba*, don't do it. Your child stands a much better chance of improving her articulation and pronunciation when she repeatedly hears words spoken correctly. Learning big words in a context and hearing you use them teaches your child more language and better ways to express her ideas and feelings.

- **Don't scold or correct your child for using incorrect language.** If your child could pronounce the word correctly, she would! She is not trying to be incorrect, so your scolding or correcting will not help. If your child's speech is unintelligible and it is interfering with her socialization and ability to communicate her needs outside the home, consult with your pediatrician, who may refer you to a speech and language specialist.

- **Less is more.** Every parent I know talks too much. *Blah blah blah*. You go on and on and on. Despite the fact that you think your child is unusually "gifted" and has advanced comprehension, you are training your child not to listen. She will become deaf to you!

  This advice especially holds true when you are saying something you *need* the child to hear. Perhaps it's an instruction, a request, or even a command. The more you gunk it up with words, the less likely your child will hear and do what you want.

  When you talk too much, you complicate the message. Your child can't possibly figure out or focus on your point. When you give your child an instruction, say it simply: *"Ruby, it's time to come to the table for dinner now,"* and not: *"Ruby, as I told you ten minutes ago, now it is time for dinner. I want you to stop what you are doing, go wash your hands now, and be sure to hang the towel up properly. You might think about making a pee first so you won't have to leave the table in the middle of dinner. And, if you do pee, don't forget to wash you hands again, and use soap, and remember to hang up that towel. Did you hear me, Ruby?"*

  Ruby tuned you out long ago. She is still playing with her Legos on the floor.

- **Be specific.** You know how easy it is to misinterpret something an adult has told you; children have the same trouble. Set your child up to be successful by being clear and direct in your expectations for your child. If you say: *"Please bring your jacket in from the car and hang it on the hook by the door,"* it is much less likely that the jacket will be dropped in the hallway, thereby necessitating more nagging from you.

- **Ask questions that cannot be answered with *yes*, *no*, or single words.** Invite conversation by saying: *"What were some of the activities that you did at Suzanne's birthday party?"* or *"Why was the piñata your favorite?"*

- **Have neutral conversations.** Most of the conversations parents tend to have with a child are about her, her day, her world. Instead, try talking about something that is not aimed at or focused on the child. Talk about something you saw and ask her what she thinks: *"Today when I was driving to the village, I saw a Dalmatian running along the side of the street, all by himself. He was running really fast. I have no idea where he came from or where he was going. What do you think?"*

Not only will you encourage conversation, but your child will feel valued in that you care what she thinks.

- **Listen to your child without immediate correction or judgment.** The surest way to stop a child from talking is to cut her off and be too quick to judge or correct her. Listen to all she has to say, and then ask questions that will help her to continue expressing herself. Doing this will also allow you to see the issue from your child's perspective: *"What are the things that Robert does that make you so mad? I want to hear about that."*

- **Honor the feelings that your child shares with you.** Consider it a gift when your child tells you how she feels. Take care not to reject the feeling: *"Oh c'mon. You don't really hate Matthew."* Instead, receive the feeling and validate your child: *"You sure do feel strongly about that. Matthew is really bugging you lately."* Even a simple statement of acknowledgment may do the trick and let your child know that she can share her "feelings talk" with you: *"I understand how you feel."*

- **Beware of "Why?"** Very often when a child (or adult) asks *Why?* she isn't really looking for an answer. She is protesting! *Why* is a cryptic way for the child to say: *"I don't like your answer!"*

  Sometimes asking *"Why?"* is a stalling technique. It buys the child time before she has to do whatever was just asked of her. If you're the one asking *"Why?"* it can be the word that shuts down communication. Sometimes a child has absolutely no idea why she did or said something. Your asking makes her feel inadequate in her not knowing, as if she is supposed to have an answer. There are times when even adults can't readily explain why they have done or said a particular thing. It can take insight and great self-awareness to be able to answer the *Why?* question. Not everyone has it all the time.

YOUR TONE OF VOICE

The tone that you use in talking to your child communicates your attitude as well as your real feelings behind your words. The tone gives a clear message, easily understood. Your tone and your words need to match, or your words are wasted.

Most parents do not have children who run in the street. Well, not more than once, anyway. Why is that? It is because you have given your child the very clear message that she *may not run in the street!* The voice you use communicates your seriousness. Saying *"Please, sweetie pie, Mommy is asking you not to run into the street"* in the same saccharine voice that you use to ask her to pick up the toy she has dropped does not send the message. When you mean business, communicate your intention with your tone.

Think about the different tones you use in a variety of situations. You have at the ready a full orchestra of tones. Choose one and make it work for you, but don't overuse your "I mean business" voice. Parents who *always* lay down the law are just as ineffective as parents who never use their tone to express the seriousness of the message.

YOUR DECIBEL LEVEL

Most people are able to control their vocal decibel level. A child can also be made aware of her decibel level and taught to regulate and use "an inside voice." The yelling and screaming child can be told to *"use that loud voice outside."*

The decibel level of your voice is a part of your verbal communication. Just like the words and the tone that you use, it can enhance or sabotage your interactions with your child. Most parents think that raising their decibel level is the best way to communicate their serious intentions. The funny thing is, most children do not respond well to screaming, yelling, and very loud voices. When parents yell, the child's attention leaves the issue at hand and goes directly to the yelling. She is not thinking, *"Mommy just asked me to turn off the television."* She is thinking, *"Wow. Mommy sure is yelling at me. She must really be mad. I don't like it when Mommy yells. I don't want to hear that voice. That voice scares me."* Mommy's words and real message are lost. Anger and the message can be expressed without yelling.

Have you ever noticed how the best teachers get their class's attention? They don't stand in front of the room, clapping and shouting, *"Quiet everyone! Quiet!"* No. The most skilled of our teachers starts talking in a very, very low voice, almost a whisper. She is patient, and she keeps talking. Someone notices that she is talking, and soon, often one by one, the rest of the children stop talking in order to hear what the teacher is saying. And the whole class is now quiet.

Yelling breeds yelling. Quiet breeds calm.

Body Language and Nonverbal Communication

You have been taught that crossing your arms in front of your chest gives the message of being closed off and unavailable in adult conversation. The same

SENSORY INTEGRATION

Some people's sensitivity to noise (or light or touch, for that matter) goes beyond what is considered to be within the range of normal. These people are *hyper* sensitive to sound. Others are in need of more input from a particular sense, and they may be *hypo* sensitive. Think about how you like your massage? Do you prefer a light touch or a deep, hard rub? Hyper or hypo? The way one's body processes sensory input is called sensory integration. If you suspect that your child's sensitivity to noise is excessive, talk to your pediatrician about having your child evaluated, usually by an occupational therapist, for sensory integration dysfunction.

holds true in your communications with your child. She may not have the language to articulate that message, but she sure is absorbing it. Open, available bodies say, *"You have all my attention. How can I help you?"* Closed bodies, which may only partially face the child, say, *"The answer is NO,"* or *"I am not available to really focus on and receive what you have to say,"* or *"What you have to say is not really that important to me."*

Facial expressions send messages that are easily read by a child. Adults often know what someone is going to say or what she is thinking just by reading her facial expressions. Children can be better at reading faces than adults. Anyone who has a three-year-old can tell the story of her young child watching her and saying, *"You happy, Mommy?"* And the mommy thinks, *"How did she know?"* Children are looking for clues and cues all the time. Your facial expression is a powerful way in which you communicate with your child. A raised eyebrow can communicate disapproval. A funny grimace you're not even aware you have made in response to a request speaks volumes to the child. A warm smile is welcoming. You can use your expression to your advantage or you can allow it to sabotage your intention when words and face don't match.

Respectful Ways of Verbal Communication

Most people don't even stop to think about whether they are *being* respectful or disrespectful to a child. Given the choice, I believe you would choose to show respect for your child. You know how uplifting it is to feel respected. Children are no different. Those who feel respected by their parents, the most important people in their lives, are more likely to be compliant and agreeable. The message of respect says, *"I honor who you are, and you are important to me."*

There are ways to interact with our children that communicate the respect they deserve. And there are things that we do that deliver a message of disrespect, saying *"You don't matter."*

Among the ways in which we communicate disrespect to our children are:

- **Talking about the child in front of the child, as if she isn't there.** At the dinner table, one parent says to the other, *"Ethan and Sammie were fighting all day long. I told them to stop, and, well, you know Ethan, he just doesn't listen to me at all. . . ."* Sammie is sitting right there. She is listening to every word you say *about* her, *in front* of her. She is no better than the plate of broccoli in the center of the table. Why not say: *"Sammie, I'm going to tell Daddy about the fighting you and Ethan did today."* And then include her in the conversation. She will feel respected.

- **Spelling in front of your child.** Do you think your child doesn't know that you are saying something you don't want her to hear when you spell the secret message to your partner? Children are quick learners. You only have to spell once or twice before she understands what is going on.

- **Using a foreign language, one not intended for the child to acquire.** Speaking a language the child doesn't understand so that she won't understand what is being said is another way of delivering a message of disrespect and exclusion. It is very different from speaking a second language so that your child will learn it (in which case you speak slowly, adding gestures and translating as needed, so that the child will become familiar with the language).

  If you would like to have a short conversation to which your child should not be privy, and it cannot wait, a respectful way of doing so would be to say to the child: *"I am having an adult conversation right now. I will tell you when I am done, and then you and I will continue talking."*

- **Name-calling, even in fun.** It is never okay to call someone a name. Not Miss Piggy for not having cleaned up her room, nor Sloppy Pants for spilling food on herself at the dinner table. As the mirror for your child, you don't want to reflect comments that will eat away at her self-image.

- **Laughing *at* the child instead of laughing *with* her.** Adults and young children have different ideas about what is funny. A sense of humor is something that a child develops. Children think that you laugh when something is funny, period. If they don't get it, you will hear, *"Daddy, why are you laughing?"* What is humor to a young child? Anything that makes *her* laugh. That would be something nonsensical, something slightly forbidden, or something ridiculous.

  Adults laugh at all kinds of things that aren't even funny. They laugh when something is cute, as when a child enters the room with her shoes on the wrong feet or when she mispronounces a word in the most charming way. As she approaches the age of four, a child becomes self-conscious and embarrasses easily. She hears you laugh, whatever the reason, and if she isn't the one trying to grab the laugh, if it is at her expense, it isn't funny at all. She may even get angry at you, hide her face, or run away in embarrassment. The child interprets the laughter as being disrespectful of her.

- **Telling tales.** Disrespectful communication also occurs when you repeat to someone on the phone the cute thing the child has said or done, while the child is right there. This act is not dissimilar to talking about a child as if she isn't there, but in this case, she will be angry or embarrassed all over again. *"Don't tell Grandma!"* the child will demand. She hated the scene once already, and now you are putting her through it again.

- **Sarcasm.** Sarcasm is usually a poorly disguised threat or put-down, which leaves a child feeling confused, bad about herself, and not worthy of your sincere and genuinely caring communication. If you are a mirror for your child, what kind of an image are you reflecting to her? Sarcasm is an extreme form of disrespect and can lead nowhere that is good.

- **Teasing.** Young children have a hard time distinguishing between what you really mean and what you don't. Teasing is confusing to them. Much like sarcasm, teases are legalized put-downs. You might say, *"Did you brush your hair with the egg beater?"* to a child with a scruffy hairdo in the morning. What the child hears is, *"My hair looks bad."* Even when you try to get out of it by saying, *"Ahh, I was just teasing,"* it still hurts, the damage is done, and the message is disrespectful. Teasing your child is not humorous to her, nor will it toughen her up or teach her to be able to "take it" later on. It is just plain unkind. You are the parent who is supposed to be supportive and loving. She has plenty of time to learn how to withstand teasing.

Listening

Listening is one of the four elements of communication, and it is the one that gets the least amount of press. Even though it may seem implausible, your child receives specific messages by the way you listen to her. Listening is one of the ways that you honor and respect her. It is a way that you build her self-image and her sense of her own value. It is a way that you encourage her participation in life and nurture the growth of her ideas, thoughts, and opinions. And it is a way of saying, *"You matter to me."*

Listening is active; it comes from a verb. But many people are hardly active listeners. How many parents claim they are listening when they are only half listening, fingers still flying across the computer keyboard? It's not that you can't multitask; I truly believe that you are able to do two or three things at once and still listen to your child. That is not the point; rather, it is how that multitasking is interpreted by your child. Is she not worthy of your full attention?

Tips and Scripts for Effective Listening

- **Don't blow your child off.** Soon enough she won't want to talk to you. Your days are numbered! Welcome this gift of talking.

- **Pay attention when your child speaks to you.** Open your body to your child. Turn toward her and acknowledge that she is speaking. Be prepared to receive her words. If it seems that what your child is saying needs more than a quick listen and you can't stop what you are doing, face your child and say: *"I want to hear what you have to say. Right now I cannot give you my full attention. I will be done very soon, so save your thought, and I'll tell you when it's time."* You can even add: *"Let me write down a hint to remind you of what you want to tell me (ask me) when I am done."*

Then, most important of all, be sure to go back to your child and tell her when it is time. She will have learned an important lesson about delaying gratification, and you will have shown respect for her need to talk to you.

- **Pay attention to your child's body language.** Just as with an adult, your child is giving you messages with her body and facial expressions about what she is really feeling and what she needs.

- **Don't interrupt.** It takes children time to form their thoughts and find the words to express them. Often their brains work faster than their mouths. Give them the time they need to get it all out.

- **Repeat what the child has said.** If you are unclear about what the child is expressing or if you aren't sure how to respond, especially if the child is talking about her feelings, it is useful to repeat what you have heard. The child will not only know that you are listening to her but also will feel validated.

- **Be an *active listener*.** Try to figure out what your child is *really* saying. There are usually two messages being communicated: the words she is saying and what is actually going on underneath the words. Take a minute to receive both. That is being an active listener.

- **Respond to the words and to the underlying message.** You can begin by responding to the words, repeating or acknowledging what she has just said: *"You really want cookies right now."*

    Take a risk and respond to what you think is going on underneath. If you are dead wrong, you will be told so emphatically! *"I think you are telling me that you are really hungry right now and you don't want to wait for dinner. You may have some carrots"* (or whatever).

    If the child says: *"But I want cookies,"* you can respond: *"Yes, I know you want cookies and you may have them after dinner* (or whenever). *Right now, if you are hungry, you may have carrots."*

    Through *active listening* you can honor the child's need, and even extend it, without giving in: *"You want a cookie so much. What kind of cookie do you want? Oreo or Vanilla Wafer? How many do you want—one or two? Okay. You want two double-stuffed Oreos. You may have them for your snack after your nap. I will put them right here where they will be waiting for you."*

Suppose you're in a toy store—(never a first choice outing when you're with a child!)—and your child begins telling you all the things she really *needs* to have. You say: *"So, which one of the Barbies do you want? What do you like about that one? Do you like that one better than this one? Is it because of the outfit she is wearing? Now I see why you want it. One day you will have that Barbie. Today is not the day we are buying it. Say good-bye to Barbie and tell her you will see her another day."*

Alternatively, you can say: *"Do you want the Lawyer Barbie or the Prom Queen Barbie? Show me. Okay. I understand. Well, let me just get your special 'gift list' out of my purse and write this down. 'Jessica wants the Lawyer Barbie on her birthday.' It is on my list. Now I will know just what to buy you for your birthday."*

Through these responses, the child feels that she has been heard and not just put off. Listening actively says, *"I really do want to know what you want and how you feel."* Sometimes just being acknowledged takes the sting out of the negative response the child is being given.

The Problem with Praise

Every time I hear a parent or teacher say *"good job,"* it makes my skin crawl. It is something that parents (and teachers) say when they want to acknowledge the child's accomplishment. It's what Alfie Kohn, the author of eight books on education and human behavior, calls a "verbal doggie biscuit." It is a totally automatic response, something a parent just tosses the child. Stop and listen to how often people say *good job*! It is used for everything. How can something be special if everything is special?

Then there is *"good thinking"*. That bit of hollow praise is just a variation of *good job*, another doggie biscuit. If there is *good thinking*, then there must be *bad thinking* too. *Thinking* is a really good thing. There is no *bad* thinking. If you are alive and thinking, then hallelujah!

Some people believe that praise will encourage and motivate the child: she has done something praiseworthy, and you hope to see it again. But there is something very final about a phrase like *"good idea"*. It is praise that communicates an end to the action. *"Now we're done with that, so we'll move on."* Is the child encouraged to keep going, to keep up the action? Will the child be motivated to try it again sometime? Nope. *"I got my doggie biscuit, and now I am done."*

When any form of praise uses the word *good, great, fabulous,* or whatever, it is a judgment. When you praise the child with judgment, you chip away at her ability to judge herself. The child comes to rely on the adult to tell her what is right or wrong or good or bad. She learns to act in order to please the adult, to meet the adult's expectation. She comes to measure her worth in terms of whether or not she has pleased the adult.

Praise that judges cultivates the child's need for extrinsic recognition and motivation. Children who become accustomed to extrinsic recognition become *Mommy (or Daddy, or teacher) addicted.* They are not intrinsically motivated. They need you there in order to feel good. A child has to learn to be her own judge, her own cheerleader, and her own motivator. If praised too frequently, the child is robbed of her opportunity to feel really good about something she has done well and bask in that goodness all by herself.

Praise-addicted children grow up to become adults who need the approval of others, or need the *good job* slap on the back in order to feel good. They are not self-motivated. They continue to look for their parents' approval, even though they are now in their forties. That is their motivation.

Tips and Scripts for Making the Most Out of Praising Your Child

- **Make your praise specific.** Stop and think about what you want to communicate with the praise you are about to deliver. Usually the praise is to encourage more of the same, in which case you need to be specific: *"You carried those groceries all the way in from the garage." "You put your shoes on all by yourself." "You worked on that painting for a very long time."*

- **Praise the action.** The most effective praise focuses on the process and the effort rather than on the product; it does not evaluate. Thus the child is encouraged toward future, independent action. She is self-motivated rather than performing for your approval. Such praise is really encouragement: *"Wow! You sure built that building high. You balanced so many blocks."*

- **Praise begins with the word *you*.** That is the first step in helping the child to look inward and to feel proud of herself for her own accomplishments. While it is not a bad thing for you to feel proud, it is not the reason for the child to repeat her success.

- **Use praise as a way of communicating your expectations for the child:** *"You came to the table right away, as soon as I called you."*

- **Praise the effort without adding your opinion.** *"You covered the whole page with paint"* does so much more than *"I love your painting."* Remember, intrinsic motivation is a goal. The child needs to feel good about what she has done even when you're not there.

- **Praise the effect of her action.** If the child has done something "other oriented," offer praise that emphasizes the effect of those actions: *"Look at Stephen's face. He looks so happy now that you shared your truck with him."*

- **Use questions as a form of praise.** Sometimes your thoughtful questions say more about honoring a child and her work than any words of praise. Your attention in the form of a question is a potent reward: *"Which part of that structure was the hardest to build?"* or *"Which color in your painting do you like the most?"*

Children's Questions

There is no such thing as a bad question. When a child asks a question it means she is thinking and her wheels are turning. Wonder and curiosity are just the things you should be encouraging in your children. They are at the heart of learning.

The way in which you respond to a child's questions communicates many important messages to her. Most importantly, it sets the tone and the stage for the questions, maybe even the *big* questions your child will ask in the future. It also puts you in the position of being the person who will always be available for your child's questions, regardless of their nature. You are the *go-to* person. Wouldn't you rather your child ask *you* than get her answers from less reliable sources?

Children usually ask questions for four different reasons: they really want to know the answer, they are trying to get and keep your attention (the prize!), they are using a question as a stalling technique, or they are trying to get a different question answered, which is hidden beneath the one being asked.

Regardless of the reason, all questions need to be honored. Unanswered questions will eventually lead to unasked questions.

Tips and Scripts for Answering Children's Questions

- **Try to determine what the child is really asking.** Either search for the question beneath the question (*"Are you wondering when we are having dinner?"* when your child asks for a snack) or ask for clarification. You can restate the question, just as your child asked it. She will tell you whether you've got it right or not: *"Are you wondering what happens to a body after it is put in the casket?"*

- **Try to determine what your child already knows or understands about the topic.** Your child might already know some information or have some preconceived ideas or erroneous information that will influence how you will answer her. You might say: *"Tell me what you know about that"* or *"What is your idea about that?"* or *"Who told you about that?"* without the slightest judgment in your voice.

- **Correct misinformation.** After your child has completely finished her question or comment, carefully and without judgment correct any misinformation she has: *"Actually, police officers don't ever put children in jail. The information you have isn't correct. Only adults go to jail."*

- **Use the *Drip Method* of explanation, giving only a little information at a time.** Children absorb and process information differently, depending upon their age, development, intelligence, and experience. Your answers should be based on your child, her questions, and what she knows. You don't want to flood her with too much information at once. If you do, it's like pouring water on a dry sponge: the information will flow away and little will be absorbed. Giving information drop by drop allows more of it to sink in. Offer a piece of information. Then pause and wait while your child gathers her thoughts. By stopping and listening for her comments or further questions, you will be able to gauge your child's understanding of your answer.

- **Provide more information as needed.** With each additional item of information, remember to pause and gauge your child's absorption and continuing interest. You might have lost her interest already, or she may be sated. That's okay.

- **Answer questions honestly and factually, and do not give misinformation.** In so doing you ensure that your child will continue to bring her questions to you, the person who will give her the straight story. Your honest responses add to the trusting relationship you have built with your child.

- **Be patient** with your child if she asks the same question over and over. She is just trying to make sense of the information you have given. With each explanation, she understands it a little better. So be sure that you are consistent with your answers or she will become confused.

- **Don't feel that you must know the answer to every question.** It's good for children to learn that parents don't "know it all." Owning your ignorance presents the opportunity for you to model and teach how one goes about finding information you don't know. Begin by saying: *"I don't know the answer to that question. We . . .*

  . . . can go to the library together and find a book that will teach us both about that."

  . . . can Google that and see if there is information about that on the Web."

  . . . can ask Uncle Louie that question. He really knows a lot about airplanes."

- **Do a follow-up check.** After you have answered a child's question, it is always a good idea to do a status check. This is another way of gauging your child's understanding and feeling about your answer: *"What do you think about what I just said?"* or *"Did I answer your question enough?"* or *"Do you have any more questions about that?"*

As mentioned, this chapter provides the foundation for the rest of the book. Everything that follows is informed by the advice given here on communicating with your child. As you delve into the later chapters, you may find it helpful to refer to this material. Just knowing the words for the answers is not enough. Remember, the manner in which you answer the questions and address the issues, and the many ways that you communicate with your child, go a long way in building healthy development. And the frosting on the cake is that you will feel like a competent parent.

❖

CHAPTER 2

"Tommy Just Doesn't Listen."

Discipline Do's and Don'ts

At some point in his young life, every child is going to refuse to get dressed, ignore a parent's request to do something, scream, whine, and engage in a host of other undesirable behaviors. And each one of these will be irritating, frustrating, or exasperating. However, the single most common complaint I hear from parents is that their child *"doesn't listen."* In all seriousness, I ask, *"Have you had his hearing checked?"* The response is almost always, *"Oh no, he can listen; he just doesn't."*

That's when I explain that *not listening* is a normal part of a child's typical development. Rather than seeing it as a *listening* problem, it first needs to be understood as an issue of developmental and deliberate noncompliance. There is always a reason why he is not listening; it's just not always evident to you. When you understand the *why* of the behavior, then the solution to the problem will come into focus.

Children are born not knowing what is expected of them, not knowing the "rules of the road." Just as a new driver has to learn what is legal and what isn't, so a child needs to learn the limits of his world. And just as the rules of the road keep all the drivers safe, the limits in the child's world give shape and definition to his behaviors and, thereby, keep him safe. A child's days are filled with testing, exploring, pushing boundaries, and testing some more. He's like a scientist using the trial-and-error methodology. These are his developmental tasks; they are part of what he needs to do in order to grow up. Here are some examples:

What happens when I drop this food onto the floor?

What sound will it make when I pound this plastic hammer on the glass coffee table?

What will Daddy do when I refuse to come to the dinner table?

Does "no" always mean NO?

There is one other element that propels your child to test limits and "not listen": *you!* You, your attention, is the prize, the thing the child wants most. Sometimes, in the absence of positive attention, negative attention, such as a stern "talking to," will do just fine. It is attention, after all.

Think of you and your child as the two parts that make up Velcro. There's the fuzzy part and the prickly part that easily catches the fuzz. You awaken each day and put on your fuzz suit. Your child wakes up and puts on his prickles. Then he spends his waking hours trying to catch you, just like the prickles hook the fuzz.

Defying you, misbehaving, or "not listening" are sure ways to get your full attention. Frankly, the child I worry about is the one who *doesn't* misbehave, who complacently sits, who never takes a step away from you, never makes a misstep, who is never defiant. I wonder if he is trying out his wings, stretching, and finding his own power. We might not like these quests and trials, but they are a crucial step in a child's development of self.

Impulse Control

Remember the cartoon character Porky Pig? When Porky was faced with a behavioral dilemma, the choice of being good or bad, he had two helpers. Angel Porky appeared over his right shoulder, wearing a white gown and a halo, saying, *"Now, Porky, be a good little pig and do what your mommy told you. Don't you take that apple. You know that isn't nice. You mind your mother, Porky."* Then Devil Porky would appear over his left shoulder, holding a pitchfork, his fat little tummy bursting out of his red devil suit, horns growing out of his head. *"You do it, Porky!"* he cries. *"You go right ahead. Yeah. You take that apple. Who cares what your mommy said. Take it! Take it!"* Young children have Angel Porkies and Devil Porkies. Angel Porky represents what he is supposed to do. Devil Porky represents the child's *impulses*, those things he is just driven to do, over which he hasn't yet developed the control he needs. In the young child, nine times out of ten, Devil Porky overrides Angel Porky. The child has heard what you have said, but he just can't resist doing what he wants.

The impulsive behaviors that characterize a huge portion of most young children's behavior will not last forever, I promise. But two-year-olds have not yet developed their brakes. They can't stop themselves. Devil Porky is too powerful. In fact, the three-to-six-year-olds are still working on their impulse control too. What's a parent to do?

Tips and Scripts for Helping a Child with Impulse Control

It takes time and practice for a child to learn how to control his impulses. Here's how you can help:

- **Save your child.** When you realize that it is asking too much of your child to stop himself, remove the object of desire. That might mean moving the child to a different place or simply removing the temptation itself. You might say: *"You really want to touch the remote control, and Daddy told you that you may not. It is just too hard for you to stop yourself right now, so I am going to put the remote control up high."*

- **Yelling won't work.** Loud voices don't work any better than soft ones when it comes to developing impulse control. Yelling can, however, frighten the child into stopping himself . . . for that one time only. Remember, lacking impulse control is not really the child's fault; he simply isn't mature enough to completely control those urges yet.

- **Keep your expectations for your child reasonable and appropriate.** By so doing, you ensure that the child is more likely to be able to meet them, and you are less likely to be disappointed. Remember that a child under four years of age is challenged by impulse control. If your child is older than four, keep your expectations appropriate and expect him to stop himself. (Consequences for noncompliance are addressed later in this chapter.)

- **Set your child up to be successful.** Try to determine whether your child's limit testing is about impulse control or about something else (such as getting your attention or not knowing what is expected). Then you can set your child up to be successful.

Many variables will affect your child's progress with impulse control, including whether he is hungry, tired, or stressed—and, of course, "lousy local conditions."

"Lousy Local Conditions"

In their book, *Becoming the Parent You Want to Be*, authors Laura Davis and Janis Keyser coined the expression "lousy local conditions." This refers to the times when a child's behaviors are magnified or even created by the conditions of the environment, such as when you take your two-year-old to visit a friend who has a crystal collection on her coffee table, or you drag your five-year-old on just "one more errand" at five in the afternoon at the end of a school day.

Simply put, it is not reasonable to expect your child to "behave" when the cause of the limit testing is lousy local conditions. He is not being set up to be successful.

Discipline

The word *discipline* comes from the Latin word *disciplina*, which means "teaching or learning." It doesn't mean to hurt, inflict pain, shame, or humiliate. Yet discipline often does just that. What it doesn't do is help the child to learn from what he has done, and to develop some self-discipline. Discipline is about *teaching* your child, not punishing him.

Your child was born in the learning mode. He started at square one, knowing nothing. And he wants to know it all. Learning in and of itself is a huge motivator. He is all about learning as he tries to figure out the ways of the world. Yet parents believe that in order for the child to learn, otherwise known in this case as "behaving" or being disciplined, he needs to be punished or threatened with a punishment or an unpleasant consequence. The child needs to be *made* to learn to do the right thing, they think. That just isn't so. What the child needs is your help in the form of consistent, clear, firm limits. That is how he learns how the world works. He can't be shamed, hurt, or even frightened into that learning, that is, self-discipline. It is through having consistent limits that make sense to the child that he grows up to be well behaved and disciplined.

Okay, Okay, you may be thinking. *We know how important limits on behavior are. But how the heck do I enforce them? And what am I supposed to do when a limit is broken?* Herein lies the real problem.

Children are born with an amazing number of working parts. Unfortunately, one of them is not a behavior navigator, a mechanism that enables the child to know what is expected of him, do what is expected of him, and to control his body. Wouldn't that have been great? That's what you are for. The child needs the adults in his life to be his navigators in the form of setting limits and boundaries. Your child's actions are saying: *"I know I need to stop, but I can't stop myself. Help! Stop me!"* And in the nick of time, Mean Mommy (as in, *"You are so mean!"*) steps in and imposes the limit. Eventually, you and your limits are internalized, becoming the inner voice that tells him what to do and what not to do. Now the child has the internal navigator he lacked at birth. This is the first step on the road to becoming self-disciplined, which is, after all, the goal.

Why Me?

Has this ever happened to you? Your children have been driving you crazy, testing limits and misbehaving. You jump at the chance to go out to a movie and leave them at home with your in-laws. Three hours later you return, prepared to see the house torn apart and the kids running wild. You walk into a perfectly quiet house, with Grandma and Grandpa watching *Jeopardy!* on the couch. *"How'd it go?"* you ask, tentatively, dreading the answer. *"They were perfect angels. No problem at all."*

Don't you wonder why you and your in-laws seem to know different children? In fact, you do. The kids your in-laws know are well behaved, as long as you are not around. Children choose with whom they are going to misbehave. And you are the winner. There are a couple of reasons for this.

Children "act out" with the adult whom they most trust: *"I can be my very worst with you, Mommy, because you are not going away. I cannot be so bad that you will leave me."*

Children also misbehave with the adult who is most likely to allow it. Your child is a keen observer; he has you all figured out. He knows that when Daddy says to stop touching the remote, he had better do it, because Daddy will act on his command. He knows that with Mommy, he might have more wiggle room. Maybe he knows that you are going to ask him three or four times, so he doesn't need to respond until the fourth time, when you might finally start to beg or even scream.

I can't think of one family where both parents practice the same parenting style, even when they are in agreement about their hopes and dreams for their children. Actually, it's not a bad thing for your child to be raised with different approaches to parenting, as long as one parent is not undermining the other and there are no mixed messages about a behavior or limit.

Goodness of Fit

Sometimes a parent and a child just don't match up very well. Experts in the field refer to this variable as "goodness of fit." Each of us is born with a particular temperament. Sometimes your child's temperament and yours don't work well together. It doesn't mean you love your child any less. It means that in some areas of your parenting, one parent will be more successful and have much less angst than the other. Keeping goodness of fit in mind with each of your children will go a long way in avoiding some of the bumps on the parenting pathway.

The bottom line? I believe that disciplined children are the products of disciplined parents. I don't mean that your own life must be particularly disciplined, but that you parent in a deliberate, thoughtful, and consistent way. If you are haphazard in your limit setting, discipline, and follow-through, your children are more likely to be haphazard in their behavior around you.

Remember, parenting is not a popularity contest. Your child does not have to like you, nor do all his friends need to think you are the best daddy. In fact, there will be countless times when your child doesn't like you one bit. You are going to have to make unpopular decisions and impose consequences that he will not like. So be it. It's your job. You are the parent. Now act like one.

Tips and Scripts for Discipline

- **There is no one right way to discipline.** You know your child best. Each child is different; each situation will, therefore, require a different response from you. What worked for one child or situation may not work for another. Ask yourself, *"Will my response (discipline) help this particular child to* learn *the limit and use it again in a similar situation? Am I teaching him what is expected, the right thing to do, and how to do it?"*

- **Stop! Wait! Pay attention to your body before you mete out discipline.** Set up your discipline process so your words are likely to be heard and received. If necessary, review the section on Tips and Scripts for Setting up a Communication, chapter 1, page 4.

- **One *yes* sustains your child through a thousand *no's*.** Your child has an amazing memory. He will not forget the one time he got you to change your mind. Giving in is a bad idea. Don't do it. Do not deliver a no if there is a chance that it might become a yes. If the possibility exists, rethink the limit. If you don't have the intestinal fortitude to hold to your limit, don't impose it in the first place.

- **Don't argue with your child!** If you have gotten to the point of needing to discipline, the time for discussion has long since passed.

- **Avoid "You're in big trouble!"** What does this mean, anyway? It's the expression that parents use when they have no idea what else to say. It means that something is going to happen, but Daddy is not sure what. Using this phrase eats away at your credibility. Know what you are going to do, and do it!

- **Discipline doesn't end with the word *okay?*** A limit or directive to a child is a statement, not a question.

- **With limit setting, always start with a *yes*, followed by the *no*.** Young children pay attention to and hang on to the first words you say. If the child has been hearing a lot of *no's* and *don'ts* and *nots*, as is pretty likely, a limit that starts with a negative just might be ignored. He knows he is going to be thwarted, so he tunes you out right from the start. In putting your "yes" first, you give him something that he *can* do.

  Sometimes the child simply doesn't know what he is supposed to be doing and needs information in order to do the right thing. Starting your *no* with a *yes* gives him the information he needs in order to do the right thing, such as: *"You really like to jump. You may jump on the bed. You may not jump on the couch. Come, I will take you to the jumping place."*

- **Grown-up choices and child choices.** As your child is learning the rules of the road, he can learn that there are some decisions that are his to make and some that are yours. Explain to him: *"There are child choices and grown-up choices. What you wear to school is a child choice. Going to school is a grown-up choice."* Then add this to your directives: *"It's time for you to go to bed. That's a grown-up choice. But you can choose what bedtime story you want. That is a child choice."*

- **The power of ambient learning.** Families with more than one child can benefit from *ambient learning*. That is, the sibling of the rule-breaker absorbs the limit reinforcement of his brother. The message is being driven home for him too.

The Four-Prong Plan for Discipline: Getting Your Child to Do What You Ask

Parents often tell me that they "count" in order to get the child to comply. *"If he doesn't do what I ask, then I just tell him I am going to count. Eventually, he does it when I count."* Counting works because no parent in her right mind is going to get to three and not follow through. *"One . . . two . . . two and a half . . . two and seven-eighths . . . two and twenty-nine-thirtieths . . ."* You stretch it out as long as you can, hoping that the child will obey and you won't actually have to do something. Once you get to three, you just can't back down; you are forced to carry out your threat, whatever it may be. Counting works. But even in counting, the child knows he has some time before he needs to spring into action.

The Four-Prong Plan for Discipline is an alternative to counting. It is a framework for structuring the regular requests you make of your child that are usually met with resistance. And it works.

STEP 1: FOREWARNING

It is really hard for a child to stop what he is doing and do something else, especially something not of his choosing. Honor that truth by giving your child some warning. See what he is doing and look for a natural break. Go over to him, get down on his level, touch him on his arm, back, or leg. Now he has received input from three senses telling him that you are talking to him. Say: *"In five minutes it is going to be time to stop playing with your Legos and wash your hands for dinner. This is your five-minute warning."*

Now if he doesn't comply, you will know it's because he would much rather continue building his Lego rocket blaster, not because he didn't hear you.

STEP 2: IT'S TIME

In five minutes, go to the child. Once again get down on his level, put a hand on him, and say: *"Now it is time to wash for dinner. Please put your Legos down and go wash now. I will save your Legos for after dinner."*

At this point, you need to wait there for a few moments. Allow for a transition time. The child doesn't always jump up and do what you say (I guess you've noticed that). Give him a moment to move to the new activity of hand washing. It's never fun to stop doing something you like and do something not-so-fun. If he does so without protest, then you're home free. But let's assume, more likely, that he doesn't budge.

STEP 3: DELIVER THE THREAT, JUST ONCE

Parents tell me all the time that this part is the hardest because they aren't at all clear about what the threat (consequence) should be. (We'll discuss consequences below.)

Try this: *"If you stop, wash up, and come to dinner now, then you will eat with the family. If you do not, then you will eat in the kitchen by yourself."* Or, " *. . . then you will eat your dinner when the rest of the family is finished."* Or, " *. . . then you will not be eating dinner tonight."*

Whatever consequence you choose, the point is that you state it clearly and calmly and are prepared to follow through if there is noncompliance. Wait a moment and see if there is any action. The first few times you do this, there probably will not be any movement toward compliance. After all, your child has never had to respond so quickly before. He is accustomed to the old ways: coercion or fight. If there is still not even a muscle twinge toward compliance, then . . .

STEP 4: LOWER THE BOOM

This is when you follow through with your threat. There is no waffling, no backing down if the child suddenly decides to scurry in and do what you've asked. His dinner plate is now on the kitchen table, and the rest of the family is sitting at the dining room table. (Or, the whole family is at the kitchen table, and Noah is alone in the dining room.) The point is that he missed the chance to join the party. There is no going back now. It's over.

When Noah wanders in five minutes later, ready for dinner on his own schedule, you say: *"Your dinner is in the kitchen. Maybe tomorrow you will come when I ask you and you will be able to eat with the rest of the family. Tonight you are eating your dinner alone in the kitchen."*

At this point you will likely have to tolerate a huge tantrum or meltdown. Yes, it's true. Noah is disrupting everyone else's dinner. But it will only happen once or maybe twice. Your child has now learned that you mean what you say. You have regained your credibility.

You can modify this technique for use with a child who is engaged in an unacceptable behavior that needs to stop immediately, such as burping at the dinner table, banging a toy car on the coffee table, spitting toothpaste at the mirror, or any of a zillion other behaviors you can name. In such cases there is no forewarning (Step 1), as the child already knows that what he is doing is not okay and has to stop right away.

In all cases you should do a revisit with Noah when the atmosphere is calm.

The Revisit

Often parents shy away from bringing up an issue once it is over for fear that the child will have another meltdown. Not so. The "revisit" is a calm review of what happened. When the child is in the midst of having limits enforced or being disciplined, he doesn't have any perspective on what's going on. In fact, his ear flaps just close right up. The revisit, when the child is no longer in an emotional state, allows you the chance to review together what happened and why. It is kind of like pouring some glue on top of the experience so it sticks. An hour or two later (or even the next morning) is usually a good time to revisit the scene: *"You didn't come to the dinner table tonight when I asked you. When you finally came, you had to eat your dinner in the kitchen, alone, and you got so angry. You had a huge fuss, but you still had to eat in the kitchen. Now you are fine. You really didn't like eating alone in the kitchen. I know tomorrow night you will come to dinner when I ask you."*

I have heard tales of children saying, *"I don't want to talk about it"* or covering their ears when you try to revisit. Do not be thwarted. You can say, *"You don't have to talk about what happened. I need to talk about it. It's my job to teach you how to behave."* And then proceed, whether or not his hands are on his ears. He hears you.

Consequences

You've probably heard that the definition of *insanity* is "doing the same thing over and over and expecting to get different results." Perhaps the particular behavior that you are trying so hard to modify in your child just keeps happening. You've taken away his dessert, his favorite truck, and you've even threatened to take away his beloved blankie. Why isn't it working?

It's not working because although these actions make the child *feel* punished, there is no connection in his mind between the behavior and the punishment. The unacceptable behavior stopped temporarily because of fear, not because of learning. There is no related cause and effect between the child's misbehavior and your response.

Consequences are the tools you use to enforce the limits you have set. Consequences are not punishments. The child understands the difference in this way: a punishment is something that your mommy or daddy does to you. A consequence is something you do to yourself. A punishment is authoritarian and requires the child to be obedient. A consequence, on the other hand, teaches the child to be accountable and responsible for his own behavior. The connection between a behavior and a consequence makes logical sense.

Implicit in the concept of consequences is the idea that the child has a choice: when you choose to behave in a certain way, you are choosing the consequence. Having such a choice is empowering and feeds his sense of competence and control.

Experiencing the consequences of a behavior is a great learning tool, but it can feel just awful to the child and the parent. Allowing the child to suffer the consequence of his actions when you could "fix it" takes tremendous strength and resolve. No one likes to see her child unhappy, especially when you know you could remove the pain. But in your fixing it, there would be no learning except maybe *Mommy can always make things better for me. I have no role in this scene.* Allowing the child to experience the unhappiness of a consequence facilitates his learning and his growth.

Too often parents sabotage opportunities for the child to learn how to tolerate disappointment or frustration. Why? Because it is really hard to watch your child be unhappy. It unlocks one of your pieces of luggage, and out flies the memory of the time Dad didn't let you go to your long-anticipated baseball game because you hadn't completed your homework. Or maybe it was the time the whole family went out to dinner and you had to stay home with the babysitter because your shoes weren't on your feet in time. You know how that feels, and your feelings are getting priority over the lesson your child needs.

I am reminded of a client whose child desperately wanted to use his own money to buy a very expensive trading card. After soliciting my advice, she allowed the seven-year-old to spend his own, hard-earned (allowance and cumulated gifts received) sixty dollars on the card. Next he wanted to take it to school. I smelled a great lesson in the making and helped Mom to discuss with her son all of the possibilities of what could happen to the card: it could get lost; it could get stolen; it could get damaged (making it less valuable); or it could come home, safe and intact. But it had to be the child's choice. So the card went to school the next day. What do you suppose happened? The card didn't come home. No one really knows why, but it was certainly no longer the jewel of this little collector's collection. As you might imagine, he was numb with grief. Mom was beside herself, blaming herself for letting him take it to school. In the after-school call I received, Mom meekly asked if I thought she should give him money to buy another card. Need I write my answer here? I feel quite sure that the lesson learned by the boy will never be forgotten.

The trading card story is an example of what is called a "natural consequence," which is a result of a particular circumstance. Here are two more examples. You tell your child not to leave the toy out on the grass because the dog might eat it. The next day, the grass is dotted with plastic red and blue pieces of the now unrecognizable water rocket. Or, your two-year-old dumps his bowl of fruit on the floor. No more fruit; all gone!

With natural consequences, the mistake or misbehavior itself teaches the lesson. The cause and effect are perfectly clear, and the child's own actions generated the lesson. An adult isn't necessarily involved. If the parent were to fix the mistake, the lesson would hardly be learned.

"Logical consequences" are related to natural consequences in that they are directly, logically, and obviously related to the crime. But logical consequences are drafted and imposed by the parent or the adult who is in charge, based on the child's misbehavior. Logical consequences make sense. Instead of happening because *Daddy is really mad at me*, they happen because of *something that I did*.

The most common mistake parents make when it comes to deciding on a consequence is grabbing one that is not related to the event. Dad wants the child to *really feel it*, so he goes for whatever he thinks will have the most power for the child. It is true that you know your child's currency, but too often that currency has nothing to do with the misbehavior; it is not logical. For example, a parent thinks, *"He loves dessert. It's the only thing I can take away that will get through to him. If he hits his brother, I will take away his dessert."*

It may well be true that dessert is his currency, and it may temporarily extinguish the misbehavior, but taking away dessert is not likely to stop his hitting his brother thereafter. Rather than being a lesson about what is expected, it is seen as a punishment imposed by the parent. It will cause resentment and perhaps fear. But there is no real lesson other than: *"When Daddy gets mad, he can take away something of mine. That is what grown-ups get to do."*

In the heat of the moment, it is really hard to think of an appropriate consequence, but it can be learned over time. The more you do it, the better you will get at it.

Unfortunately, there is no one-size-fits-all script for which consequence fits which misbehavior. Depending on the crime and the child's particular temperament, age, and development, different consequences will be appropriate. Keep this reality in mind when your older child, who carefully scrutinizes how you treat his younger brother, whines, *"That's not fair. When I did that, my consequence lasted for two weeks."* Your answer is, *"I have different children, and I treat you differently."* (For a discussion on this topic, see "It's Not Fair" in chapter 6, page 115.)

- **Neither natural nor logical consequences work with two-year-olds.** They are plum in the middle of being victims of their own impulses, which are difficult to censor. Depending upon your two-year-old and his development, age-appropriate responses would be those that can be immediately implemented and are very short in duration, such as handing him a ball to throw and taking away for a half hour the puzzle he has just heaved, or taking him out of the sandbox where he has sprinkled sand on his friend and directing his play somewhere else for fifteen minutes.

- **Consequences must be suited to the child's age and development.** Asking a three-year-old child to clean up everything in the playroom is simply not a reasonable expectation or consequence. *"You need to pick up and put away everything that has wheels"* makes sense.

- **Beware of overkill.** The four-year-old who has left the tops off many of the family markers . . . again . . . will learn from having no markers for a day or two. Taking all the pens away for a week is overkill. If they are his own markers, when his favorite green pen dries up from having been uncovered, be sure not to replace it right away. Say: *"Oh well, I guess you have learned what happens to pens that don't get covered."* And possibly for a five- or six-year-old, *"Maybe we could talk about how you can earn (some of) the money to buy yourself a new green marker."*

  The five-year-old who leaves his jacket on the kitchen floor day after day when you ask him to take it to his room will learn a fine lesson from going to school with no jacket, just layers of sweaters on an icy cold day (and he won't catch cold!). No jacket for a week is overkill.

- **Don't punish yourself.** In the heat of the moment, the parent may reach for a consequence that she thinks will really mean something to the child: *"Okay, then. We are not going to the beach today."* But if you have been looking forward all week to going to the beach with your friend and her daughter, it probably isn't a good consequence for your child's not having his shoes on at the appointed time. You shouldn't suffer the consequence of your child's misbehavior.

- **Stick to your guns.** If the consequence is appropriate and powerful enough, while the child will not like it, it will seem fair to him. He can tell you that you are mean, that you are the worst mommy in the whole world, even that he hates you, but these are just diversionary tactics. He will try his best to get you to change your mind, but who wouldn't?

Diversionary Tactics

Once you have gathered your thoughts, framed the consequence, developed the plan, and dropped the bomb, your child will not be happy. Now is when he will try his best to get out of the consequence, regardless of its size or appropriateness. Children develop some pretty powerful, sometimes even creative approaches for trying to get you to change your mind—from apologizing and arguing to whining and complaining, screaming and crying. None of these should work! Here is where your intestinal fortitude comes into play.

Tips for Dealing with a Child's Diversionary Tactics

Some children are real fighters. They want what they want when they want it, and they will say whatever they think it will take to get it. Parents are often thrown by these nasty comments and fall back on the old *"You may not talk to me that way. . . ."* In place of that useless and ineffective comment, try using one of the following phrases to refocus the attention on the child and the consequence for her behavior:

1. Do I look like the kind of mommy who is going to change her mind?
2. I have made my decision, and I am not going to change my mind.
3. Regardless of the names that you call me, you still . . .
4. Regardless of how you feel about me, you still . . .
5. You choose your behavior (not putting your shoes on), you choose the consequence.
6. In spite of your thinking that it is not fair, you will still . . .
7. You are responsible for what your body does, and now you will . . .
8. We don't change the rule after it has been broken.

And finally, my personal favorite:

9. *I am done talking about this.*

Threats

Threats are the ploy most commonly used by parents. Here is a typical scenario: Mom tells six-year-old Justin that it's time to put on his shoes for school. Nothing happens. She tells him again . . . and five minutes later, again . . . and again. After the fourth request, Mom looks at her watch and sees that now they are going to be late. She gets serious, her irritation is leaking, and she adds the threat: *"Justin, put your shoes on right now, or I am leaving without you."* Justin doesn't pay attention and goes right on playing with his Super Transformer. Now Mom is yelling: *"Justin, I mean it. Right now. Shoes on, or I will leave."* Justin drags himself over to his shoes, sits down, and gets distracted by his magic flashlight pen on the floor next to the shoes. *"Okay, Justin,"* Mom says. *"I am leaving. I am walking to the car right now. Bye-bye, Justin. Here I go."* Justin hears Mom gathering her purse and keys, and screams, *"No, wait! I am coming right now. I am putting on my shoes. Wait! Don't go!"* Of course, Mom waits. Justin runs to the car, tripping on his untied shoelaces, pouty and crabby, whimpering: *"Why were you going to leave me?"*

The lesson Justin learned here? Mom doesn't mean what she says. Justin has learned other lessons too: that he will usually have a few chances to do what Mom asks of him, and that Mom is full of hot air. She may threaten something or other, but it is not likely that she will follow through. Justin can always save himself at the last minute.

Many parents suffer from this wet-noodle syndrome. They threaten and threaten and never follow through. In fact, they look for ways *not* to follow through, for if they do so, it is sure to ignite a firestorm of a tantrum, and no one likes to deal with those.

When my children (triplets, remember?) were in preschool, it was quite a production to get everyone up, dressed, fed, and out the door to school. One of my daughter's best attention-getting devices was dillydallying while getting dressed. Going to school was not a choice; I could not leave her at home as a consequence for noncompliance. On the day I decided I had had it, after suitable warning, I said, *"Jessie, this bus is leaving for school, and you are going to be on it. You can wear your clothes or just your undies. It's your choice."* So I carried a screaming, kicking, flailing Jessie to her car seat, dressed only in her underpants. Once we arrived at school, Ina, the world's best director, took the cue as I handed her the bag filled with Jessie's school clothes I had hastily grabbed before leaving home. *"Oh, Jessie,"* she admonished, *"all children who go to this school must wear clothes."*

No hollow threats and no more problems with Jessie getting dressed for school. That consequence was one she long remembered.

I have found that parents who work outside of the home, in addition to their work as parents, often have the hardest time following through on their warnings. They figure, *"I have so little time with my child. I want the time that I have to be pleasant."* That thinking is short-sighted. Following through will not only lead to extinguishing the behavior at the time, but with an appropriate consequence, it will likely make that behavior go away altogether, and your time together will be more pleasant.

Tantrums

As much as we hate them, tantrums are very much a part of almost every child's development.

As soon as children are old enough to hold an idea in their head, that is, to remember what it was they wanted, they are old enough to have a tantrum about not getting it. Tantrums can begin as early as six months, but you don't usually see the classic tantrum until the child is around fifteen to eighteen months old. When they end is a bit less predictable, as that variable has to do with your child's development and with you, but they usually begin to ease up after three or three and a half years, and they certainly diminish in frequency.

What causes a tantrum? Usually it is due to frustration or anger. In their mission to learn about the world, test limits, try out their autonomy, and be in control, young children will be thwarted at every turn. Their frustration level is certainly exacerbated by their lack of language skills and their inability to make things work the way they want.

Tantrums are completely normal. And they really do make sense when you keep the young child's agenda in mind: *I know what I want. Yesterday at the birthday party I had ice cream. It was great. I want it again . . . now.* You explain why ice cream is not a choice, and he has a screaming fit. But he hasn't forgotten, and an hour later he tries again. *Yes. Ice cream. That's what I want.* And each time he asks, you thwart his desire, over and over again, until he is exhausted and totally frustrated. Here comes the tantrum.

It is universally accepted that the worst time of day is from around 5:00 P.M. to 7:00 P.M. or so. Many a parent complains about her child's behavior being particularly challenging then. Your house becomes a "whinery." I call it the "Piranha Hour"—that's when mothers want to eat their young!

At the end of the day, everyone in the family is at his worst. Your children have held it together all day, either at school or home, accepting various limits and basically doing what is expected of them. But this can only go on for so long, and there comes a boiling point. The limit testing, the sibling fighting, the back talk has to come out sometime. At the end of the day, it's game over. Get ready, here it comes.

You too have held it together all day long. You were your professional, polite, patient self. Or you were the good parent all day long, tolerating whatever was thrown your way by your children, the broken washing machine, your mother-in-law. By the end of the day, you are spent. Like the horse that begins galloping as soon as he sees the stable, you are in a race for your children's bedtime. Nothing will deter you: *"Just eat your dinner, have your bath, and get in bed! Don't cross me, because I will surely explode."*

Even your caregiver might have had it. She did her job with your children all day just as prescribed by you. She is wiped out too.

So, what we have is a convergence of exhausted, burned-out, spent people who live in your house. Of course it is the Piranha Hour!

While you have the maturity to know that soon you can relax, the children will be asleep, and the dishes will be done, your child does not. He has no resources left. Without the ability to withstand any more frustration, he collapses into a heap, yielding to a full-blown tantrum. He is neither happy nor comfortable, and he wants just the thing that always makes him feel better: You! How can he get your attention now, when you are so crabby? He'll act out and misbehave, even tantrum, and like always, he will get your attention. That brings the mommy he knows, even if she is angry.

Tips and Scripts for Handling a Tantrum

There are many different theories about how tantrums should be handled. What works for one child might not work for yours. Moreover, what worked for your firstborn might not work for your second or third. Keep in mind the goal is not only to end the tantrum but also to support your child when he's gone to the dark side.

- **Don't reason with your child when she is having a tantrum.** In fact, say as little as possible. Children's little ear flaps close right up when they are in the midst of a breakdown. Save your energy and your talk for later.

- **Keep it safe.** If the child has collapsed into a tantrum in a place where he might hurt himself, move him to an area where he will be safe—an open, carpeted area, away from the glass coffee table. A child in the midst of a tantrum often flails, grabs for things to throw, or reaches for people to hit. Keep the child away from everything, including your body.

  Sometimes very young children feel totally out of control and will need you to contain them. Sit on the floor and gently but firmly hold your child's back to your front, on the floor between your legs, both arms crossed in front of him. This is not an angry hold, but rather one that says I am keeping you safe. Soon (or maybe not so soon!) he will stop resisting you, relax a bit, and take it down a notch to crying. This hold should not become a physical battle. It is, instead, a form of support and safety that you provide for your child.

- **Do not leave the child alone.** There are those who believe in sending the child to his room to have the meltdown. I believe the child is better served by your not abandoning him to his out-of-control feelings and behavior. Stay close by. Even though you are not talking to him, he knows you are there, and your presence *is* comforting. He might command you to *"Go away"* or *"Leave me alone,"* but he doesn't mean it. Sit in a chair across the room and pick up a magazine. If the child is holding on to your leg, try to ignore it. In fact, try to ignore him altogether as best as you can. You can say: *"You are really angry right now. I will wait until you are done."* Or, *"Let me know when you are done."*

  If the child is trying to hurt you, hit you, or grab at you, stand up and step away. Tell him: *"I will not let you hurt me. Let me know when you are done, and we can talk."*

  When you are standing, your legs are the only target he can reach. He'll wrap his arms around your calves in a death grip. Ignore it. It will end eventually, I promise.

- **The End Save.** You can usually tell when the tantrum is winding down. When you hear and see that your child is starting to come back down to earth—his crying has calmed to sobs, his breaths are broken and quick, he is sniffling a bit—it is a good time to step in and accompany him on his journey back. Scoop him up and say something diverting, like: *"C'mon, Sam, let's go see if there are any squirrels outside."* By this point, most children are ready to be saved. They just don't know how to do so gracefully. A paradigm shift offers the child the chance to reenter the world and save face.

Public Tantrums

Handling your child's tantrums at home is a piece of cake compared to handling public displays of the same behavior. Here the whole world is your judge, as the neon sign over your head flashes PARENT IN TROUBLE. There is an unspoken expectation that children are supposed to "behave" in public and that it's your fault if they don't.

While no one likes a child to act out in public, parents are their own harshest critics. Here are some suggestions for how to cope.

Tips and Scripts for Handling Public Tantrums

- **Discuss your plan in advance.** Be clear and precise about what will happen and your expectations of the child: *"We are going to the toy store, where I am just buying a birthday gift for cousin Seymour, nothing else. You may look at all the toys and even tell me what you like, but I am only buying one thing and that is a gift for cousin Seymour. If you need to have a fuss, we will leave the store and I will go to the store without you."*

- **When all hell breaks loose in the market (or any store)** . . . Don't worry; it's bound to happen sometimes. Your child desperately wants the fruit roll. You say no, and it's curtains. Here are your choices:

  1. Tolerate the tantrum, but do not walk away from the child or threaten to leave him there alone. Stand and wait calmly. Smile at your audience to let them know you are in charge (even though it may not feel that way!).
  2. Get down on your child's level and quietly say, *"You have only one chance to stop now. If you stop, I will not have to take you home."*
  3. Pick up your child in a football carry (under your arm). Wheel your basket to the nearest checkout. Tell the cashier your name,

that you will be back to finish your marketing, and ask her to wheel your basket into the big refrigerator in the back. This is not an unreasonable request. The staff are glad you are taking care of business. If someone is at your house, drop the child off and return to the grocery store without him. If no one is home to stay with your child, phone the store manager and say you will return as soon as possible (and hopefully without your child, as that is the logical consequence for misbehavior in the grocery store). Be sure to do your *revisit* (see page 30) and remind your child of your expectations before his next visit to the store.

- **When all hell breaks loose in the restaurant**... Tantrums in restaurants are more difficult because, unlike the grocery store, patrons are there to enjoy themselves. When your child has a tantrum, it can ruin other guests' dining experiences. It most certainly is your job to restrain and contain your child. Make sure your expectations are realistic, though. Some children do not belong in restaurants. Period. They are simply not mature enough.

1. In advance, tell your child the plan and your reasonable behavioral expectations for your restaurant visit.
2. Bring extra nibbles and distractions to keep your child busy while he waits for his food to arrive.
3. If you have a child whom you think might have to be removed at some point, and the party involves more than the three of you, be sure to take two cars. That way, when the child needs to go home, you can follow through without ruining everyone else's experience. If child number two gets to stay at the restaurant with Mommy, then the impact is even stronger.

   At the very first sign of a disturbance, remove your child from the table and take him to a private area. Get down on his level and reiterate your expectations, as well as what will happen if they are not met. Be calm and clear. Use few words: *"In this restaurant you may not yell or cry loudly. It needs to stop right now. This is your only warning. If it happens again, you will be taken home."*

   If it happens again, take him home! Now, here is the kicker. Make sure that you and your husband or you and the baby go out to dinner the very next night, or even breakfast the next morning. Yes, hire a sitter! Tell the child: *"Daddy and I are going to a restaurant, but we are not taking you with us. Last night you were not able to use your inside voice, you had a tantrum at the restaurant, and I had to take you home. So you may not go with us today. We will try again another day."*

Then go! And finally, the day after that (yes, three meals in a row or three days in succession), invite your son to try again at the restaurant. This method may stretch your budget, but it gives the child the chance to feel the consequence of his initial restaurant tantrum and then have the chance to be successful.

- **Comebacks for the public's rude judgment.** It is amazing how often complete strangers feel free to make judgmental remarks about our parenting. If you're stumped for a response, try the following:

  1. To the woman who criticizes the way you are handling (or not handling) your child, say, *"Thank you for your opinion."*
  2. To the person who lets loose on you with a tongue-lashing, you just may need to say, *"Do you feel better now?"*
  3. Just to make yourself feel better because you are embarrassed, say, *"You must remember what it is like to have a three-year-old. Being a mom is really hard work."* Then throw up your hands and move away.

- **Learn this mantra:** *"I don't know these people, and I will never see them again."* Remember this: your first job always is to be your child's protector and his advocate. He is absorbing whatever you do. He is more important than any stranger you meet in public. Do what needs to be done.

CHAPTER 3

*   *   *   ❖   *   *   *

"It's All Molly's Fault!"

Sibling Issues

Your expectations for your children's relationships are highly influenced by what you bring to your role as parent. It's what you have packed in that set of Samsonite previously discussed. What did your parents say to you and your brother when you were growing up? How were you punished when you hit your sister or grabbed her toys? Were you forced to share your clothes? Did you share a room? Were you spanked? The template you use for dealing with your children's relationships came with you in your two-suiter.

In retrospect, you are really glad that you had siblings when you were growing up, right? But at the time, every now and again, you probably wished that the little creep would fall off the planet. The rivalrous feelings and uneven nature of sibling relationships are the stuff of family folklore. Everyone has tales to tell.

While single children grow up to be happy, well-functioning adults, there are few people who question the benefits that having siblings brings to a developing child. Sibling relationships provide a ready-made scrimmage for the sport of interacting with others. They offer continual practice for many of the social skills that your child will use when she is out in the real world. Siblings necessarily learn about taking turns and sharing, giving and taking, standing up for themselves, giving in, and compromising. Living with siblings presents regular opportunities to learn to delay gratification and to tolerate frustration, two of the most important lessons young children must learn. In short, living with a sibling introduces, educates, and sensitizes the child to relationships of all kinds.

Every parent longs for a peaceful household where siblings enjoy being together, respect one another and one another's possessions, and play happily together for hours on end. Wake up! There is no such thing. The truth is, all siblings squabble. In the produce section of the market, where news is spread and conversation happens, you *never* hear the following: *"My four-year-old and my six-year-old get along just perfectly! They are the best of friends; they never argue, and they always share!"* What you are more likely to hear is: *"My children are driving me crazy. The big one picks on the little one; the little one worships the big one. I just can't handle it. I can't believe I actually wanted two children."*

Sibling Rivalry

For the first two years of your firstborn's life, she was the center of your world. Whatever she wanted, she pretty much got, right then and there. No one else was there with needs to be met. Then the second baby arrived. Wow, was Number One in for a surprise!

Sibling rivalry can begin the moment the second child comes home from the hospital. Sometimes you won't see evidence of it until the younger child begins to encroach on the first child's life, reaching, then crawling, and then walking into her space.

Sibling rivalry is natural and inevitable. In fact, it is just so normal that perhaps it needs a different name. There is something about the expression "sibling rivalry" that implies that it shouldn't be happening . . . if only you did the "right thing." While there certainly are things you can do to encourage positive sibling relationships, the bickering, fighting, and competition are just part of what happens among siblings. When you choose to have more than one child, you have entered the zone of *"sibling shenanigans."* It encompasses the good, the bad, the ugly, and the fabulously unforgettable.

At the core of most sibling issues is every child's normal and natural desire to have her parents all to herself. Even if the second child arrives when the first is still "too young to know better," even if both parents work outside the home and the child is accustomed to being with a caregiver full-time, the parent is still the treasure, and the child still wishes to have her all to herself. Learning to share their parents is not unlike any of the other kinds of sharing that children need to learn, but the stakes are higher. Once the child sees that she has to share her most precious possessions—her mommy and daddy—the shenanigans spring forth.

Couple this desire to have Mommy and Daddy all for herself with the child's still-immature ability to delay gratification, and there is trouble brewing. *"I want my mommy, and I want her NOW!"*

Sibling issues are fueled by other aspects of your child's development as well as some forces of life and nature. One of these is the child's very basic fear that there will not be enough. Your egocentric little one just looks out for herself. She wants what she wants, when she wants it, and she wants all of it. She is just learning to recognize that other children have needs and wants too. And when she understands that other children might have wants too, her needs become even more immediate. Her priority is getting herself filled up, getting enough.

Watch preschool children at a Play-Doh table. One child sits down and grabs all four balls of Play-Doh. She wants it all for herself. A second child comes to the table, and the first makes absolutely no attempt to share. If she has to give up even a tiny bit, it's a huge sacrifice. You would think you had asked her to give up one of her hands for her friend. Among siblings, the child's having enough usually means that she has more than her sibling.

Another factor that can lead to sibling shenanigans is every child's basic preference for receiving over giving. The joy that comes from giving and from sharing comes with age and experience. It is a grown-up pleasure, one that needs to develop over time, alongside her ability to empathize. To expect that a child will feel pleasure watching her baby brother receive a gift is simply not reasonable. She wants all those gifts for herself . . . even if she doesn't *want* them!

To happily give up something that she loves so her sibling can have a turn is, well, a ridiculous thought. That doesn't mean, however, that you should stop encouraging sharing and caring; it means that it is well within the range of normal for the child to balk and resort to some form of sibling shenanigans in retaliation.

Dealing with Sibling Fighting

There are four things you must understand in order to successfully to deal with your children's fighting.

1. Life is not fair!

I think that you already know this, but you are still trying to make it fair. Understand that nothing you can do will make it that way, not in the eyes of your children, anyway. Remember, your child wants enough of the good stuff, and that isn't always possible. So she sees life as being not fair.

It is incumbent upon you, the parent, to *try* to make things fair. Your children need to see you exert the effort. Leading your children to believe that life is fair by working overtime to make it so, however, will certainly not prepare them for reality. Fair doesn't mean that things will work out the way you or your children want them to.

The problem comes when you, the parent, equate fairness with equality. Very often being fair means that things are not equal for your children. For example, one of your children needs shoes, and so you buy them for her. Your other child complains, *"That's not fair! I want shoes too."* You know that you will buy your second child shoes when he needs them. That is being fair, but it is not being equal at that moment.

2. Your children have different parents.

You are a different parent to each of your children, and your spouse is too. There are reasons for this truth. Your firstborn is your "practice child," and everything you did was the first time with her. You are an old pro by the time you have the next child and are a very different parent by virtue of experience.

In addition, each of your children has a different temperament, and you respond and relate to each based on who she is. In fact, you are a different parent to each child because each needs you to be so. You have different children, so you treat them differently.

3. In every family there is a "rotating pill."

In every family in which there is more than one child, someone is always being a "pill." This reality certainly isn't written anywhere, but it sure is true. At any given time, one child is more demanding, needier, or going through a difficult stage. That child is in the "pill position," otherwise known as the "rotating pill." The amazing thing is that almost never do you have two children in the pill position at the same time, unless both are ill. When one child is in the pill position, the other one is a perfect angel: *"Look at me, Mommy, I am being good."* Expect that at some point, each of your children will have a turn in the pill position.

4. It will all come out in the wash.

This was one of my mother's expressions. I offer it as reassurance that, in the end, each of your children will get as much of you as she needs. The attention, time, and love that you give each of your children on any given day will vary. The child in the pill position will need and get more. If you were to keep a tally sheet, you would see that, in the end, there *is* some kind of equality, if there are no outstanding problems or issues.

So, why do siblings fight? The simplest answer to this question is also the most obvious. Siblings fight because they can . . . and they will! They'll fight over possessions, territory, and out of boredom, or because it's a habit. They may even find it empowering to squabble. The closer in age they are, the more they'll fight. There will also be some sharing, laughter, and great times, of course. Those aren't the times that drive you nuts. It's all that bickering!

Tips and Scripts for Dealing with Sibling Fights

Each family will have different feelings and a varied tolerance for sibling fighting, based in part on what is in their luggage. But a clear policy about *no hurting* is crucial; children need to feel protected. Children younger than three will be challenged by that rule and will need help not only with their impulse control but also with expressing their powerful feelings acceptably.

- **Use a timer; it's magic!** Since many of young children's fights are over property and territory, and since the young child's ability to share is underdeveloped, a kitchen timer may be useful, especially when the young children are close in age. In the eyes of the child, the timer is fair, insuring that each child gets a turn. This also relieves you of the job of deciding whose turn it is. Explain: *"When the bell rings (or when the sand on top runs out), it will be Ruthy's turn to use the eggbeater. And then, Robert, it will be your turn again. And then Ruthy's, and then yours. We will set the timer for every turn."*

  At first, the children's attention will be on the timer, watching and waiting for the turn to be up. Since it was the timer and not you who said it was the other child's turn, giving up the toy is usually easier. Then you can quickly reset the timer for the next turn. Make sure the timer is set for a very short period of time, just a minute at the most, at first. The toy or item of interest needs to change hands several times in order for each child to grasp the concept that she will get another turn soon.

- **Unless there is blood, butt out!** When both children are older than three, stay out of their fights. Left to their own devices, getting no attention for their fights, siblings will find a way to coexist, and that will likely include fighting now and then. Of course, I do not believe that real physical fighting should be tolerated. When you hear one of your children scream, *wait* before you run in. Do not call out anyone's name. (If it is an emergency, you will know it after a second or two, but let those few seconds pass.) Your children might actually work out whatever is going on. After the initial pause, you may state: *"I hope everything is okay in there."*

If it isn't, you will certainly hear about it, but do not invite an explanation or tattling. By making this statement, you are letting your children know that you are close by, but you are not jumping in to solve their problem.

If you see that someone is hurt, help her first, as needed. In so doing you model what is most important to you: physical safety. Attend just to her hurt, ignoring the tattling and complaining. Say: *"Let's get some ice for your boo-boo."* Or, *"Do you need a Band-Aid?"*

Make no comment about what has happened or what one child did or didn't do. Do not give attention to the aggressor. She may not be the child who is at fault. Remember, it is likely that you do not know the whole story; you only heard the ending.

Because it is almost never clear what really happened in physical fights, it may be best to separate the children. Tell them: *"I don't know what happened, and I do not want to know. I do know that we have a no-hurting rule in this family. The rule was broken, so now you may not be together. Hilary, you go in your room, and Phoebe, you go in your room. You both need to cool off. I will let you know when five minutes are up and you can try again to be together without hurting."* Ignore all protests.

There are occasions when one sibling, completely unprovoked, is dangerously aggressive with the other. It may be the result of an issue that the sibling is having that has absolutely nothing to do with the other child. In this rare case, the aggressor must be separated. Tell her: *"I do not know what happened. I do know that we have a firm rule of no hurting, and you have just broken that rule. You have lost the privilege of being with your sister. Cool off in your room for a while. You can come out when you think you can follow our rule."*

Leave it in the aggressor's court about when she comes out from her *cooling off*, even if it is only one minute later. She is the one who has to be responsible for her actions, not you. *"You may come out when you think you are ready to be with your sister without hurting."* If it happens again, then *you* will determine the length of her stay.

Take pains not to pay any attention to the victim, unless there is real physical damage that needs attention. Now it is only about the unacceptable behavior of the aggressor. By sympathizing with the victim, you are behaving like a judge, and while you will not tolerate hurting, you do not take sides. Neither the victim nor the aggressor must see that the victim is "getting you." Such a response will merely perpetuate the effectiveness of fighting as a way to hook you in.

If a child is repeatedly unable to curb his physical fighting, it is a good idea to seek help from a mental health professional. This behavior is now beyond the bounds of typical sibling shenanigans.

- **Do not single out one child.** Resist the urge to call out one child's name (and that's usually the older child, isn't it?). If you are unable to stop yourself, then you may say: *"I hope you are able to work out your problem in there."* Such a comment lets your children know that you are aware that something is up and that you expect them to work out the problem without your showing favoritism or labeling one offspring the aggressor or "bad child" and the victim the "good child."

- **Teach *conflict resolution* . . . (but it may not work!).** Knowing how to compromise is not a skill with which children are born. Children need to be taught how to resolve a problem so that both children are satisfied and no one feels like the loser. Conflict resolution techniques only work when both children are able to articulate their story and their feelings.

> The lesson starts with your nonjudgmental, calm involvement using only one word: *"Stop!"* or *"Wait!"* and getting between the children. Put them in different chairs across a table or on opposite ends of the couch, if necessary. Each should have her own space.
>
> Make no comment on what you think happened. One child's needs cannot be put above another's. Both children must be acknowledged. One at a time, turn to each child and say, *"Tell me what happened."* Insist that each wait while the other talks.
>
> Then repeat what you have heard. *"Amanda says that she was*

playing with the whirligig and you took it from her. Is that correct, Amanda? And Matthew says that the whirligig was on the floor and he picked it up to use it. Is that correct, Matthew?"

Wait for the responses and corrections, repeat them, and then ask, *"What should we do about this problem?"*

Remember that conflict resolution takes time and patience. The children need to know that you have all the time in the world, that you will wait until they come to some agreement. Usually each child just wants to win; neither really cares about the whirligig at all. The fight has been about getting your attention, but you did not take sides. More than likely, the fight will fizzle out; one child or the other gets bored or is ready to move on when the thrill is gone.

Even if you have taken the time to repeatedly teach conflict resolution, one or both of your children may not be able to use those skills in a given situation. One may be too tired, the other may be too hungry, or both may be spent. After all, they are at home, the very place where they can let it all hang out.

If you have two tenacious children, you may have to wait it out, even suggest a possible solution if no one seems to be coming up with one. *"Shall we use the timer, so each of you gets a turn with the whirligig?"* Of course, in the service of fueling the fight, someone might now bicker about who gets the first turn. You can draw straws, you can pick a number, or you might just make the call. The children have learned two things. The first is a compromise technique. The second lesson is that there isn't a payoff to Mommy or Daddy getting involved. It takes time, it's kind of boring, and there is not much attention to be gained.

- **Send each child to a different room.** While your first reaction to fighting should always be to ignore, ignore, ignore, if it gets to the point where you absolutely cannot tolerate the bickering, you can send each child to her separate bedroom or to any two different rooms for a cooling-off period. This is not a time-out or a punishment. The message is that there needs to be a break in the action, a cooling-off period. Tell them: *"I don't know what is going on, and I don't want to know, but clearly you both need to cool off. Jason, you need to take five minutes in the den, and*

Hannah, you need to take five minutes in the laundry room. I will let you know when the five minutes are up."

- **Send both children to the same room.** Once again, your first response is to ignore, ignore, ignore, so your children will learn that there is no payoff to their fighting; it is their job to solve their conflicts. But if you cannot take it, in the service of putting the ball solidly in their court, another option is to send them away together to work it out: *"I don't know what is going on, and I don't want to know, but your bickering is driving me nuts. Both of you go into that room* (a small room that is neutral) *and work it out. You may come out when you are done."* I give them less than a minute.

- **As a last resort, remove the object of the fight.** Only as a last resort, and only if all else has failed, you may need to remove the toy over which the children are fighting. Say: *"I am going to remove this train until you can solve this problem so that you are both happy."* It is crucial that you not act angry or fed up when you step in and remove the toy. You are looking for a solution, not a punishment.

- **Give yourself a time-out.** In case you haven't clearly gotten the message, the best response to fighting is to ignore it. However, if that is just impossible, another option is to *remove yourself* from the scene. Say: *"I don't know what is going on, and I don't want to know, but I can't take the noise of the bickering. I am going into my room alone where it is quieter."*

  I can guarantee that as soon as you have closed and secured your door, you will hear frantic footsteps down the hall. *"Let us in, Mommy. We're done. Let us in."* This is the point at which you open the door and come out, as if nothing has happened. No finger wagging, no tongue-lashings about getting along and not fighting. It is done. Go back to what you were doing.

Car Fighting

The close quarters of a car magnify sibling fights to the point of driving any parent nuts. Since you probably don't have a chauffeur screen in your car—the kind that separates the limo driver's seat from the passengers in the back—chances are at some point your children's shenanigans in the backseat will be a call to arms. Of course, the best thing to do is ignore it; it will stop eventually. But that's really hard, I know.

Tips and Scripts for Handling Car Fights

- **Be consistent in your reaction to car bickering.** Each of us has a different tolerance level for car fighting. Regardless of what yours is, you must be consistent about it, and you must make your children aware of it. Tell them: *"If you two fight that is none of my business. But you may not be so loud in your fights that you distract me from driving safely."*

  Do not let it go one day and jump down the children's throats the next. If you are having a particularly bad day and cannot tolerate even a small amount of typical car fighting, let your children know in advance: *"I have a huge headache today and I will not be able to stand any fighting at all. I need you to cooperate and control yourselves in the car. This is your fair warning."* If you say it like you mean it, they will get the message and comply.

- **When the fighting hits your limit, you must react.** Pull your car over to the side of the road. Stop the engine, turn around, and say, *"I cannot drive safely with the noise and distraction from your fighting. Do you think you can stop?"* Wait for a response. If you get an obligatory but insincere yes, and you see that the fighting seems to be on the verge of continuing, you may add: *"I will wait until you are going to stop."*

  Then pull out your book, rummage through your purse, but do not move, look back, or pay any attention to the fighters. When the fight appears to have genuinely stopped, get going again. If it continues, pull over to the side of the road again. Stop the car, get out, close your door. Go to the rear passenger door, open it, and say: *"I will not drive anywhere while this loud fighting is going on. I am going to wait until you are done."*

  Then stand by the side of the road, not looking at your children at all. Turn your back on the car. Breathe. Go through your wallet . . . anything. When it seems that things have calmed down, get back in the car and continue. Regardless of how late this action will make you, follow through. It gives your children a very clear message about what is and isn't acceptable in your car.

- **Work hard not to appear angry.** If you let your exasperation show, you will take the car fighting to a different level. Children may not fight in the car because it is the rule, it isn't safe, and it is within their control. Do not pollute the message by making it be about pleasing you.

Tips and Scripts for Avoiding Sibling Fights

While fighting among siblings is to be expected, there are a number of things you can do to minimize them.

- **Allow children to own their own toys.** When children feel a sense of ownership, they are usually much more willing to share what they have. Give each child a bin for her toys and allow her to control these items. Label all toys. (I can hear you groaning, but do it! Use initials or color coding.) Make it clear that each bin is off limits to the other child. The child will be less threatened by the presence of the sibling when she knows that her things are hers.

- **Give each child her own space.** In the same way that each child deserves to own her own things, each child needs to have her own space in your home. Just like adults, children like to "nest." Even if you live in a tiny house and three children share a room, there is still a way to identify each child's space. Designate separate drawers for each child. Divide up the closet by hanging cloth or ribbons from a hanger to show that the hanging space beyond that point belongs to a certain child. Sometimes an older child who shares a bedroom needs a small desk in the corner of your office, just for her. Having her very own place emphasizes and reinforces a child's sense of being an individual.

- **Do not force children to share.** It is unreasonable to expect a child under the age of three to share, and it may be hard for four-, five-, and six-year-olds as well. Genuine sharing comes from the heart, and it takes a long time to cultivate. Insisting that a child share causes the child to hold on more tightly to the desired object and often creates resentment, which can lead to that dreaded bickering. Try saying: *"That flashlight belongs to Mimi, and you need to give it back to her. Then we will ask her if you can have a turn. I think she might let you try it out for a quick minute."* You may need to help her give it back, replacing it with something else.

   In saying this, you are not only confirming Mimi's rightful ownership, but you are also reassuring Mimi that Melissa won't have her flashlight for very long. Then you turn to Mimi and ask, *"Mimi, can Melissa have a short turn with your flashlight?"* My guess is that Mimi will say yes. Melissa will have her turn and Mimi will quickly grab it right back. That's okay. At least she gave her a turn. And if she says no, you can say: *"It looks like Mimi doesn't feel like sharing right now. Maybe later she will. Let's go see what else you and I can find to play with."* You have validated Mimi, you are supporting Melissa, and you are avoiding an explosion.

- **Be an advocate for the older child.** Even though I am a middle child, I am a strong supporter of the oldest child. Sometimes she really needs to be protected from the younger one, the marauder. This poor girl has had to cut up her portion of her favorite thing—you!—time and time again. And each time, her share of the Mommy and Daddy booty gets smaller. Support your oldest child by being her advocate.

   1. **Allow the oldest child privileges that the younger ones don't have.** In most families, the oldest child has more responsibilities than the others because she can handle them; allow her plenty of privileges to offset all those responsibilities.
   2. **Never say *"You are older, you should know better."*** While the older child usually does know better, it discounts her feelings. At the same time, it will surely take the thrill out of being the oldest and cause resentment toward the younger one.
   3. **Never defend the little one by saying, *"He's just a baby, he couldn't help it. He didn't know any better."*** This comment, while it may be true, puts you in the position of siding with little Jack and not understanding the older child. You would get a whole lot more mileage out of saying, *"Look what Jack did. I sure wish he would get bigger and learn to be careful of your special buildings."*
   4. **Help her to protect her things from the littler ones.** Provide a high shelf for storage, or suggest and provide a high table on which to work, since it is not possible to get the little one to keep his hands off anything he can reach.
   5. **Do not insist that the older child include or play with the younger one all the time.** Doing so can cause resentment and impede their developing a spontaneous and pleasant relationship. Let the children play together on their terms, not on yours.
   6. **Teach the older sibling to remove herself when the little one is bothering her, rather than run to you for help.** She can say, *"I don't want to play with you when you bother me,"* and go to her room and close the door, if necessary. What the younger child wants most is the attention of his older sibling.

7. **Empower the older sibling to take control of her own privacy in "legal" ways.** Help her to make a sign for her door that says KEEP OUT on one side, and COME IN on the other. A drawing of a traffic light with the red colored in on one side and the green on the other works for the child who is not yet a reader. The older sibling will feel powerful and protected.

8. **Identify and acknowledge how hard it can be to have a younger sibling.** *"Little brothers sure can be a bother sometimes, can't they?"*

• **Give children enough time alone with you.** Try to spend separate time with each child every week. In a perfect world, I would recommend you do this every day, but you and I know that is just not possible. Giving the child the attention she craves and deserves will go a long way toward calming sibling battles for your attention. Separate, or "Special Time," does not necessarily mean going out, spending money, or having a field trip. In fact, it is more effective if spent *in* the home. The idea is that you are choosing to spend time with your child over everything else—the phone, the laundry, the dinner preparations, the computer, and especially the other children. Do something that your child values. Sit on the floor of her room, even if she isn't. That position makes you more available. Ask her what she wants to do. If she doesn't know, suggest: *"I want to do whatever you want to do, because I just want to be with you and no one else."*

Just a chat is good enough! Twenty minutes is sufficient. The message is clear: *I want to be with you, and nothing else is that important right now.*

• **Avoid comparisons like the plague.** While comparisons in families with more than one child are inevitable, they are poisonous. If you must make them, do it out of earshot of your children. Negative comparisons leave a child feeling that in your mind, she is somehow inferior to her sibling. While parents feel that a negative comparison might motivate the child, it usually backfires, causing resentment toward the child to whom she has been compared. Positive comparisons can be just as bad. Holding one child up to the other only makes her feel that her position is tenuous and that, when the other child rises to her level, they will have switched places.

• **Offer praise to each child when praise is due.** Don't feel as if you have to praise them both in the same breath. You may compliment one child on the way she has controlled her body at the dinner table, and the other one pipes up with, *"What about me?"* You say, *"Right now I am just talking about Shelby."* (For a discussion about praise, see chapter 1, page 15.)

- **Allow your children to have separate relationships outside of the family and at home.** Each child deserves to have the run of the play-room and toys sometimes without having to include the sibling. You can say: *"I am going to make sure that you and Mandy can play by yourselves when she comes to play. I will watch little Davey, and I will not let him bother you. But I would like you to include him for a little while. Would you like to do that at the beginning or at the end of the playdate?"* Then you need to keep your word and occupy little Davey. Likewise, when one sibling is invited to a birth-day party or a playdate at someone else's house, do not drag your other child along.

- **Take children out separately as well as together.** In most families, the older child has a pretty busy schedule, and the younger ones either get dragged along or left at home. Each of your children deserves to have an experience with you outside of the home without the other children. This is easy to do with the firstborn, but most families cringe at the idea of taking out the younger one and leaving the older sibling at home. Your oldest child needs to learn that, just as you take her to ka-rate alone, so you take her brother to Music and Mush all by himself. It's a hard but important lesson and will go a long way toward helping your children see that each is valued and gets some of you, the trea-sured booty.

- **Allow your children to be angry at one another.** Allowing your children to be enemies also gives them permission to be friends. Sib-lings getting angry at one another is a big part of growing up in a family. It only becomes a problem when parents don't allow normal anger to surface, run its course, and dissipate. Anger that has not been expressed causes resentment. Sometimes allowing the child to be angry enables her to get over it. Honoring and validating her feelings often helps to diffuse them. When your children are angry at one another, acknowl-edge it but don't try to make it go away. Say: *"You are really angry at your brother. You didn't like it when he spoiled your game. That was lousy. After a while, maybe you won't feel so angry."*

It is a mistake to insist that your siblings "kiss and make up." In order to get along, siblings need to experience being together during all kinds of weather, good times and bad, angry feelings and happy.

Do not force your children to apologize to one another. In so doing you are, actually, teaching them to lie. Most times the child is not at all sorry. She is glad she hit her brother. It would be more effective if you insisted that the aggressor find a way to demonstrate her apology, rather than falsely stating it. Say to the older child who has transgressed: *"You need to find a way to help your brother to feel better. You can bring him his blankie or you could sit and look at a book with him."*

Say to a younger child who has caused the problem: *"You need to help your sister to fix her picture. You can bring her a new piece of paper or help her to put the caps on her pens."*

In so doing, the child is not losing face but is learning the lesson of helping to repair the damage she may have done.

- **Catch your children getting along.** When you notice your children treating one another kindly, let them know how terrific you think it is. Then take it a step further. Chances are your children have heard you on the phone sharing your frustration about their fighting. Do an about-face and make sure your children hear you bragging about how well they get along.

- **Share stories about you and your siblings when you were growing up.** Children love to hear stories about their parents, especially ones that demonstrate that you've felt the same things they feel—the hurt and rage at being picked on by an older sibling, the annoyance of having a baby sibling who was a pain. Sharing how you felt about these experiences helps your child to know that her feelings are understood, and that she is not alone.

Tattling

No one likes a tattletale. They are perceived as weak and wimpy by their peers, and they are annoying to their parents. The funny thing is that though tattling is easy to stop, parents are the ones who perpetuate the behavior.

Children love to tattle because it works: you are once again hooked in as the person who solves the problems. The responsibility of working it out is no longer with the child.

There is a good reason why tattling usually begins around the age of four. This is when the child's conscience begins to develop. It is also when children really grasp the idea of rules and have a strong interest in who follows them and who doesn't. So sometimes when a child tattles, she is checking out the rules. *"Simon took more than two crackers"* is really Julia's way of saying, *"I followed the rule; I took only two crackers."*

Sometimes tattling is the child's way of confirming the rule. *"Simon is going outside without his shoes on."* There should actually be a question mark at the end of that tattle, because she is really asking, *"Is it okay for us to go outside without our shoes on?"*

Of course, among siblings, tattling can easily be a way of getting a brother in trouble or making the tattler look good by comparison, thereby gaining points with the parent. You remember that trick, don't you?

Tattling works in multiple ways at once. When Julia says, *"Simon ate a piece of Halloween candy and you told us we had to wait until after dinner,"* she is reminding herself of the rule. In addition, she is letting you know she is following it; she is checking to make sure the rule still applies and to see if you are being consistent; she is getting her brother in trouble; and, best of all, she is hooking you in. Tattling can be powerful stuff. It's no wonder that children do it!

Tips and Scripts for Eliminating Tattling

- **Make the decision not to accept tattling.** This sounds much easier to do than it is. You have been receiving your children's tattling for a long time. It is a habit for them and for you. You don't even stop to think about it. It happens and you automatically respond. Ending tattling has everything to do with your decision not to receive it.

- **State the rule: *There is no tattling.*** Tell your kids: *"In this family there is no tattling. I only want to know if there is danger, an emergency, or something is very wrong."* Then you offer an example or two. *"If your baby brother puts a small toy in his mouth, if someone is badly hurt, if the toilet bowl is overflowing, then I want you to tell me about it. These are emergencies."*

- **Know that it will take time for the children to learn the difference between *reporting* (because of danger) and *tattling*.** As your child adjusts to the new system, you may need to point this out to her:

"That is not something I need to know," delivered without reprimand or anger, is a clear message.

- **Do not reprimand for tattling.** Remember, your child is just learning a new system. Reprimanding her for tattling will not teach her, it will make her feel bad. The point of the lesson is not to tattle, and the reprimand will shift the focus from not tattling to not making Mommy or Daddy angry.

- **Respond to tattling with one word.** The absolutely most effective response to tattling is the following, stated blandly and very matter-of-factly: *"Oh."* This response tells the child you have heard her and you are not responding. Take pains with your tone in answering. There is no question mark at the end—*"Oh?"*—because that implies that you are asking to hear more. And there is no exclamation mark (punctuated with raised eyebrow), *"Oh!"* because that offers a judgment. You must not absorb any of what your child has said.

- **Be consistent.** Not responding is difficult because it is easy to let down your guard and fall back on your old habit of solving your children's issues.

- **Follow up later.** You may need to follow up on something about which your child has tattled. But since you are working on not responding to tattling, it must be done later. A good deal of time later, you might want to say: *"You are correct, Julia. It is never okay to go outside without shoes on. You do know our rule."* Here, the emphasis is on Julia and not on her rule-breaking-brother, Simon.

Tips for Encouraging Close Sibling Relationships

The greatest antidote to sibling shenanigans is to create a solid family base.

- **Create regular opportunities for just your family to be together.** While it may be more fun for *you* to go on outings and vacations with another family, it is not always in the best interest of your family. When you go somewhere only with your family, your children are left with just one another. It is amazing how well the children will get along if there is no one else with whom to play. You will also be creating family memories of great times (because who fights in Hawaii or at Disneyland?) together *as a family.* Even today, all three of my adult children will tell you that their favorite memory and still their favorite thing to do is to go on a family vacation. There is just nothing like it!

- **Create family rituals.** Family rituals also make unforgettable family memories, from Thursday Game Night and Sunday Morning Bagels to rainy day movies and making snowmen after the first snow. My family used to pile in the car in our pajamas every Christmas Eve and comb the city for the best Christmas lights. This ritual lasted until our children went off to college!

- **Allow your children to have secrets together, behind your back.** Sometimes, for the sake of building their relationship, you need to turn your back and allow the kids to break the rules together. Partners in crime are, after all, partners. A client of mine tells the wonderful story about her three children who stole gum out of her purse, right behind her back, as she sat on the stairs. She knew full well what was happening, but she also knew what fun the children were having, so she pretended not to know as she heard them giggling and sneaking around. Imagine the memory those children have of the time they got away with stealing the gum out of Mommy's purse.

. . . ❖ . . .

CHAPTER 4

"How Many Bites 'Til I Can Get Dessert?"

Children's Eating Habits and Behaviors

For most of us, food is about a whole lot more than nutrition. Food and eating issues are packed away in one of the pieces of luggage you are hauling around from your upbringing. Inside are echoes of your parents begging you to eat, forcing you to eat, not letting you leave the table until your plate is clean, or bribing you with dessert. There are scenes from your childhood dinner table, admonishments about putting your napkin on your lap and not burping out loud, squabbles about who gets to sit in the "good chair," and warnings about having to stay seated until everyone is finished.

Then there is the misguided notion that your skill as a parent is confirmed by the foods your child consumes. Somehow you think that if the child eats three somewhat square meals a day, including a small representative from each of the five food groups, then you are a good parent. *One baby tree of broccoli? Hey, it's green, he ate it, and I am scoring big in my mom job.*

Each of us has food associations. Eating certain foods reminds us of specific people (Grandma's chicken soup), events (hot dogs with pickle relish on the Fourth of July), and holidays (what's Christmas without fruitcake?). And while your child might rather eat worms than try lima beans now, later on he may eat them because they remind him so fondly of what you made every Sunday night. My friend Ralph tells me that he absolutely hated okra as a child and wouldn't be found dead eating it. But okra was a part of the Sephardic culture in which he was raised. Now he loves it and begs his wife to make it. It reminds Ralph, now eighty years old, of his childhood. You just never know what kind of an eater your child will be when he is an adult. At some point he will take risks and eat food he previously never even smelled.

In truth, most parents don't really have a clue about what is reasonable for a child to eat or how he should behave at the dinner table at each age. Food, love, and control seem to be inextricably connected. It's really tough to view each as separate and exclusive from the others.

Food and Control

With young children you can call it *control* or you can call it a *power struggle*. At this age, they are the same thing, often manifesting in the same way. At the root of a child's thrust toward growing up is growing away. From the earliest signs of movement, the child begins to move away from you, crawling off to explore uncharted territory.

John Bowlby, the renowned British psychologist who gave us "attachment theory," likened the child's movement away from the parent to the petals of a daisy. You are the yellow part in the center, and the child's path away from you traces the lines of the white petals: away and back to check in. Away and back to check in. As the child grows, the petals get longer, as the child takes bigger risks, moving farther away from you: *I am figuring out who I am. I am moving away from you, but I always keep you in sight.*

One of the growing child's greatest tasks is learning to be separate from you, both physically and emotionally. It is what becoming an individual is all about. Separateness is something that evolves, one baby step at a time, built on repeated, successful experiences of practicing one's growing autonomy. This effort goes on and on and on, from toddlerhood all the way to the child leaving for college, and even beyond for some adult children these days.

In the growing years, a big part of that practice at being an individual comes in the form of needing control and power. And boy, does it ever come! It's not fun. For a preschool-age child, one of the biggest ways to exhibit his power is to show his particular—and I mean very particular—desires. They fall into four general areas: eating, sleeping, talking, and eliminating. In fact, even older children who have "control issues" usually exhibit them in one of these areas. Notice that these are all activities where one person absolutely cannot control another person. Think about it—you cannot force another person to eat. You can put the food in his mouth, but you sure can't make him swallow. When you are four years old, there aren't a whole lot of areas where you can dig in your heals and insist on having it your way, but food is one of them!

Food is also a way for your child to engage you. Your child craves your attention in any form he can get—negative attention, positive attention, it's all attention. The food wars will certainly attract that.

So remember, in discussing the stuff that kids will or won't put in their mouths, often it isn't about food. It's about control and about getting your attention. Hear this: Don't fight about food! Don't even go there. You are not going to win.

The Food They Eat, aka Nutrition

One of your goals as a parent is to help your child to develop a healthy relationship with food. It is a worthy goal, one that is influenced not only by your childhood experiences but also by your own tastes and ideas about food.

The nutritional needs of young children, who grow in ways that are predictable and distinctive from adults, are different from those of adults. Experts worry most about children getting the amounts of iron and calcium their growing bodies need. But getting a child to eat just what she needs is no small task, nutritional requirements aside.

Although picky eaters drive most parents wild (see page 72 for more about Picky Eaters), being a picky eater does not put a child at risk for overall nutritional deficiencies. While these children might take in fewer nutrients than more adventurous eaters, their nutritional needs somehow get met, except in extreme cases.

The one thing that I can tell you for sure is that most toddlers enter toddlerhood (at twelve to fifteen months) eating a wider variety of food than they will eat when they leave toddlerhood (around three and a half years old). In fact, it is amazing how most American preschool-age children subsist on some version of the "Orange Diet": macaroni and cheese, pizza, grilled cheese, plain pasta with butter, chicken nuggets, Cheezits (or Cheetos or Goldfish), and carrots, the lone vegetable!

When I was a preschool teacher, preparing each day's snack was always one of the morning activities in which the children could participate. How funny it was that the child whose mother claimed she *"didn't eat anything"* was always the first at the cooking table, helping to prepare raw cabbage, green peppers, celery, cucumbers, zucchini, and so on. She then gobbled up those veggies and begged for more, even the purple cabbage! The fact that children often will eat various foods in different environments or when they are with different people certainly speaks to the reality that issues about food are often not about food.

Lack of knowledge and unrealistic expectations often contribute to a parent's frustration in trying to get their child to eat. Somewhere along the line, most parents have come to believe that in order to be healthy, children need to sample each of the five food groups every day. Sound the buzzer, please: this is false. What is important is that you look at the nutritional picture over the course of a few days or even weeks. A much more reasonable view, according to Pam Siegel, nutritionist and family therapist, is that children ought to eat a variety of foods, perhaps including a sampling from each of the five food groups, over a seventy-two-hour period. So, relax. If Robbie ate some salad two days ago, he is still good to go for veggies.

One of my favorite ways to reassure parents is to tell them about my son, Lucas. Now there was a picky eater. Today Lucas is a healthy, strapping man. But when he was growing up, he would not eat anything green, and I mean *anything*. The greenest thing that passed between his lips was lime yogurt. So much for green vegetables every day.

Young children also don't have adults' sense of timing about food. Tuna salad tastes just as good in the morning as it does at noon. Scrambled eggs are just fine at night. They learn food timing from daily life. It's a mistake to limit breakfast, lunch, and dinner foods to those times of day. If your children had more choices about what they could eat at various times, there might be fewer battles about food.

Children can be very fickle in their tastes. Food that was previously adored can be violently rejected almost overnight. One day your child looks at his lunch and screams, *"I hate peanut butter!"* to the same peanut butter and jelly sandwich on white bread with the crusts cut off that he has eaten every single day for the last six months. And that about-face is usually for a reason about which you have no idea . . . nor does he. One day your three-year-old loves pickles, liverwurst, curry, and calamari; the next day he won't touch any of them.

On the opposite end of the spectrum, children can be bingers too. They discover something that they like and they want it every day, maybe even every meal. They don't seem to tire of it. The amount of food that children eat can also vary tremendously. One day a child can put away as much food as a sumo wrestler. The next day he may have no appetite at all, and it isn't because he is full from the previous day. Often before a growth spurt, your child will eat voluminous amounts. He is ravenous and asks for food all day long. Then abruptly, his appetite falls off. Fatigue and sleep levels affect appetite too. Tired children are hungry children. At a loss to know what ails them, children will go for whatever they imagine will soothe them. Mood, as we all know, can affect appetite. Physical health will too.

Remember when your mother used to say, *"Your eyes are bigger than your stomach?"* She was right. Children aren't so good at measuring. Your child sees things in black and white, he wants a whole lot or a tiny bit. There is no in between. So, if macaroni is being served, and he is hungry, he wants an enormous mountain of mac.

Young children usually take the short view on food and eating. They have a limited ability to wait, and they want the food that catches their eye. The food that is most appealing to them is not at all necessarily the food that is best for them. It just doesn't get much better than a chocolate cupcake piled high with three inches of frosting.

Speaking of sugar, perhaps your first child didn't have any refined sugar until he was three years old. In fact, he didn't have any bleached flour, preservatives, or unnatural anything. His nutrition was carefully calibrated and very sound. You were in control until someone brought him a cookie with rainbow sprinkles on top for his third birthday. The cat was out of the bag. *"I love sugar!"*

Then your second child was born. While child number one didn't have sugar until he was three, child number two has her first lollipop before she takes her first step! It is much easier to restrict the foods that your first child eats than it is with your second or third child. Even parents with the best of intentions have to stop and reconsider the situation. Different kids, different ages, different circumstances, and different things work. You need to know what you are up against. It is darn near impossible to allow your five-year-old the gumdrops while offering your three-year-old the raisins.

Then there is salt. People are not born with a taste for things salty (or sugary); these are acquired tastes, and most of us love them both. There is a time and a place for children to have these foods . . . in moderation. The boundaries differ for each family. Strictly forbidding a food that the child is already aware exists will create a craving later on down the line. It will also set you up for plenty of power struggles with your child. Children who are given unreasonably strict limits about food (unrelated to allergies) will search out the forbidden fruit elsewhere. Learning to live within your reasonable limits about food is a lifelong lesson. Not only will the child learn to accept the limits, but he will, hopefully, acquire some lifelong nutrition habits as well.

Tips for Managing Your Child's Nutritious Food Intake at Home

- **Toddlers love plain food.** According to Leann Birch, Ph.D., professor and eating specialist at Pennsylvania State University, the child's preference for bland foods is likely a carryover from primitive times, when not eating potent-tasting foods prevented children from ingesting toxic substances. Your child is not alone!
- **Keep foods separate.** Most children don't like foods touching one another. I wish I could explain it, but I can't. Anything that is poured over toast is the kiss of death and will certainly go untouched on the plate. Save your casseroles for company. Children like to know what it is they are putting in their mouths.
- **Prepare a snack box.** Decide what "carb" snacks are okay for your child and package them in grab bags, ready to go. Keep a variety of grab bags in a snack box in the pantry right at your child's level. When it is snack time, bring out the snack box and allow him to choose from it. Often it is the power of being able to choose the food and grab it for himself that makes it tastier.
- **Remove the enemy.** Purge your pantry of the foods you do not want your child to have. If that is not possible, at least place these foods totally out of your child's sight, and be sure not to go after them when your child is around. Why do you think grocery stores put the sugary cereals at a child's eye level?

Teaching Children about Food

Soon after you brought your brand-new bundle of joy home from the hospital, you learned that the way to soothe him was with food, a diaper change, and sleep (his and yours). Already food consumption had a definition for the baby: *it makes me feel better.* And thereafter you stuck various things in his precious little mouth to stop that outrageous screaming—breast, bottle, juice, Cheerios, Goldfish, and so on as he got older and louder. Yes, the mouth is the center of the world for the infant. It is where he gets his needs met. Food and love come in via the mouth after screams and complaints have gone out.

Tips and Scripts for Teaching Your Child about Food

There does come a time, fairly early on, when parents need to teach children about food and its purpose in people's lives. A lesson might sound like this:

"We eat food when we feel hungry. Our stomach tells us that it is hungry, and so we eat. When we have eaten enough, our stomach gives us the signal to stop. That's what being full is."

"Eating food helps all the parts of our bodies to grow and work well. It helps us to grow muscle, to be fit, to feel good and strong. It helps our brains to be alert and to learn."

"Just like cars use gas to work, bodies need food to work. If we put juice into our car, it sure wouldn't run very well! We need to put foods into our bodies that help all of our parts to work well and that let our bodies grow to the size they are supposed to be."

Tips and Scripts for the Parent's Role in Eliminating the Food Battles with Your Child

Know that *you* play a role in the drama of food choices, mealtimes, and eating behaviors. Becoming aware of your contribution is the beginning of the lesson about how to stop the food battle.

- **Model the eating habits you want your child to have.** Parents spend a whole lot of time focusing on what the child should and shouldn't eat, and hardly give their own eating a thought. At four in the afternoon, you are ravenous and grab a handful of whatever is closest. You're thinking, *"It doesn't matter what I eat as long as Sarah is eating well."* You are your child's most powerful food model. Your child is watching and will want to have what you have and do what you do. So if you don't want your child to eat certain foods, don't eat them yourself (within her sight, earshot, or awareness). And if you don't want your child to drink soda, then you'd better change your own soda-drinking habits.

    If you stand at the counter to eat your meal, if you grab a snack from the car, you are teaching your child to do exactly the same thing. It is difficult to teach your child the importance of eating well and purposefully as part of being fit, to teach him the manners that surround our eating habits, if you do not model the ways in which we do that.

- **Have rules about where food is eaten and stick to them.** In this crazy-busy world, the leisurely meal eaten at the family dining room table accompanied by friendly chatter is but a tale from the past. Parents want their children to be mindful and not absentminded eaters, but they rarely do much to encourage that. Children who eat in front of the television, as they are rushing out the door to school, in the car, or as they are leaving school, aren't paying attention to eating. They are engaging in mindless, automatic eating that is an accompaniment to another activity. Eating needs to be purposeful. It is an activity in and of itself. The entertainment is the pleasant or interesting discussion that happens among people while you eat. Children should eat in the kitchen or dining room, at the big table or at their little table in the kitchen.

- **Do not ever make food a battleground.** When you fight with your children about food, the fight becomes the focus, rather than the food. Sometimes the child will actually refuse food he might otherwise eat (or want to eat) because the battle over it has begun. Not making food a battleground does not mean you have to give in, for example, allowing him to eat a dinner of his choice: it simply means you are not going to go to war. Insisting that a child eat a particular food, or just take a taste, is a call to arms for some children. You can refuse to fight and say, *"This is the dinner I have made. You can eat it or not."* No engagement. No battle. (And no worries, please, that your child will starve!) The child can focus on eating what you have offered or not. It need not become a battle with you. (See The Special Meal Chef, page 70, for more on this topic.)

- **Stop talking about food.** Serve the meal, sit down at the table, put your napkin on your lap, and talk about the weather! Don't talk about the meal. Hold your tongue. Your child will not eat as a result of anything you say. Your pre- and post-meal comments will only complicate the issue, taking it out of the realm of food and right into the realm of control.

- **No more "clean plate club"!** Coercion isn't a sound form of parenting. Not only does it set you up for a power struggle, but the child also learns to rely on others to tell him how much to eat and not pay attention to how full he feels.

- **Food should never be a reward or a punishment.** Every human being deserves to be fed. Making food of any kind a reward or punishment adds a symbolic and emotional component to this most basic need of life. Food needs to be kept neutral. Coercion is neither a productive nor lasting form of child rearing.

- **Small children need small amounts.** Children want to be successful in their eating. They like to eat it all up: *tah dah! I ate it all!* A whole apple can be daunting, but he might be likely to eat a few slices of it. Instead of piling the food on the plate, give a small amount of each item and wait for him to ask for more. Children are not necessarily thrilled at having mounds of food the way many adults are. It may, in fact, serve as a turnoff. (If your child is still in the stage of wanting the *whole* thing—rejecting the pieces—then buy very small apples!)

- **Refrain from *"Please, just take a bite."*** It is close to impossible to get a three-to-five-year-old child to *just take a bite.* You might as well be asking him to eat worms. The child would rather be right, would rather have the power to decide what he eats, than give someone else control over what he eats.

  Some kids will agree to have a taste if they are also permitted to *spit it out if you don't like it.* Allowing a child not to eat it at all may be just what is needed to get him to give the new food a try, though I can't promise that this method won't create a new issue—the spitting-peas-across-table issue.

- **Allow for snack time.** Human beings are the only species who practice the habit of eating three square meals a day. Most other creatures nourish themselves in very different ways, all of which respond to actual bodily needs. There are the grazers, who eat tiny amounts of light vegetation all day long, and the predators, who search out their meal when they are ravenous, eat until they are full, and then don't eat for a few days. According to nutritionist Pam Siegel, M.P.H., M.F.T., people would do much better to eat small, nutritious meals several times a day. Yet parents worry that snacks will spoil the child's appetite. Instead, welcome the snack and give smaller meals! Just make sure that your offerings are foods that make a difference and are not "trick foods." (See below.)

- **Children should not necessarily have free rein of the pantry or refrigerator.** You are allowed to have an *only adults open the cupboard/ refrigerator* rule. When your child is old enough to be safe (not climbing on or into the refrigerator or pantry shelf or dropping the pickle jar as he is exploring) and to make the right choices, you can adjust your rule.

- **Teach your child about "trick foods," aka junk food.** Junk food is one of the big battlegrounds of the food wars. One person's junk food poison is another man's finest feast! Each of you has different ideas about what food is junk and what is okay for your children to eat. Here again, if you look into your Samsonite, you are often able to see where and whom your ideas (misguided or not) come from.

    Here is what I know for sure: when eating "properly" becomes important to your child, he will do it. My son, Lucas, whose green food was lime yogurt, now eats all kinds of vegetables. He is health conscious and well aware of the role food plays in his body shape, musculature, and overall well-being.

    Most people call food that isn't particularly nutritious "junk food"; I call it "trick food" because it tricks you. The explanation goes like this:

    "We eat food, and our bodies use all the parts of the food that are helpful. Some of it goes to help our blood, some goes for our bones, some goes for our skin or our muscles or eyes or teeth or hair, and some of that food helps our brains to grow. The helpful food makes us feel full, and if we eat helpful food we aren't hungry for a long time afterward. The part of the food that our body doesn't use turns into pee and poop, and we get rid of it in the toilet.

    "Some of the foods that we really like are foods that aren't helpful; they don't do much good for our bodies. They taste really good, but they don't give our bodies any fuel. Those foods are called 'trick foods' because they trick our bodies into feeling full. Usually, after you eat a 'trick food' you are hungry again soon, and your body still needs food to help it to work well."

- **Beware of becoming the Special Meal Chef.** Mealtimes and menus present a problem for the parent-chef. You want your child to learn how to read his own body signals and eat what he likes when he is hungry, yet he needs to learn to conform to a house standard. There is just no way that the parent-chef can possibly cater to everyone's individual needs, tastes, and timing. Most parent-chefs think that is their job. I think it is an impossible task. Different families handle this challenge in different ways: some parent-chefs provide everyone with the same meal, saying, *"This is the dinner I have made. Eat it if you would like. You are in charge of what you eat or do not eat."*

Many of us in the field of child development believe that children will eat when they are hungry—hungry enough. You might have to tolerate a whole lot of complaining and whining, but a healthy child will not starve himself. (A child who is heading in the direction of starvation has issues that are not about food. In this case, you must seek help from a mental health professional.)

Some parent-chefs prepare just what they know each child will eat to ensure that everyone gets exactly what he wants (hence the name Special Meal Chef).

Some parent-chefs search for the middle ground. They make a menu that has at least one food that appeals to each palate: salad that this one likes, pasta that he likes, bread for her, meat for him. Everyone has something, and there are no fights. No one starves.

Some parent-chefs provide flexibility for the child who is older than five: *"If you don't want what we are eating, you may fix yourself something else."* (Only offer acceptable choices, perhaps a bowl of cereal or a bagel.)

The only wrong choice is to do something that you *don't want to do*, about which you feel resentful. Your resentment will leak, and the meal will be laced with those unpleasant feelings.

• **Have a default food on hand.** Since eating or not eating often has to do with power and control, you might want to have a default food at the ready. This should be a food that your child *will* eat, but not something that you have to put any effort into preparing. Half a peanut butter and jelly sandwich, some cheese and crackers, or a bowl of Cheerios are good examples. The default food is placed to the side of the child's place setting *every night* and not just on the night when you are serving something you know he will refuse. When the child sits down and exclaims, *"I hate chicken!"* you can reply, *"Then you may eat your cheese* *and crackers,"* saying no more than that. Do not engage; do not discuss; do not react.

- **Have a clear policy about after-dinner snacks.** When there has been an issue over dinner, it is not uncommon for the child to need a nighttime snack desperately, proclaiming his extreme hunger. Children also use nighttime snacks as a stalling technique at bedtime. In both cases, the easiest way to deal with the request is to allow the snack; however, never allow it after the bedtime routine has begun. It should be the same two choices every night. I am a big fan of the following because they represent sound nutrition and they are a defined amount of food, each coming in its own package. Tell your child: *"I hear that you are really hungry. You may have a* banana *or some* string cheese, *just like every night. Take your pick."* Discussion over. Do not engage.

Picky Eaters

If you have a child who is a picky eater, know that you are in good company. It certainly is a common complaint among my clients. Experts say that possibly half of all two-year-olds fall into this category, and there is evidence to suggest that for some it can continue through adolescence. Some children actually have a "neophobia"—a fear of the new—and it reaches its height between the ages of two and six. Steering clear of new foods may again reflect ancient biology at work, which protected our ancestors from eating abundant and potentially poisonous vegetation.

It is important, however, to keep trying when it comes to introducing new (healthy) foods. Researchers have said that it takes repeated and consistent exposure, likely ten to fifteen tries or more, before a child might even taste a new food, but parents often give up after two or three tries. Children whose parents give up entirely and stop introducing new foods are those who are less likely to become more adventurous eaters later on.

Preschool-age children are particularly prone to being picky eaters for a variety of reasons. They are trying out their independence in all kinds of ways, and being picky about what they eat is just one of the ways they assert themselves. As adventurous as they might be in other areas, food is not usually one of them. They like the foods they like, so why bother with anything else? Some children (and adults) are particularly sensitive to food textures or even colors. A child may not be willing to try a food just because of the way it looks.

Getting your picky eater to sample new foods reminds me of Charlie Brown hitting his head against the wall. Good Grief!

Tips and Scripts for Dealing with Picky Eaters

- **Stop talking about it; stop worrying about it!** The harder you try to force food on a child, the less likely he will be to eat it. The more you talk about it, the more tightly your child will hold her lips closed. Do not comment on what the child is or isn't eating. Not one word.

- **Use different plates.** In addition to offering small portions, serve your picky eater on smaller plates and use small utensils. Bread plates are less threatening. Occasionally serve a meal or a snack on a party plate. In so doing the emphasis is taken off the food and put onto the fun plate.

- **Offer a few choices.** Smorgasbord snacks and meals, including bite-size servings of a variety of choices, make the child feel powerful in choosing for himself. Too many choices can be overwhelming, so offer two and no more than three.

- **When introducing a new food item, don't put it on your child's plate.** Instead, place it on a separate plate away from him, and don't make a big deal about it. He may or may not be willing to give it a try, but you won't have sabotaged the possibility by showing your investment in his trial. If by some miracle the child wishes to try the new food, give him a very tiny taste.

- **Introduce new foods when your child is definitely hungry.** Hungry children are more likely to risk trying something new.

- **Invite "guests" to join you.** Occasionally invite a favorite doll, stuffed animal, or puppet to join you for dinner. Allow the child to encourage the guest and model how to eat.

- **Serve food in special ways.** Mickey Mouse pancakes taste much better than plain old rounds. Rice-cake children (cream cheese faces and raisin features) are a treat.

- **Involve the child in the preparation.** This might make him more willing to give it a try. Daddy exclaiming, *"This is delicious. Who in the world made it?"* can be a real motivator.

- **Read one of the books for picky eaters.** (See Related Books for Children, page 224.)

Sweets and Dessert Foods

In my office, I keep a large glass canister filled to the brim with a zillion different kinds of candy. There are parents who come for sessions and dive into that candy jar like, well, kids in a candy store! Everyone has stories about the role that sweets played in their growing-up years. Though most parents agree that they don't want sweets to play a big part in their children's lives—and they know the deal with sweets, nutrition, and dental health—somehow it just always creeps in and becomes a problem.

No matter what you serve the children and what rules you set up, if desserts and sweets are a big part of your life, your children will get the message about the role that sweets play. This doesn't mean that your child will grow up to be a sweetaholic, but it's pretty darned likely that sugar will play a starring role.

Metabolism plays a part in everyone's consumption of food. It also has a role in one's desire for sweets. Some children are less interested in sweets than their peers; others absolutely crave them. We do know that there is an addictive quality to sweets: just try to cut sugar out of your life!

As with all people, each child has a unique eating style and habits. Some children are able to delay gratification; but most have a hard time doing so. Some children eat sweets and still eat nutritious food. Others eat sweets and then refuse healthier fare. It is important to keep your child's particular style in mind when deciding if and when to offer sweets.

You should also consider what role you want sweets to play in your child's life; in addition, it is crucial that you separate your issues, past and present, from your child's issues (or lack thereof) with sweets.

Sweets are used in lots of ways throughout the world. Sometimes candy is thrown at thirteen-year-old children who have just finished reading from the Torah for the first time. This is a way of wishing them a sweet life now that they have become adults, according to the Jewish faith. At a Persian wedding

I attended, candy was thrown at the bride and groom so that they would have a sweet life together. Sweets are used to celebrate, to show affection, to show appreciation, and as rewards.

Tips and Scripts for Handling Sweets and Treats

In these times, when eating disorders abound, it is of critical importance that you do nothing to contribute to that potential in your children.

- **Do not use sweets (or food) of any kind as a reward or as first aid.** In doing so you may inadvertently set the child up to *need* to be rewarded or soothed with a sweet. Sweets are then given emotional significance. This is different from having a celebratory meal for a graduation, an accomplishment, or a milestone. On these occasions food, and not just a sweet, is the common ground that brings people together to share good feelings, good conversation, mutual support, and good food.

- **The One-Sweet-a-Day Rule.** For children who constantly ask for sweets, a good idea is to limit the sweets to one per day. First, you must figure out the equivalencies, such as two chocolate kisses equals one cookie—equals three gummies—equals five jelly beans. To make this choice easier for the child, package the choices and have them ready to go. Allow your child to choose to have the sweet *whenever* he wants it. He can have it at 6:00 A.M. when he awakens, at morning snack, or before bedtime. It is his choice, but he does have to brush his teeth afterward.

  The one-a-day plan can be very effective because it puts the control in the hands of the child. The young child, who is just learning number value and timing, might have a harder time with *just one*, as well as with *you've already had your one for today*. Combine that with lack of impulse control, impatience, and extreme desire, and enforcing this rule might be hard. But the four-to-six-year-old gets it.

  There will be those days, such as when there is a birthday party or other special event, when the one-a-day plan will be challenging. Some children will be able to handle the conflict and make the choice of not having their usual daily sweet so that they can have birthday cake later on. For others, it is just asking too much. It's not worth fighting about, so forget it on these days. The one-a-day plan is for your regular days.

- **Limit the sweets that are on hand.** If your cupboard is filled with sweets, cookies, and candies, it will be really hard for your child to focus on other foods. If you don't have any sweets in the house, he'll just have to pick something else. There will be some complaining, but what's new about that?

- **Desserts: beware of the *"How much do I need to eat in order to have dessert?"* trap.** If eating dinner is all about getting to dessert, your child will hardly taste what he is eating, let alone learn to enjoy it. The focus will be on the goal, dessert. In addition, the child who is allowed to negotiate his food intake will attempt to use that tool for other things he doesn't want to do.

  For some people this is a radical notion, but here it is: eliminate dessert. I am not saying *not* to have sweets. I am saying don't associate dessert with a meal. That way there is no bargaining for sweets at mealtime. *"Two more bites of string beans"* shouldn't lead to the sweet reward . . . or any reward for that matter. Remember, I said *don't fight about food*. This is just what I meant. Dinner needs to be about dinner. Your child needs to learn to eat until he has had enough and be done. It is his choice, not yours.

Table Behavior

Dinnertime at Robert Anderson's house in the old television show *Father Knows Best* is a far cry from most people's reality today. The peaceful family meal is a worthy goal, but with young children it is more dream than reality. Aside from not always being hungry at mealtimes, children eat different amounts at a different pace from adults and their siblings of different ages. To top it off, their attention spans are less than half that of an adult's. All of this makes staying willingly at the table a challenge. The child has little interest in any conversation in which he is not directly participating. He would rather sprawl in your lap, eat off your plate, explore the trajectory of peas, see what tone the half-filled milk glass makes, and hang off the side of the chair. Eating is just not so exciting for him. He wants to eat (or not), be done, and get on to the next adventure.

Tips and Scripts for Mealtime Behaviors

Having expectations that are thought out and reasonable for your child's table behavior will go a long way in eliminating mealtime battles.

- **Set the stage for the meal.** Turn on the answering machine and turn off your BlackBerry, the television, and your work brain. Put down the newspaper and have your kids put away their electronic games. Make it a rule that phones are not answered during dinner. These small acts give your children a clear message about the importance of the family meal.

- **Meals happen at a table.** Mealtime should be about food, socializing, and sharing. When it happens at a table, together with parents, it can be a pleasant activity, one that is eagerly anticipated, that creates happy memories and positive associations. Discussions and learning will abound, and table behavior will be modeled.

- **Include your child in the conversation.** Mealtime conversations ought not be about admonishments, rule following, or behavior reviews, and the conversations need to include everyone in the family. Save your grown-up conversations for later. Talk to one another. Tell stories. Laugh! Ask questions: *"I heard a story in the news coming home tonight, and I wonder what you think about it. A man was keeping a whole menagerie of wild animals in his house, and his neighbors didn't like it. They complained to the authorities, and now the man has to give his animals away. Do you think that was okay?"*

  Studies abound that link children's success staying "on track" through the teenage years with having family meals that are filled with conversation. It is through such activity that parents have a direct opportunity to share their opinions, ideas, and values, which children need to hear over and over as they grow up. You could say: *"I was driving home from the office and a man yelled some really nasty things at me. That really wasn't okay. I can't stand it when people use bad language."*

- **Stop feeding your child.** Although there are cultures where feeding a child well into his elementary school years is common practice, I don't support it. Feeding a child who can certainly feed himself (those over eighteen months) gives the clear message that he is not in charge of his eating. The only thing it feeds is the food power struggle. In feeding himself a child is given the message that he is an individual and has power. If he doesn't eat, he doesn't eat.

- **Model the table behaviors you expect your child to learn.** Watching Daddy put his napkin on his lap and Mommy ask politely for items to be passed are lessons your child doesn't miss. A parent reaching to sample food off the child's plate teaches the child that such behavior is acceptable. Thundering burps that receive laughs will surely be copied.

- **Expect your child to sit in his own chair and eat food off his own plate.** The first time you allow a whining child to sit in your lap and eat off your plate will be the first of many times to follow.

    Young children fidget; it's hard for them to sit still in a chair. Decide what is most important to you—that the child is *at* the table, he is *eating* his meal, and you are actually *having* a family meal, or that he sit still and upright in his chair. As long as there is some semblance of being in his chair—sitting on his knees, or just being wiggly—it counts. My vote is to let this one go.

- **Set clear limits around mealtime behavior . . . and be prepared to enforce them.** Decide what behaviors are the most important to you and let your child know ahead of time that you expect them to be followed:

    "Everyone at our dinner table is going to sit in his own seat. You are too. After dinner you may sit in my lap. But during dinner you need to sit in your own chair."

    "Inside voices are used at our dinner table. Children who need to scream will be excused from the table, and they can finish in the kitchen" (laundry room, den floor, wherever you are not).

    When a child does anything with food other than eat it, give a clear message about what is and is not acceptable:

    "Can you stop squishing your peas, or should I clear your plate?"

    "When you throw your food you are telling me you are finished. If you are done, you may be excused."

Then do it and put up with the ensuing screaming. It will only happen once. (For a detailed discussion on consequences for noncompliance, see chapter 2, page 31.)

For too long my client Corey had been telling her five-year-old daughter to eat with a fork and not her hands. Finally Corey told her daughter that since she didn't use her fork, Corey guessed she didn't need utensils and took them away . . . for several meals. The kicker came at dessert one night when ice cream was served. Her daughter pleaded, *"When can I have a spoon again?"* as she ate the soupy ice cream with her fingers. It was a mess. When Corey finally allowed her daughter to have utensils again, her daughter picked up her fork and exclaimed, *"I love you, fork!"*

- **Have realistic expectations for how long a child should be able to sit at the table.** Although there are no definitive rules, as it depends not only on the child's age and development but also on his temperament, generally speaking, my advice is to aim low and be thrilled when you get more!

  A **two-year-old** child may actually be able to sit longer than a four-year-old child, as he will be a slower and more distracted eater, entertained by having everyone there together. Consider five minutes a success.

  It is reasonable to expect a **three-year-old** child to sit at a dinner table for five to ten minutes. Some will have much greater staying power than others.

  A **four-year-old** should make it ten to fifteen minutes.

  A **five-year-old** usually can last fifteen to twenty minutes, and the same is true for a **six-year-old.**

  Needless to say, the length of the stay will depend upon variables such as how tired the child may be, what the day was like, and what is next on the agenda.

- **Meals should end before they need to.** Allow his meal to end when the child begins to show signs of being finished eating. Don't let your mealtime deteriorate into "dinner hell."

- **Stalling should not be honored.** Some children are naturally slow eaters. We aren't talking about them here. Children who are "stallers" often do so as an attention-getting device. When you recognize that you are being manipulated, give this child some warning: *"It is almost time for dinner to be over. It seems to be taking you some extra time tonight. I will sit with you for five more minutes. Then I am getting up."* When the time is up, and you know who is now holding the reins, say: *"I am done with my dinner and it's time for me to clean up the kitchen. You may stay at the table until you are finished."* Get up and leave. Be sure to be matter-of-fact and have no anger or hostility in your voice. I would place money on your child being done as soon as you leave.

- **For tips on restaurant behaviors, see chapter 2, page 41. For a longer discussion on manners, see chapter 5.**

CHAPTER 5

❖

"Get Your Finger Out of Your Nose!"

Dealing with Boogers, Burps, Farts—Manners and Social Graces

Brunch with the in-laws who have just arrived from London is about to begin. Four-year-old Jimmy and two-and-a-half-year-old Jennifer, impeccably dressed, hands washed, are seated at the table. You're holding your breath. Glancing at your children, you are horrified to see Jimmy harvesting the morning's boogers, his finger up his nose almost to his eyebrow. *"Jimmy, not at the table!"* you hiss, teeth clenched. *"I want the jelly,"* announces Jennifer as she hoists herself up, one knee on the dining room table because she is going to reach for it all by herself. And you know your mother-in-law is thinking, *"These children have no manners at all."*

There isn't a parent on the planet who wants to raise a child who is unmannerly. But teaching manners can be much harder than you imagine. You have one idea, and your independent preschooler has another.

Every society has its own language of manners. They bring a degree of civility to our world and help to order experiences, new and old. They are a kind of protocol. Manners are scripts that ease the way, provide transitions, and demonstrate respect. Manners actually empower children by giving them the scripts for how to make their way in the world.

We think a child who is not well behaved around an adult is not showing *respect*. The parent says, *"You may not talk to me that way; it is disrespectful."* Yet having respect for someone has little to do with manners: *"I really respect Oprah Winfrey for what she has made of her life."* Respect is a very difficult concept to teach a child. It is only by getting to know the concept in context that a child ever figures out what it means and might even be able to practice it.

"Respect" is used as a shorthand of sorts to describe an expectation for the way in which the child interacts with an elder. *"Daddy gets mad at me when I tell him he is a poo-poo head."* The child doesn't say it again not because it is disrespectful; it is because Daddy got mad. It is a parent's job to teach the child the boundaries of acceptable and unacceptable behavior. In so doing the parent helps the child expand her repertoire of social skills and her ability to get along with peers and adults. Through repeated experiences, the child learns that manners are one way that we show people respect.

In order to practice respect, a child must be able to consider another person's point of view and think about someone else's feelings. Bearing in mind how children come into the world, this is a daunting task. As a vulnerable infant, the child is focused on her own survival. Her egocentricity makes sense. Allowing for another's needs and feelings is something that comes with growth and development. Thus, there is a developmental component to learning manners. Using manners entails taking someone else into consideration. Children must develop this capacity. Herein lie the roots of a young child's tendency to be disrespectful. It's not her fault!

Young children between the ages of two and four years are impulsive. They think it and they say it. They haven't developed internal censors. A client told me that on her new babysitter's first day, her three-and-a-half-year-old son declared for the world to hear, *"I don't like her. When is she leaving?"* The young child doesn't stop to think about what he is saying; he just says it. Young children lack diplomacy, and they are just beginning to learn its usefulness. That includes learning manners.

The young child will first use manners because she learns that they are the key to getting her needs met. It's pretty darn selfish. She isn't motivated by an understanding of the need for or true meaning of manners, but by knowing she won't get the juice until she says, *"Please."* As the child's egocentricity becomes less useful for her, she is also beginning to be able to consider and value others' points of view and is starting to cultivate some empathy. That is when she might unsolicitedly begin to use manners as signs of respect. What a relief it is when your child says *"thank you"* to Aunt Shirley without your prompting.

Many an adult feels that an unmannerly child is a poor reflection on the parent. *"Can't those parents teach that kid some manners?"* is not an uncommon refrain. The child refuses to say thank you after the playdate, and the neon sign over the parent's head lights up: BAD PARENTING JOB! While it *is* the parents' job to teach the child manners, this task is complicated by the child's development, as discussed. Asking a two-year-old to use *only* her fork and spoon and not her fingers just isn't developmentally appropriate, even though it is mannerly behavior. Asking a three-year-old to sit up and sit still at the table isn't reasonable for her wiggly little body. The child's innate limitations must be understood and accepted.

Another part of the story is the child's temperament. With some children, you can push and beg and cajole and bribe and get nowhere at all. She is just not going to budge. The shy child might be reluctant to greet or respond to a new person, or even an old family friend. Some children are like porcupines. They become very prickly when they feel threatened or when you are asking too much of them. The tender or uncomfortable child may blurt out, *"I don't want to say Hi,"* right in your boss's face. Each child's unique temperament plays a role in his willingness to practice those mannerly greetings and farewells.

And finally, there is you. While many parents acknowledge the need for manners, they may not be modeling the very behavior that is expected of the child. Your child watches you constantly. She is learning how to *be* in the world from everything you do and say to everyone with whom you come in contact.

When I was a school director, I used to stand at the school entrance every day and greet all two hundred children and their parents by name. It was not uncommon for a child not to greet me because of his temperament or mood. That I understood. But I was amazed at the number of parents who didn't display the good manners of greeting me or even responding to my greeting. Need I remind you that polite parents will likely raise polite children, while rude parents will certainly raise rude children?

Tips and Scripts for Encouraging Your Child's Use of Manners

- **Catch your child doing the right thing and reinforce it.** When your child uses the manners you want, sing her praises. Be specific, though, saying:

  "You remembered to say please *this time!"*

  "You greeted Mrs. Sanders so nicely. I know you made her feel good when you said good morning."

  She will know how happy you are just by the tone of your voice. You want her to feel good about herself for doing the right thing and not just for making you proud.

- **Work on one area at a time.** The young child has a greater chance of succeeding if she is not overwhelmed. If you have decided that telephone behaviors are your priority, then work on them and let the others slide a bit. But do remind her (once is usually sufficient) if you notice she's not using those telephone skills.

- **Plan ahead.** If you know you will be in a situation that will call for manners, let your child know what will happen and what you expect of her: *"We are going to see Grandma and Grandpa and their friends, Mr. and Mrs. Berman. When you are introduced to them, it will be nice if you will find something to say to them like, 'Nice to meet you.' Do you have any ideas of what else you might say?"*

  My friend Sally tells the story of taking her six-year-old son, Eric, who had never seen an infant, to visit a friend and her week-old baby. In the car on the way over, Sally explained to Eric, *"You are going to see Mary's brand-new baby. You know, new babies look different from bigger ones. They are tiny and wrinkled up and look kind of funny. You need to think of something nice to say to Mary about the baby, something that will make her feel good."* Upon seeing the tiny baby, a wide-eyed Eric stared at the baby, looked up at Mary, and proudly said, *"He has a really big head!"* Clearly Eric had given some thought to what would make Mary feel good.

- **Practice!** If you know that you are going to be in a situation that will demand manners, practice the behavior you hope to see. Use stuffed animals or dolls and act out the situations. Be playful but be specific. Take turns playing different roles and be sure to act out your pleasure at hearing your child use the manners you are practicing.

- **Never embarrass your child.** If you are in public or in the presence of someone who is not part of your nuclear family, get down on your child's level and whisper the prompt or correct her ill-mannered behavior. (Depending upon your child's temperament, mood, and the situation, she may or may not respond. Remember, this behavior cannot be forced.) Remove your child from the scene altogether before you discuss her behavior. Embarrassing her will only add to her resistance and likely create anger toward you.

- **Respond immediately.** Keeping in mind the embarrassment factor and the need to remove the child, respond to her lack of manners immediately. Young children do not learn well after the fact.

- **Use different approaches for insisting upon manners.** Giving the same direction over and over again will teach the child to not listen to you, as will long-winded explanations. Show your child, literally, what you expect her to do, or try offering her a one-word reminder, like *"Elbows."*

- **Don't expect perfection.** Most people just don't use their most polished manners all the time, so don't expect it from your child. There will be times when she will actually choose *not* to use her manners. As is always the case, pick your battles.

- **Give your child information.** While it seems obvious, parents often forget to explain to the child why she needs to use manners. Remember to use only a few reasons so the point won't be lost.

> *"When you say* thank you *to Brittany and her mom, it makes them feel good. It is one of the ways that we have of being kind and showing that we care about someone else."*

> *"Granny spent a lot of time looking for a sweater she thought you would like. It would make her feel good if you would say* thank you.*"*

> *"I feel like getting you that glass of milk when you say* please.*"*

Please, Thank You, Excuse Me, and Other Social Graces

Children are parrots. That is the way in which so much of their learning happens. They hear you talk and they mimic you. Have you ever accidentally said a swear word and later heard your child repeat it, with exactly the same intonation? It happens. The first rule for *please, thank you,* and *excuse me* is to model saying those words all the time, when they are appropriate to the situation. Your child is taking it all in.

There will be situations, however, when attaching *please* or an *excuse me* to a given behavior isn't effective. For example, even though your child says *"excuse me"* because she wants to talk to you when you're in a conversation, *excuse me* might not make the interruption okay. That goes for you too: if you are furious at a particular behavior and an immediate command is in order, do not spit out a *"please"* through your clenched teeth. *"Feet off the table now!"* will do. In fact, I believe the hissed *please* actually detracts from the child's learning its real use.

Neither *please* nor *excuse me* are magic words. They are social necessities that all children need to learn to use. Getting them to say *please* all the time is a common struggle for parents. As mentioned, it isn't reasonable to expect that your child will always say it. Remember, it takes practice. If you become too focused on this issue, it can become the basis for yet another power struggle. *"Okay, I am not going to say* please. *You can't make me. I don't care if I can't have the juice. I didn't want the juice anyway. And I hate you. You are a mean mommy."* And on it goes. All this for a *please*? Sometimes when you stop trying and relinquish the control to your child, the very thing you are hoping for happens.

Tips and Scripts for Eliciting *Please* from Your Child

- **Refrain from being the *Please* Police.** Nagging a child is not an effective form of parenting or teaching. In the same way that you detest your child's whining, she detests your nagging. In fact, your reminder may backfire by teaching your child that *not* saying *please* gets your attention.

- **Create a signal.** A simple signal such as tugging your ear or pinching your nose is a different way of reminding your child to say *please*. Explain to her the plan: *"We are going to have a signal to tell you that you have forgotten to say* please. *When I do this, it means you need to add a please to your request."*

- **The nonresponse.** When all else fails, it will work simply to ignore your child's request. This method works best when you explain to her: *"When you ask me politely, I will do what you are asking, if I can. When you don't, I will not respond at all. That is the way you will know that you need to ask again, this time politely."*

  Before she realizes why you are not responding, your child is liable to get frustrated and yell at you, as if you didn't hear her. Turn around and give her a quizzical look. She will figure out what is necessary.

- **When it is appropriate, encourage your child's friends to say *please*.** This one is tricky, as some people agree with it while others do not. But when your child has a guest who does or doesn't say *please*, you can say, *"In this family, we try to say* please *when we ask for things."*

Mainly, this comment serves as a reminder to your own child. She also learns that good manners ought to be used by all people. Conversely, when the guest is polite (and they usually are, à la Eddie Haskell), use the opportunity to point it out to both children: *"You sure have nice manners. Thanks for remembering to say* please.*"*

Thank You

In order for a child to say *thank you* she must possess a degree of development that comes more slowly to some children than others. Unlike saying *please*, which actually helps the child to get her needs met, *thank you* gets her nothing. It is just a plain old have-to.

Voluntarily saying *thank you* means that the child is developing empathy, knows how her words make another person feel, and has achieved a degree of emotional intelligence. She must be able to recognize, experience, and share her good feelings and at the same time understand that they are the result of something someone else has done.

Finally, being able to say *thank you* requires that the child be able to predict the future and remember the past. When I receive a gift, for example, I know that some time in the future I am going to enjoy using that lovely crystal bowl. I have served food in beautiful bowls before, and I know how useful they are. I also know that my friend likely went to a lot of trouble to find me just the right crystal bowl. Not so with the young child. She lives only in the moment. She hasn't necessarily had experience with the gift, so she doesn't know the pleasure to come. How can she be grateful? Nor does she think that Granny tried to give her something she would like and went to a lot of trouble to do so. She opens her birthday package and sees a tea set. She doesn't think, *"Someday I will get pleasure out of that tea set."* Perhaps she thinks, *"I don't like this gift!"* She is in the moment and lacks impulse control. Instead of an appropriate (and albeit hollow) *thank you* to the gift giver, she screams, *"I don't want this! I hate tea sets!"* And you want to duck under the nearest table.

The brilliant, now deceased, comedian Danny Kaye once recorded a song called "The Thank-You Note." In the song he mimics a five-year-old-boy who is writing a thank-you note to his aunt for the underwear he has received from her as a gift on his fifth birthday. In the same sentence that he thanks her for the obviously unwelcome underwear, he adds how much he will enjoy wearing his new underwear when he receives the skates he really wanted for his birthday.

The birthday boy got the idea of showing gratitude, but just barely.

Fear not. Over time, in time, and with practice and your encouragement, your child will learn to say *thank you* appropriately.

Tips and Scripts in the Event of Noncompliance

Remember, you cannot force a child to talk, and that includes saying *thank you*. If you have forewarned your child of the expectation and she is not willing to voice her gratitude, it is probably for one of the following reasons:

- **She is "shy" and not able to express thanks.** It is too uncomfortable for her. (See the box on page 90.)

- **She is exhausted after a long day, and it is lousy local conditions.** (See chapter 2, page 24.)

- **It has become a control issue, and she is exerting her power.**

- **She is engaging you negatively.** (Remember, any attention will do.)

In all of these cases, it is best that you simply voice the *thanks* and not get into a battle with the child then and there: *"Amanda is not able to say* thank you, *but I want to say thank you so much for the lovely time she had at your home."* Now leave.

At a later point when Amanda's energy and attention are no longer on the battle and she is able to take in what you are saying, you might say: *"Part of going on a playdate is saying* thank you *at the end. If you are not able to say* thank you, *then you will not have the playdate."*

Here is the tricky part. Either concoct a scenario where the friend calls for another playdate that very same day or fake a phone call within earshot of the child: *"Oh hi, Mrs. Wexler. Jennifer would like Amanda to come over for a playdate? Well, I don't know. Today Amanda wasn't able to say* thank you *after her playdate with Samantha. Our rule is that Amanda needs to use her manners and say* thank you *at the end of the playdate or she may not have a playdate. Let me ask Amanda."*

My guess is that Amanda will want to have the playdate and will agree to say *thank you*. Make the playdate for as soon as possible. And, of course, on the way to the date, be very clear about your expectations: *"I know you are going to be able to say* thank you *at the end of your playdate today. Yesterday you were not able to, but you have agreed that it is something you will do today. Good for you!"*

It is anyone's guess as to whether Amanda will or won't say *thank you*. If she doesn't, then turn down the next playdate request, restating the reason right in front of Amanda.

You may have to fake a few telephone requests for playdates, all of which you turn down, saying: *"I am so sorry. Amanda is not having a playdate because she hasn't learned to say* thank you *to her hosts. Maybe another time."*

If it is not the child's temperament that is inhibiting her ability to say *thank you*, this method will work. The child will learn that it was her behavior (or lack thereof) that led to the consequence of no playdates. She will find a way to say *thank you*.

In the event that your child is "shy" and is temperamentally challenged by having to say *thank you,* it is important that you find some way that she can show her appreciation. Take the time to brainstorm with her for ways that she might be able to express her appreciation: *"I know that it is hard for you to say* thank you, *but it is important that we find a way for you to let Mrs. Leonard know that you appreciate going to her house. What might we do to let her know?"*

No doubt your child will shrug her shoulders, but you must persist. Suggest some alternatives to the traditional *thank you*: give a wave, offer a smile, nod in agreement to the *thank you* that you, Mommy, express verbally. What is important is the acknowledgment and even the smallest show of *thanks*. Sooner or later, with repeated playdates at that house and, therefore, an increased comfort level, Amanda will spontaneously say *thank you*. Taking the power struggle out of it will also invite the response. It is not for *you* that Amanda says *thank you*. It is for Mrs. Leonard and because it is a common courtesy that is expected.

Burps and Farts

While children need to be taught to say *excuse me* when they burp or fart, it is not something that easily rolls off the tongue. At first, the child has no idea that there is something about her that's not okay. Burps and farts are just things that bodies do. Then she sees the response these releases get from her peers, older siblings, or even from Uncle Pete. She gets lots of attention. She made everyone giggle and laugh. *Wow! There must be something really great about my farts!* Now they are fun and funny. She has no idea about the social unacceptability of these acts. And, once again, the child is egocentric, so she first thinks about herself and not about what effect her noises and smells may have on others or

THE SHY CHILD

While sometimes shyness is a stage through which a child passes, more often being shy is an inborn temperamental trait. Often the parent who worries that her child is shy recognizes that either she or the child's father was shy, too, as a child. The parent still feels shy in certain situations. Sometimes the child even gets a double dose: shy mother and shy father.

Some children do "come out of their shells" as they mature; others merely learn to cope, developing ways to help themselves feel more comfortable when necessary.

As the word *shy* has a rather negative connotation, I suggest not labeling your child "shy." Telling your child she is shy gives her both an excuse and permission to behave in shy ways. Find other words to describe her to others and for her to use: she is "sensitive," "reactive," or "introverted." It takes her a little "time to warm up."

(See Related Books for Children, page 224, for books for the shy child.)

about the prevailing social rules. Kids of all ages love these bodily functions. (I know some grown-ups who do too.) They are funny not only because they are usually unexpected, but also because they make the child feel powerful.

In addition, the child doesn't receive consistent messages about burps and farts not being okay. The parent works hard to help the child feel that everything about her body is acceptable. Yet out comes that fart when you least expect it. And it is a hoot! Older preschool and elementary-school-age children are especially susceptible to the fart giggles. Toilet skills are near and dear to them. All bodily functions have taken on a new meaning and have great power. While young children have been taught to say *excuse me*, the implication being that there is something not quite okay about that fart, it is just much more fun to crack up with your buddies. Therein lies the mixed message: your friends think farts are great, while Daddy and Grandma tell you that you need to say *excuse me*.

Occasionally Daddy himself lets loose with a beer burp or a bean fart—and he does it right at the dinner table too! Mommy shoots him a dirty look, but Daddy is rather proud of himself, and while he delivers a half hearted *excuse me*, he continues to laugh. The child wonders, *"Are burps and farts okay or not okay?"*

You may be fighting an uphill battle when it comes to saying *excuse me* following the release of a burp or a fart. Yes, it is important that your child learn the appropriate response to her behavior. But it will be many years before she actually wants to extinguish the behavior and willingly says *excuse me*. It's too cool to burp and to fart.

Interrupting

Parents teach children that when adults are talking they need to say *excuse me* before interrupting. The child can actually learn this lesson quite easily, as it is another tool for her. But teaching a child to say *excuse me* when Daddy is talking to someone is only a half-solution. Requiring a child to say *excuse me* does not teach her not to interrupt. Instead, she learns that interrupting is okay, as long as she says *excuse me*. But *excuse me* doesn't always work. Daddy might not want to be interrupted at all, *excuse me* or not.

An aspect of learning to delay gratification is learning how to wait. Sometimes that means not interrupting and having to wait your turn. You can tell your child: *"Yes, I know you said* excuse me, *but I do not want to be interrupted. You need to wait until I am done with this conversation."*

Do everything in your power to ignore your child, who is likely to be waiting impatiently. Neither her interrupting nor her *excuse me* can work if you want your child to learn not to interrupt. But be reasonable with your expectation. Finish that conversation in a hurry and then acknowledge that she did wait and you appreciated it.

Greetings and Farewells

Instilling the social graces of expressing greetings and farewells is not usually as challenging as *please* and *thank you*. Most children learn to say *hello* and *good-bye* fairly easily. In fact, little ones love doing so. The toddler in the shopping cart is the store's official greeter, waving and shouting *hello* to anyone in the vicinity. The same holds true for waving *bye-bye*.

As the child gets older and the thrill is gone, it becomes another chore for her, especially depending upon her temperament. Asking the very shy child to say *good morning* to the school director is not unlike asking her to do a back flip right then and there. She just can't do it. Since children need to learn the importance of the mannerly greeting, do not let go of the expectation. Rather, adjust your expectation to the child's ability. You might say as you walk to the school doorway, *"You need to find a way to say* good morning *to Mrs. Elson that is comfortable for you. Sometimes it is hard for you to say the words* 'good morning.' *Let's talk about what else you can do. You could wave* good morning; *you could smile* good morning; *or you could nod to say* hello. *(*The older child might feel proud to wink in acknowledgment.*) Which do you think you will do today?"*

Giving the permission *not* to say the words often gives the child the strength to say them when she is ready. Once again, you have removed the power struggle from the lesson. It isn't about you. It is about teaching the child the manners that are expected.

Kisses and Hugs

There are some parents who believe that it is important, even mandatory, for children to kiss and hug certain people when they greet them or say *good-bye*. I am not in this camp. Certainly grandparents expect a kiss and a hug from their precious grandchild. And I know too well that they are easily offended when they are not granted that gift from the child. You might hear: *"Well, if you don't give me a kiss, my feelings will be hurt."* Or worse, *"If you don't give me a kiss, I won't bring you a present anymore."* The only lesson to be learned from this scene is that kisses and hugs can be used for bribery. Children need to learn that kisses and hugs are expressions of our deepest feelings of love and caring. They are not to be dispensed willy-nilly.

In these times when child sexual abuse is more prevalent, it is crucial that you teach your child that she is in charge of her body and what she does with it. That includes the dispensing of kisses and hugs.

Tips and Scripts for Kisses and Hugs

I know you experience a wave of terror at the thought of asking your mother-in-law not to insist on a kiss from her grandchild, but the lesson here is more important than the selfish feelings of the relative.

- **Give your relatives information.**
  "We are teaching Justine that she is the boss of her own body. Being able to say

NO to a request for a kiss gives her permission to say NO to someone who may try to steal a kiss at a different time. I know you want her to grow up to be powerful and in charge of her safety. We do too." You can add, *"This is not about you, Grandma. Please don't take it personally. This is about keeping our Justine safe."*

- **Ask for a kiss or a hug.** Encourage close family members and friends to *ask* for a kiss or a hug rather than insist or demand them: *"Justine, I am so glad to see you. May I give you a kiss?"* If she says NO, you can try, *"Well, how about a hug, then?"* And if the person is further rejected, *"Okay, then. You are the boss of your kisses and hugs. You can let me know if you want a kiss later on."*

  Chances are she'll come running when Grandma gets involved with someone else. All children love Grandma's attention!

- **It's about control.** Withholding kisses and hugs is a stage through which most children pass sometime between the ages of two and six. Power, control, being in charge of everything, including their kisses and hugs . . . that's a big part of these years.

I'm Sorry

While everyone seems to have her own idea about the importance of this act of civility, everyone agrees that it is a crucial part of the manners lesson. It is important in the big picture. Religions give specific guidelines for being genuinely contrite. Courts of law make rulings and impose sentences based on the guilty person's show of remorse and contrition. And it is important in the small picture too. Friends make up after a fight when the transgressor expresses his apology. The woman into whom you accidentally banged your grocery cart forgives you when you apologize.

Parents teach children to apologize because we want them to learn to be courteous, to be socially appropriate, to show respect, and to demonstrate some accountability for their actions. We also know that learning to say *I'm sorry* is one of the rules of the game. If you want to get along with people, you need to learn to apologize for your mistakes and misdeeds.

Children come to believe that *I'm sorry* works even more magic than *please*. It is supposed to make fault go away and everything "all better."

Having been repeatedly warned by her teacher to keep her hands out of her juice, four-year-old Lizzie couldn't resist. Noticing that I, the school director, was watching her do it yet again, she exclaimed in rapid fire, "Sorry sorry sorry sorry." She couldn't sell *sorry* to me, though she sure thought it would work, just as it must have worked at home.

Children need to be taught that being sorry means something, that it entails more than merely saying the words *"I'm sorry."* The children who learn this lesson are those who have seen it modeled for them. *I am sorry* needs to be a true expression of remorse and regret. The real *I am sorry* says: *"I feel for you. I regret having done what I did because of the way it affected you."*

Then there is the parent who insists that his child say *I'm sorry* to her sibling or to a playmate when, in reality, the child isn't sorry at all. This is the parent who feels embarrassed or uncomfortable about what his child has done. He feels social pressure to make the child play by the rules and apologize. If the child doesn't, then he is a bad parent. Actually, by insisting that the child say she is sorry, the parent is teaching the child to lie. She absolutely meant to grab the toy from her brother or tear up her playmate's picture. She is not sorry! But Daddy says she has to *say* she is sorry. Sometimes the child is ordered to say she is sorry before she really knows what happened and what her part in the action was. She is just parroting what her parent says. I am not at all sure that is a message you want to teach your child. (For advice about dealing with inappropriate behavior, see chapter 2.)

Directing a child to apologize is not going to make her a compassionate person. The child who is raised in an environment where contrition is genuinely shown, where *I'm sorry* is said with empathy and heartfelt meaning, where she can see that the apology is deeply rooted and sincere, is the child who will learn to say *I'm sorry* when she truly is. Yes, a child needs to learn for manners' sake that when we make a mistake or hurt someone's body or feelings, we need to apologize. But forcing a child to apologize when she doesn't feel sorry is a mistake.

Tips and Scripts for Teaching *I'm Sorry*

....

- **Teach your child to say *I'm sorry* when you feel she is genuinely sorry.** *"You see how sad Nate is that you took his toy. Look how big his tears are. You might want to tell him you are sorry. You could even find him another toy that he likes to play with."*

- **Help the child to find a way to show she is sorry, rather than insist-**

ing on the apology. Children who are given the opportunity to help the other child feel better come up with appropriate, sensitive, and often right-on-the-button ideas for consolation. Moreover, sometimes a child needs a way of saving face. She feels sorry but can't (or won't) say the words.

> *"You need to help Anna feel better. You pushed her, she fell down, and now she has a boo-boo. What do you think might make her feel better?"*
> or
> *"Come, let's get Anna some ice to put on her boo-boo, and you can sit with her until she starts to feel better."*

Being proactive, being able to *do* something about the harm caused, is an important step in feeling contrite.

For the younger sibling Amelia has just clobbered "accidentally," you might try: *"You really hurt your brother. Now you can help him to feel better. Why don't you get him his blankie, find one of his books, and sit and look at it with him while he starts to calm down and feel better."*

Being sorry, even genuinely sorry, is only part of the story. Just as we offer the "shy" child gestures that work for her to be mannerly in her greetings, so we need to help the child who has taken the misstep find ways to change her behavior. This is the second aspect of the apology: helping the child to recognize that she may need to stop herself before her behavior creates the need for an apology.

> *"How might you stop yourself next time you want the toy that Nate has? What will you do?"* Her answer may be, *"I will ask Nate for a turn"* or *"I will ask you for help."*

When the child has the opportunity to make a plan and to learn from the experience, she is making amends by changing her behavior. After all, that is the desired result.

Telephone Manners

Children love and hate the telephone. They love it when it is theirs to play with. They love it when they can hear your voice when you aren't home. They hate it when it is the thing that takes you and your attention away from them.

The phone, be it cell or landline, is not a toy, though your child might take issue with that fact. Many a parent has given the phone to a child for the purpose of placating, soothing, distracting, bribing, or buying time. What a confusing message that is to the child: *"Sometimes I can play with Daddy's phone, and sometimes I can't. I am going to spend lots of time trying to figure out the rules for this one. I will just try to play with it all the time."* The phone is not a toy, and it never should be used as one.

I know that not all people feel this way, but I find it off-putting to have my phone call answered by a young child who shouts into the phone, *"Who is it?"* That is not the way a phone should be answered. Then I have to spend some time convincing the child, *"Hand the phone to Mommy"* or *"Tell Mommy that Betsy is on the phone."*

Children are old enough to answer the phone when they are able to write down a message clearly or *remember* to give you one. Your child can't write yet, you say? Then she is not old enough to answer the phone!

I know, I sound like an old fuddy-duddy, but I do believe in telephone manners. Why don't you?

There is also a safety issue at stake here. That is the reason for my insisting that the child not answer the phone until she is old enough to say, *"My Mommy is not available right now"* or *"My Mommy can't come to the phone."* It is too easy for the young child to give out information over the phone that no one should have. *"No, my mommy isn't home, but my babysitter is."* If you are not home, you certainly don't want anyone knowing just who is or isn't there. You never know who has your phone number or your address.

The phone is your child's enemy: it takes you away from her. Isn't it interesting that as soon as the phone rings, your child needs you?

Tips and Scripts for Conquering the Enemy Telephone

- **During the times of the day when your child is with you, limit your phone conversations to very short ones.** Remember, you are setting your child up for failure if you have anything longer than a short conversation.

- **Tell the child your plan.** Describe the behavior you expect from your child while you are on the phone. Say: *"I am going to have a very short phone* *conversation. I do not want to be interrupted, but I will be right off. Show me what you are going to do while I am on the phone."*

- **It takes time to learn not to interrupt phone calls.** You may need to follow through with a logical consequence for her interrupting: *"I will finish this conversation in my bedroom* (door closed) *since you keep interrupting me."* Try again soon and give the child a chance to be successful. (For a detailed discussion of logical consequences, see chapter 2, page 31.)

Dealing with Rudeness in Public

You're waiting in line at the post office and in walks a dwarf, or "little person." His size is kind of fascinating, but of course it isn't polite to stare. Then your child shrieks with wonder, interest, and curiosity, *"Mommy, look how little that man is! Why is he so small? Look, Mommy, look!"* You want to melt into the floor.

The way in which you respond to the child's question or exclamation will have as strong an impact on her as your actual answer. Immediately shushing her, saying, *"That isn't a nice question to ask"* is likely to confuse the child, even create some guilt: *What part of that wasn't okay? Asking the question? Pointing it out? Saying it loudly? And is there something wrong with being a little person, or being fat, or having a big nose? Just what is the problem here?*

You want your child to come to you with her questions, whatever they may be. You want to be the go-to person in her world. Telling her *"That isn't a nice question to ask"* will undermine that goal. Further, a child's curiosity is natural, and it is good. You don't want to give her the message that there is something bad about her wondering. Children ask questions and make comments about people who are different because they want information.

As your child grows up, she is going to see many things she will have never experienced before. Certainly you want your child to accept differences or different-looking people as a normal part of life. By not addressing her comments or questions about the *difference* she has spotted, an additional message about *difference* is delivered: *"Maybe that wasn't an okay question to ask. Maybe there is something wrong here."* Children don't have a judgment about the difference, just a curiosity. It is the adult who has had years to develop his judgments. Parents need to take pains not to pollute their children with their own and others' negative judgments. This is a lesson from which the whole world would benefit. *Difference* isn't bad; it's just different. Answering questions directly and honestly or acknowledging comments about difference is another step in teaching your child to be open-minded and comfortable with difference.

While you want to encourage your child's curiosity and welcome her questions, she needs to learn the when and where of the asking. Herein lies the *manners* part.

**Tips and Scripts for Dealing with
"Those Public Exclamations and Questions"**

....

- **Always respond to your child's question.** You may need to get down on your child's level and, modeling an appropriately quiet voice, say: *"Yes, that lady is very small. I will tell you about it when we are outside of the market."*

- **As soon as you can, answer the question directly and honestly.** Immediately upon walking out of the market, finish your conversation:

   "Did you notice that I used a quiet voice in the market when you asked about that small lady? I used that voice so that neither you nor I would hurt her feelings. We don't know how she feels about being small, and we don't want to hurt her feelings by mistake.

   "You were right, she is unusually small. She is called a dwarf or a 'little person.' Usually people are not that small, but sometimes a person's body stops growing and doesn't get to be very tall. She is different in that way. Your body has not stopped growing. People come in all shapes and sizes, but they all have the same body parts and feelings. They are still people just the same as you and me."

Addressing your child's comment or question is a *teachable moment*. It is an opportunity where your child not only learns the answer, but she is also exposed to your values (there is nothing bad about *difference*), and she learns that you will always tell her the whole, true story. The young child may not fully understand the reasons behind your instruction to whisper or to wait with her question, but she will have learned what to do next time.

- **At a later time, you will need to address the effect the child's**

question may have on others. In order for a child to become sensitive to this, you will need to revisit the issue at a time when she is not consumed by what she has seen:

> *"Sometimes, when you see something that surprises you or that is different, you wonder about it or have questions. And I sure am the person you can ask. But you need to remember that maybe that person isn't so comfortable about her body, or maybe she doesn't like it when people talk about her. I know you don't want to hurt her feelings. So it would be a good idea to talk to me about what you see, or ask me your questions, using a whisper voice. Thinking about the way your words affect another person is part of being polite and courteous."*

- **Create a signal or a code word that will let your child know that his question or comment needs to wait until you can be private.** Sometimes in these kinds of situations, when your son has just blurted out an astute observation about the man's really shiny bald head, for example, you don't want to say anything else. You and your child can create a special signal, a tug on your ear, for example, or a simple code phrase, *Later, gator,* that lets each of you know to talk quietly or not make a comment or talk about it in private. In so doing, the child will feel acknowledged and respected but not ignored. (For information about teaching the concept of public versus private, see chapter 7, page 132.)

- **Model a direct approach if it might be appropriate.** There will be times when, if you are comfortable enough, you will be able to channel your child's question or comment into a useful interaction with the subject. Many times I have heard from handicapped people, for example, that they much prefer a child's direct questions to the adult's averted glances and hushed comments. You might say: *"My daughter noticed that you are in a wheelchair. She is very curious about that. May she talk to you?"*

  Approaching the person like this models for your child a polite way to interact. It also puts the subject matter out in the open and gives the person the opportunity to respond or not.

Boogers and Nose Picking

Older children and adults know that nose picking (or rhinotellexomania) is something that is considered impolite and is done in private, but everyone does it. Your child is no exception. Very young children discover nose picking as they explore all of the openings in their bodies: *Look, here's another place for me to put my finger!* Your two-year-old picks her nose because, well, it's there and she can. As the child gets older, nose picking continues for different reasons. Perhaps the child excavates, as my family called it, because she has allergies that create an overabundance of mucus, which turns crusty. Maybe the child is bored and it's just something to do. Most likely, she has the feeling that there is just something up there, and she wants to get it out because she can.

In reality, there is nothing bad about nose picking. One can actually feel quite accomplished after the successful removal of whatever extra crusty business was up there. The danger in nose picking is the transference of germs and dirt from finger to nose or overzealous harvesting, which can cause bleeding. It's public nose picking that is socially problematic.

Children learn early on that nose picking is *disgusting*! (Even more *disgusting*—actually horrifying to parents—is the child who practices mucophagy, the act of eating her harvest.) They can be guided to acceptable nose-picking practice until that time when a classmate hollers out, *"Eeewww. You're picking your nose!"* and the habit dissipates rapidly.

Tips and Scripts for Dealing with Nose Picking

- **Give information.** Without judgment or disdain, let your child know how and where to pick her nose. *"I know that it feels good to get the dry mucus (boggers, if you prefer) out of your nose. That is something that you do in private, in your own bedroom or when you are in the bathroom."* (For tips about teaching public versus private, see chapter 7, page 132.)

- **Teach nose blowing.** The satisfying sensation of a good nose blow can be a good substitute for nose picking. *"It seems like there is some dry mucus (dried boogers) in your nose that needs to come out. Let's give it a good hard blow into this tissue. It will feel better."*

- **Say as little as possible.** After your child knows the booger lessons and your expectations, your best bet is to say nothing at all. Nagging your child, brushing her hand away from her nose, or making disparaging comments won't help, as the child probably doesn't even realize that she is picking her nose. Shaming is not a positive form of child rearing.

- **Beware of nose picking as a means for getting your attention.** Negative attention is attention, after all.

- **Have your child checked for allergies.** If you notice that your child has a continuous stream of mucus, it is a good idea to consult your pediatrician or an allergist. A continuously loaded nose is no fun at all.

Your child will learn manners, and she will actually begin to *use* them too. Exactly when and how is a mystery. What is known, however, is that learning to use manners, like everything else, takes time and practice. Someday the playdate's mother or your child's teacher will report that you have an incredibly polite child. At first you will wonder if they are talking about your offspring. And then you will realize that all of those reminders are sinking in. She does know her manners. And then sometime, I promise you, your child will come forth with a *thank you* right from her heart, and you will know you have done your job.

CHAPTER 6

❖

"It's Not Fair!"

Day-to-Day Parenting Dilemmas

When I was a kindergarten teacher before I had my family, I could hardly wait to have my own children. I absolutely loved and could tolerate everything about my students. It wasn't until I had my own family that I realized just why I had loved the children in my classes so much: at the end of the school day, they all went home.

In the course of just plain old daily living, children do things and say things that drive you mad. Sometimes you can stomach these things, but then there are *those* days when the whining drives you crazy, and the ninth *"That's not fair"* sends you right to the chocolate cupboard. What's a parent to do? These are the day-to-day dilemmas, and for each of them there is a script.

Whining

There is no behavior more universally disliked by parents than whining. Simply stated, it is intolerable. Like chalk on a blackboard, it grates in the worst way. It doesn't even matter what the child is saying: if it's in that whiny voice, you can't stand it. The very sound of that voice brings out parenting behaviors that you swore you would never use. Whining is not a developmental milestone. But it sure seems that way, as every parent commiserates about the problem. As is the case with tantrums, we know when it begins—as early as two and a half or three—but when it ends has everything to do with the way whining is handled.

An aspect of whining that is developmental, however, is the child's learning to tolerate *not* getting what he wants. Learning to tolerate the frustration that follows a NO response is a big part of growing up. It takes time and experience. Being able *not* to whine often includes being able to tolerate NO for an answer.

Whining is hard for parents not only because it is so annoying but also because it comes with a question mark. Sometimes the request within the whine is actually reasonable. You wonder, *"Why shouldn't I just give him the water and ignore the whining? It's hot out, and he's tired."* Sometimes whining feels like an indictment and you think, *"Well, maybe he's right. I did spend more time with his sister than with him. That's why he's whining."* Your child senses your ambivalence and thinks, *"Maybe this is going to work."* And he keeps on whining. The icky, whiny tone is overlooked and the content gets your attention. The child outsmarted you. Whining worked.

Children whine for a variety of reasons—they are tired or hungry, frustrated or bored, or the environment is too loud or too chaotic—but all the reasons lead to the one most powerful reason why a child whines: for your attention.

Have you ever wondered why children don't whine in school at all? Your child holds himself together there, reserving his worst behavior for you. He knows he can be icky with you, and so he is. You will not stop loving him. Further, there's no whining at school because your child doesn't crave his teacher's attention like he craves yours. He is accustomed to sharing the teacher with other children. It's you, dear parent, whom he doesn't want to share (with a sibling, with a parent, with the phone . . .), and he will do whatever it takes to get your attention, positive or negative. Your child whines because it works.

Tips and Scripts for Dealing with Whining

- **Resolve not to respond to whining.** This is the most powerful way to eradicate whining. Do not respond at all—not with one single comment, word, or sound. Remember, children whine to get your attention. Do not give it to them. It is crucial that you be scrupulously consistent in your nonresponse. In order for whining to stop, it cannot *ever* work. If there is any chance at all that you are going to give in, do it *before* the whining starts.

- **Notice when whining most often occurs.** In most families whining happens at the end of the day or in the morning when families are hurrying to get going. Keep track of when the whining happens so you can figure out which of your child's triggers is the cause and anticipate the possible antidotes for those that are unavoidable. For example, your child may need to have shorter playdates, eat dinner earlier, or be allowed more time to get dressed in the morning.

- **Whining is often a habit.** Children become so accustomed to using their whiny voices—and getting what they want—that they don't even know they are doing it. Your child is not trying to be annoying; he is trying to get his needs met. If whining has always worked in the past, it is what he will continue to do. The habit needs to be broken.

- **Teach your child about his different voices.** Telling your child not to whine doesn't work because it doesn't teach him what he should do instead. Your child needs to learn the difference between a whiny voice and a regular (acceptable) voice. This lesson needs to be taught only when you and your child are not in the heat of a whiny moment. At a quiet time, have a chat with your child about his different voices. At that time, and at that time only, you can imitate his whiny voice for educational purposes only. Try saying: *"Sometimes you use a voice with me that is a whiny voice. It sounds like this_____. Do you recognize that voice? That voice does not work with me. When you want my help or attention, you need to use your regular voice. That is the voice I will listen to and that will work."*

  You can also practice using different kinds of voices with your child at other moments that are not heated. When you are reading a story together, use a whiny voice for one of the characters and invite your child to do the same. Point out the differences so that he will become aware of them.

  It may be more effective to record the very voice you dislike. Let your child hear it along with his regular voice. Make sure you tell him: *"THAT is the voice! That is the voice that works! That is your regular voice. I love it. It's music to my ears. When you use your wonderful regular voice, it is easy to hear you and give you the attention you need."*

- **Explain the change.** Let your child know what is happening. He is accustomed to whining and getting what he wants, or at least getting your attention: *"You know how sometimes when you whine I ask you to use a* *different voice? Well, there is a change that you need to know about. I am no longer going to respond when you whine. Whatever it is that you want, you will not get it if you use a whiny voice. That is not a voice I want to hear, so I will say nothing at all. You will need to use your regular voice if you want my help or my attention."*

- **Develop a signal.** As whining is a habit, some children will need to be reminded over and over to use a different voice. In order to spare you both frustration, develop a signal that reminds him to use his regular voice: *"You and I are going to have a special signal that means you are whining and need to use a different voice. When I tug on my ear like this, it means 'Start over with your regular voice.'"*

- **Catch your child *not* whining.** When you are working on breaking the whining habit, it is crucial that you praise your child for using his regular voice in place of the whine. When he does, you can't praise him too much. It is a powerful motivator and strengthens your child's ability *not* to whine. You can extend the praise to include telling your partner at the dinner table (or when you're within earshot of your child while on the phone): *"I wish you could have heard how many times Penelope used her regular voice today. There was no whining at all!"*

- **Take time immediately to answer the nonwhiny voice.** This will help him learn that his regular voice really works. If you are unable to grant his request at that time, give him an ETA as to when you will: *"You asked me with your great regular voice! I know that you are waiting for me to help you with your building. I am going to help you very soon, after I finish folding the laundry."*

  Even if the answer to a request might be an outright no, you must still respond right away, but do so in a kind and understanding way, leaving the child with some hope: *"You used your regular voice so well. You really want to play outside right now, and I see how disappointed you are that you can't. After lunch you can play outside for sure."*

- **Give your child information.** Children are capable of understanding what might have been lurking underneath a particular whining incident. At a later time, you can chat about what you think caused the whininess. In so doing you will help your child to learn to express what he was really feeling that caused the whining: *"I think you were really angry* *at me when I wouldn't take you to the park, and so you used that whiny voice with me. Next time, you could tell me, 'Mommy, I am so angry at you. I want to go to the park.' And I will understand how you are feeling."*

- **Do not respond to public whining.** Whining is whining wherever it happens. If you are in public and you have a whiner, he should get the same nonresponse as he would get at home.

Persistent whiners are usually the ones who have figured out with whom their whining works. Children are quick learners, and it is your job as the parent to teach them how to get their needs met without whining.

Back Talk

Back talk is one of those behaviors that is difficult because it feels like it is a challenge to your authority, and it makes parents feel powerless and even incompetent.

Most children talk back to their parents. You probably remember doing it—as well as the back of the hand that followed. In the old days back talk was not tolerated. The punishment was immediate and often severe. The back talk stopped because the children were terrified.

As discussed, you are dragging around the luggage that holds the template for your approach to parenting, but seldom do you use your parents' methods.

The parenting pendulum has swung from acceptance of using fear as a tool to the idea that children should always *like* you; they shouldn't feel angry at you, nor should they feel discomfort. So when they talk back, you are not really sure what to do.

Children talk back for many reasons. Back talk may result from a child's being tired, hungry, overloaded, or just from needing your attention. The most common reason that the young child talks back is to assert himself. It is no coincidence that back talk begins to fully flower after the child turns four, the age of Tarzan chest pounding. He is testing his separateness from you, playing with his independence. It is not unlike a peacock spreading his feathers or a predator peeing in another animal's territory: *I'll show you.*

Of course, you view back talk as being disrespectful. But back talk is not necessarily a sign of disrespect for you. (Understanding respect and all of its nuances requires a broad understanding of the different relationships different people have with one another. That takes lots of experience. See the discussion on respect in chapter 5, page 81.)

When your child first started to talk back, did you notice how that first sassy phrase was delivered with kind of a question mark on the end? *"Just get it yourself . . . ?"* Or maybe he said it slightly under his breath, or mumbled it, with his chin down, speaking into his chest. These are sure signs that he's trying back talk on for size: *let's just see how this works.*

The good news is that rarely does a child talk back to a teacher or a coach. If he demonstrates the ability to hold himself together at school or karate class, to treat adults with the respect that is expected, then you don't have a whole lot to worry about. Back talk usually happens with the people the child trusts the most, in the environment in which he can let it all hang out. That doesn't make it okay, but it is a big relief.

So what can you do about the back talk, regardless of where it happens?

Tips and Scripts for Dealing with Back Talk

- **Remember that children learn by testing limits.** In order to know what is and isn't acceptable, children need to try things out. The first time you hear it, let your child know that he is talking back and that it is unacceptable: *"The way you just spoke is called back talk. It is not acceptable, and I will not listen."* And add: *"I want to hear what you have to say, but you need to find a better way to tell me. You need to change your tone."*

   When the waters have calmed, have the conversation about back talk. Learning and change do not happen in the heat of the moment.

- **Mind your anger.** You want your child to learn not to use back talk, that it is unacceptable, and to learn that it doesn't work. If you overreact, raise your voice, and show intense anger, your child will not only focus on the anger, but he will also see the power of his words, having gained the attention he craves. Allow the lesson to be learned. Be composed. Speak slowly, clearly, and firmly. Let your tone indicate that you mean what you say, without raising your voice.

- **Do not engage when your child talks back.** Your child needs to learn that back talk is not an effective or acceptable way of communicating. Do not empower him. Stand up, walk away, flash a look, but do not engage. There is no chance that your child is going to change his feelings as a result of your explanation. Do not explain your point of view. It is not a battle of wills. There is no battle to be won; there is only one lesson to be taught: *it is not acceptable to use back talk with me. I will not listen or engage with you.*

- **Be done with it.** As infuriating as back talk is, when it is done, let it be done. State your expectation and move on. In so doing you sap the back talk of its power over you.

- **Give your child permission to disagree with you respectfully.** Let your child know not only that you don't expect him always to agree with you, but that there are appropriate ways for him to express his disagreement: *"You don't have to agree with what I say, Rachel. I even like that you have your own opinion. But you need to tell me your opinion in another way that isn't disrespectful. You could say, 'Daddy, I don't agree with you. I think you are wrong. I think I should be able to stay up late tonight.' But when you use back talk, I cannot hear your opinion and the discussion is stopped."*

- **Defiance in the form of back talk should be ignored.** As a show of independence or testing his limits, the five- or six-year-old may defy you with a big fat *"NO!"* or *"You can't make me"* when you give a directive. This too is a form of back talk. Maintain your composure and let your child know exactly what you expect. Get close to him, down on his level, which will underscore your seriousness, and say: *"I told you to pick up your jacket, and I expect you to do it."*

  And then walk away. That is as much attention as he should receive. You will be surprised to see that in his own time and likely with a tremendous amount of attitude, your child will comply . . . eventually.

- **Choose your battles.** There are going to be opportunities for you simply to turn your head. Take them. If your child walks out of the room, mumbling under his breath that *"you stink,"* you may just need to ignore it. At least he didn't scream it in your face. That is a step in the right direction; he is learning that he may not talk that way to you. There will be face-saving eye rolls and *tsks* and exasperated exhalations that you should choose to overlook; at least he got the message. Everything cannot be a battle.

Swearing

Does it seem to you that swearing is much more common today than ever before? I think so. Foul language, as our parents used to call it, has become part of our culture's lexicon. We hear it so much that sometimes we don't even hear it. I hope we are not becoming immune to it.

Like the use (or not) of manners, children's swearing is seen as a sign of poor parenting. But it's not about you: it is part of a child's development.

The young child, in his egocentric state, doesn't give much thought to other people and his effect on them. As he grows, with development and maturity and appropriate coaching from you, he will learn how his words affect others and will take that into consideration. But he is not there yet.

Young children learn language from the world around them—the grocery store, the playground, the car pool. They are not only absorbing the words they hear around them but also learning when those words are used. They notice the intensity with which they are delivered and the power they have. Your child is fascinated by words. It is another of the ways in which he explores his world: *"This is what I just heard. I think I will try it out and see how it sounds and what happens."* By age three, he has already developed an expansive and sometimes very colorful vocabulary of about two thousand words. He has been busy absorbing everything he hears and trying much of it on for size, and he discovers that words are magical and powerful. There is a cause-and-effect aspect: *I say this word, and that happens. Wow!*

Your child mimics what he hears friends, older siblings, and characters in the media say without really knowing what they are saying. He learns which words seem to have more power than others. Those swear words are just added to the collection. Whether or not they become part of his daily verbal repertoire depends, in part, upon you.

While most adults agree that certain words are definitely swear words, especially those with four letters, others extend the category. For some, uttering religious words, like taking the name of God in vain, is a form of swearing. Others feel that words that refer to sex or body parts are also in this category. Even within some families there is disagreement about the use of swear words. One parent may openly swear while the other cringes at the thought. Before you begin to address the issue of your children's swearing, it is important that you and your partner come to some agreement about what words are unacceptable. While older children are capable of learning that you can say the "*f*-word" with Uncle Jon but not with Daddy, the inconsistency is confusing for young children. Children ought not to be given mixed messages within the home environment.

Tips and Scripts for Dealing with Swearing

- **Decide which words are never okay to speak and stick with that rule.** This applies to everyone who lives in your house . . . including you. If swearing is part of your particular style, don't expect your child *not* to swear.

- **Spread the word.** Enlist the help of all the adults who come into regular, extended contact with your child, as well as your relatives, young and old. Explain the bad habit your child is picking up and ask them to eliminate swearing and model the use of appropriate language. The older siblings should be asked to curb their language in the presence of your young child, even when you are not around. You might be surprised how well they will comply when they feel that you and they are on the same team.

- **With young children (two- to four-year-olds), continue to ignore the word.** As your young child is busy testing the limits of his world, it is possible that he will use the word again and again, as he looks for a response. Ignore, ignore, ignore. Not getting a rise out of you, the child will soon stop using the word. And the swearing will be over . . . for now.

- **Do not overreact.** If your child's use of a swear word brings an explosion of a reaction from you, you'd better believe his swearing will not stop. If you get angry, he is reminded of just how much power he has. If you laugh, it will only encourage a repeat performance. Give your young child a calm, clear message about the unacceptability of his language, and be done with it.

- **Older children (five- and six-year-olds) may require a different response.** The older child uses swear words for different reasons. He may be trying them on for size and to see your reaction, or he may truly be expressing a strong feeling . . . just as he has seen you do. If it is the former, first set a calm, clear limit about the unacceptability of his language. If it continues, get down on his level, look him straight in the eye, and say: *"I will not be with someone who uses that language."* And walk away, giving him no more attention at all.

If your child's swearing is a result of anger or frustration, validate the feeling and help him to explore a more appropriate way to express it, but mention at a later, calmer time: *"When you used swear words before I think you were really frustrated that the puzzle wouldn't fit. If you had asked for my help, I would have helped you. But I will not listen to bad language."*

- **Suggest alternatives to swear words.** Sometimes a child will accept a substitute swear word. Words that are funny or have a special zing can do the trick: *Fooey-spitooey! Rats! Dang it! Oh, potato chips!* Even pretend words can do the trick. I once had a preschool student who used to scream "Becca!" when he was really angry. Using those words yourself legitimizes their use and gives them power too. Remember: monkey see, monkey do.

- **Never wash out a child's mouth with soap.** You're probably thinking that people don't really do that anymore. You are wrong. In the heat of the moment and without a clue about what to do, many a parent resorts to that archaic and abusive form of punishment. Causing fear and resentment is not sound parenting.

- **Comment on the language that you hear.** When others, not even people you know, use swear words within earshot, make a comment to your child: *"I am sorry that man doesn't know any better than to use swear words. I don't want to be around people who talk like that."* Your child will learn that your standards are consistent and not just for him.

The good news is that as children get older and their self-control increases, swearing usually lessens until it becomes a "big kid" problem. And that's a whole different story.

The Word *Stupid*

All parents dislike swearing, but many absolutely cannot tolerate the use of the word *stupid*. (And, frankly, it is easier to eradicate swearing than it is the use of this word.)

The problem is that *stupid* is a marginal word. It isn't really a swear word, but it isn't a nice word to use either. Adding to the problem is the fact that parents model the many uses of the word *stupid* all the time: *"Look at the stupid man, crossing right in the middle of the street,"* or *"That was such a stupid thing to do,"* or *"I shouldn't have done that. I just feel so stupid."*

If you cannot bear the word, if ignoring it doesn't work, if *stupid* is running rampant in your family, then:

- **Reform your ways and remove *stupid* from your own vocabulary.** Treat it like a swear word, if you so feel. *"In our family* stupid *is not a word that we use. Let's find other words that say how angry you are."*
- **Give information.** *"Stupid is a really unkind thing to call a person, and I want to tell you why. Stupid means that someone's brain isn't working well, not the way it is supposed to. And that would be so terrible and sad. It is a hurtful word. That's why I never call a person stupid."*

  With this explanation, you are giving not only information but also a lesson in empathy, helping a child think about how someone else would feel if you called him that name. Depending upon both your tolerance of the word and your child's ability to regulate his usage, you can add: *"It is okay to call a thing* stupid—*stupid table, stupid car—but it is not ever something that we call people."*
- **State your limit and move on.** Once your child knows how you feel, just flashing a look can be reprimand enough. As with swearing, back talk, and whining, too much attention might be just what is needed to fuel the behavior.

Potty Talk

"Potty talk" is a stage through which most four-year-olds pass, especially boys. In light of development, potty talk makes sense. Kids this age are very interested in their own bodies and in all their parts, especially the ones that are covered by the bathing suit. The toilet skills they recently (or almost have) mastered bring forth all kinds of new words and inventive ways of using them. In their mastery, children step back and tease about those parts that were only recently the object of so much attention.

Four-year-olds also are still working on figuring out their limits and boundaries. What is okay to say and do and what isn't? Potty talk pushes that limit. *It's not really bad; it's only a little bad. Just months ago, all my parents talked about was my pee pee and poop and tushie. Now I'll try it.*

In addition, the four-year-old's sense of humor is just developing, and right now it is pretty basic. There is nothing quite as hysterically funny to a child this age as a friend asking, *"Please pass the poo-poo crackers."* Since kids love an audience, the jokes, aka the potty talk, just keep on coming. And we all know some adults whose humor has never gone beyond this stage!

Tips and Scripts for Dealing with Potty Talk

- **Give information.** Explain to your child: *"I know that you really like to say words like* poopie *and* pee pee *and* tushie. *Those are words that you may say with your friends who want to talk that way or when you are in your own room. Those are not words that grown-ups want to hear."*

- **If at all possible, ignore the potty talk.** Attention of any kind (including laughter) will only fuel it, as it feeds on an audience of absolutely anyone who will listen, especially another child. Enlist the help of the older siblings by asking them also to ignore and not fuel the potty talk by egging on the younger sibling.

- **Mind your own use of real words for body parts and processes.** When adults use made-up, cutesie names for body parts and bodily functions, the child gets the message that there is something not quite okay about those parts or functions. Using correct names and labels gives the child permission to talk comfortably about these things, to ask any questions he may have and not feel embarrassed.

- **Teach your child other ways to be funny.** At the same stage when children are indulging in potty talk, they are beginning to cultivate a sense of humor. Buy a joke book and help your child to learn why some jokes are funny. Teach him about riddles and knock-knock jokes. Four-year-olds think they are an absolute hoot. (It doesn't get much funnier than: *Knock Knock? Who's there? Mickey Mouse's underwear!* That's the best of both worlds—jokes and potty talk!)

As children get older, potty talk usually lessens, though for some it never totally loses its punch. Look at your own friends for proof!

"It's Not Fair!"

In the eyes of the child, the things that life dishes out are supposed to be equal for everyone, but they seldom are. Someone will always be shortchanged. In his dream of fairness, however, what your child is really thinking is, *"I want the most, the biggest, the best, the first."* No matter what you do, no matter how hard you may try to make things fair, your child is likely to find a way to see that it isn't fair. That is because fairness is subjective. What seems fair to you will not seem fair to him. In his egocentric little shoes, unless it is all about him, it isn't the way it should be, and that isn't fair.

"It's not fair" becomes a euphemism for *"I don't like what you have just said."* In that respect it is not unlike the *"But, whhyyy?"* response. (See chapter 1, page 8.) "It's not fair" is a protest. Listening to the words only and not hearing the message of protest and desire, parents respond as if *fairness* were something they should be facilitating.

What is being fair? As discussed in chapter 3, fairness means that everyone gets what he needs at the time. In order for a child to understand that idea, he first needs to accept the reality that each person is unique. Therefore, each person has different needs at different times and will be treated differently. That kind of difference is difficult for a child to grasp. With growth and experience, he will begin to accept that reality. The words your children need to hear over and over are: *"I have different children, and I treat you differently. You each have different needs, and I give you just what you need at the time. That is being fair to you."*

Tips and Scripts for Dealing with "It's Not Fair!"

....

- **Eliminate the "That's not fair" from your own daily usage.** Pay attention to the things that you say. You will be surprised at how often adults say that something isn't fair. Replace those words with the real protest you are feeling.

- **Do not perpetuate the fairness myth.** From your children's earliest ages, stop yourself from trying to treat them equally. If one child needs new shoes, only buy shoes for him. Trying to be equal in your treatment only fuels the child's belief that life is supposed to be fair and that somehow he is being wronged. It sets the child up for many disappointments in the years to come.

- **Acknowledge the feeling, but allow your child to be disappointed.** Learning to tolerate disappointment is one of the most important lessons of childhood and one that is crucial for independent adulthood. While you can acknowledge the child's feelings, do not sabotage his learning by taking away the disappointment: *"You really want to get some new shoes too, and you're so disappointed that I am not getting them for you. When you need new shoes, I will buy them for you."*

- **Acknowledge the desire.** Some feelings can be assuaged by giving them life: *"Tell me what it is you need, and let's make a plan for how it might happen."*

  Have the conversation and honor his desires and "needs," as outrageous as they might be. Then take out a pen and paper and write: *"Jeremy wants new red high-tops the next time he needs new shoes."* It doesn't mean it will happen. It means the child has been heard, his desires validated.

- **Tolerate the protest.** When your child protests that he is not getting shoes and it isn't fair, keep calm and do not allow the comment to get a rise out of you. If you get agitated, you are giving the child the message that he was right: life is supposed to be fair. Instead, you can say: *"Yes, I know. Life sure isn't fair."* It's okay for your child to be unhappy. This too shall pass.

- **Let it go.** Learn not to respond to "It's not fair!" Sooner rather than later, your child will learn that the comment won't change anything. You can even say, *"Do I look like the kind of mom who is going to change her mind when you say that?"*

- **Guard your guilt.** Life is not fair, so don't feel guilty about not making it so. Allowing the guilt to have a voice will only make you vulnerable to being manipulated by your children's cries for fairness.

"I Hate You."

My husband grew up in a family where he was not allowed to "hate" anything. Hate was considered a very strong feeling and a word that should not be used or taken lightly. "I hate you" has particular power for many parents, in part because they have internalized their own parents' feelings about the word.

Another reason why parents react so strongly to "I hate you" is because they suffer from the misguided notion that their child is supposed to like them as a friend. The truth is, your child has friends, and you are not one of them. You are his parent, and that's a much bigger and more important role. Sometimes being a parent means that your child doesn't like the things you say, the decisions you make, or you. Underneath it all, I promise you, your child loves you, even when he says he hates you. If your child didn't feel secure in your love, he wouldn't feel safe saying that he hated you. That would be way too risky.

"I hate you" is an expression of powerful emotion that gets boiled down to three little words. Young children are filled with powerful emotions, and they are just learning the acceptable and unacceptable ways of expressing them. Hate, in particular, is an expression that the young child hears being used all around him, often through gritted teeth. It seems to have real power. *"I hate this traffic." "I hate it when we run out of hot water." "I hate my boss."* There is a lot of hating that your child hears about. Given the opportunity, he is going to try it out.

Young children feel small and powerless, so they look for ways to feel big and powerful. Expressing a strong feeling is one of the ways. Spewing "I hate you" packs a whole lot of power, and it usually elicits a big reaction from the target. The unsuspecting parent, never having had a four-year-old who hates her, is shocked and devastated by such a comment. It's understandable. You have given this child your heart and soul, and what you get in return is a declaration of his hate! It makes you feel really sad. But your child's hate is not about you.

Part of your child's development is learning how to recognize, label, and express his emotions. He needs to learn that it is okay to have strong negative feelings, including anger. Your child isn't stopping to think, *"How will Mommy feel when I tell her I hate her?"* He is thinking only about himself: *"I am angry, really angry. Mommy wouldn't let me have that cookie. I hate Mommy because I really want that cookie."*

Forbidding the use of the expression "I hate you" sends the message that it isn't okay to have those strong feelings. Even when you suggest that he find another way to express himself, the child gets the message that his feeling was not okay. But all feelings have to be acceptable. They are feelings, not actions.

Young children see the world in black and white. It is the way they interpret and organize the world. *Are you a boy or a girl? Are you Christmas or Hanukkah? Are you happy or sad?* It takes maturity in many areas to understand the nuances of gray. There is no room for middle ground yet. How can it be that it is okay to be happy but not angry? *"How could I love Mommy but hate what she is doing (or not letting me do)?"* It's confusing.

As your child matures, he will learn the power of his words and the effect they have on others. That is part of his growing emotional intelligence. But children under six are not there yet. They are all about themselves.

When your child says "I hate you," it is not a forever thing. In fact, it is hardly even momentary. You say, *"No television."* Mikey gets angry, really angry. He says he hates you because you got in the way of his desire: TV. Then he spies his favorite train. Minutes later he calls out to you, *"Where is the caboose?"* It's over. He doesn't hate you anymore.

Here is the good news about children who say "I hate you." Saying "I hate you" is a sign of the child's positive development. Not only is he becoming aware of his effect on other people, but he is also learning to use his words and not his actions to express his feelings.

Tips and Scripts for Dealing with "I Hate You."

- **Teach your child that it is okay for him to be angry at you.** Do not confuse saying "I hate you" with being disrespectful. The two are quite different. By your nonresponse, your child learns that it is safe for him to express his feelings to you; that you will not stop loving him, despite what he has said.

- **Speak to the feeling.** Respond calmly to why you think the child is angry, without commenting on his hate. Remember, calm begets calm: *"You are so angry at me for not letting you watch television now. You know you can watch it later, just like I promised."*

- **Don't try to prove him wrong.** Your child is feeling what he is feeling, and that is powerful stuff. In the heat of the moment, it is impossible to talk anyone, adult or child, out of his feelings. Telling your child that he doesn't mean what he says denies him his feelings. Right then, for that tiny moment, he means it. But the young child doesn't really know the meaning of what he is saying. He is merely expressing a strong feeling to a person with whom he feels safe.

- **Resist the urge to say, *"You hurt my feelings."*** You are the adult, and you are in charge of your own feelings. A child should not have that much power over your feelings. It is way too threatening and scary for him to think that you, his lifeline, are not in command of yourself and the situation. As he matures and gains empathy, he will learn the unkindness of what he says and how his words affect you. For now, he needs to be accepted, warts and all. Besides, with his friends or siblings, your child is already learning the power of his words. If he tells a friend he hates him, the friend is liable not to play with him. That's a natural and powerful consequence. He is learning some important lessons and social skills.

- **Resist the urge to say, *"Well, I love you"* in response to your child's *"I hate you."*** As his parent you are trying to help your child deal with his feelings. Turning his words around will only shame him, as well as give him the message of his expression not being okay.

- **Introduce the existence of that middle ground.** You can suggest to the child who proclaims his hate about something (not a person) previously loved by saying: *"I think you are telling me that peanut butter is not your favorite. Saying 'It's not my favorite' is another way of saying you don't really like it."*

- **If you absolutely cannot stand it, walk away.** While this would be my last-choice response (because it gives the child too much power), if you are falling apart at the pronouncement of hate and truly cannot deal with your child at that moment, say: *"I don't choose to listen to you talk like that, so I am going into another room. We can talk about what you are feeling when you have cooled off."*

Lying

The first time a parent "catches" his child in a lie, he is horrified, fearing that his little angel is going to grow up to be a psychopath or an untrustworthy human being. Wrong, wrong, wrong. Lying is not uncommon, even among young children.

Learning to be a moral person takes maturity, experience, and time. Like all other aspects of development, it is a process that is complicated and requires a parent to be consistent and patient. If you accept that your child is "in process," you'll be able to respond in a helpful and appropriate way to his exploration of telling the truth. Learning to tell the truth is just that . . . a lesson to be learned.

We all know successful, well-adjusted adults who do not adhere to the truth 100 percent of the time. Everyone tells "white lies" sometimes. Yet when a child tells a lie, regardless of the reason, parents assume the worst—that their offspring is on the road to moral decay.

Calling it lying is overkill and is not really applicable to what young children do. Lying as you know it implies some malice and calculated premeditation or intent. Young children are neither developed nor experienced enough to bring into play all the forces of grown-up lying. For that reason alone, I prefer to call it *bending reality to meet one's needs at the time* because, in essence, that is at the root of a child's lying.

Lying is usually not a serious problem in children unless it becomes habitual. If this is the case, you should seek the guidance of a mental health professional.

Children bend reality for a variety of reasons, depending on their ages and stages.

The two- to three-year-old is just beginning to distinguish fantasy from reality. He doesn't have the slightest idea that he is not telling the truth. This child doesn't know what is real, what is really possible, or what is pretend and couldn't happen. Have you ever tried to convince a three-year-old that the monster under his bed is pretend? No can do! Regardless of your guarantee, there is still something really scary under there that may come out and get him in the middle of the night.

Toddlers also engage in wishful thinking. Something that they want badly can morph into something that really happened. How embarrassing is it when your child's preschool teacher calls to congratulate you on the birth of your new baby girl . . . and you just got a new puppy. Instead of telling it like it is, the young child tells it like he wishes it would be.

Your young child has an incredibly active imagination. He has a hard time distinguishing between the things he has imagined and what really truly happened. He creates stories and events that rival the best fiction writers: *"And then my daddy grabbed the alligator, and he threw him in the garage, and . . . and . . . and . . . and the policeman came and he chopped off his head!"* The tall tales they tell! It is very much a part of typical child development. I used to caution the parents of my preschool class students, *"Tell you what, I won't believe the stories your child tells me about you, if you promise not to believe the stories he tells you about me!"*

Sometimes toddlers are so busy that they actually don't remember all that they have done. When you ask, *"Did you put your jewelry box in the bathtub?"* the child may genuinely not remember having done so. Maybe she's not lying; maybe she is just not remembering.

Toddlers are motivated by wanting to please Mommy and Daddy (or the person in authority). Doing what is "right" means doing what will make you happy. They are masters at reading the signs that tell them what you are feeling, observing your glare or upside-down smile or hearing the sigh in your voice. This child will respond with whatever it is that he perceives to be the answer you want to hear and that will make you happy or take your anger away. When you ask, *"Did you put your toys away?"* He'll say, *"Yes, Mommy!"* regardless of whether or not he did.

The young child is in the midst of developing empathy, while still being "all about me." Being able to consider how someone else feels or is affected by his actions or words is just coming into focus. Telling the whole story requires the child to hold two thoughts in his head at the same time: *I want it now*; and *someone else wants it too.* Wanting something so badly that you changed the reality (*"I had it first!"*) in order to have it, sometimes gets in the way of the child's telling the whole story, (*"He had it first, and I really wanted a turn, so I took it."*) which acknowledges another's feelings. That can be hard stuff for the egocentric young child.

Around the time that they turn four, children begin to understand the difference between truth and fiction. Reality gets twisted for other reasons. The child rewrites history in order to get out of doing something he doesn't want to do. *"Did you brush your teeth?"* Of course he didn't, but he says yes because just maybe you will believe him and he'll get out of doing it.

Another common reason for the four-year-old to rewrite history is to protect his tush! He wants to avoid punishment. This child usually knows full well that he has done something that's not okay. One: he may bend reality in the hope that saying it didn't happen will undo the deed. He denies the truth and constructs reality as he knows it should have been: *"I didn't use the paint in my room. I was carrying it to the playroom, and it accidentally spilled on my bedspread."* Two: he engages in out-and-out denial. He knows he has blown it, and he doesn't want to get in trouble: *"Nope. I didn't do it."* This brand of reality bending will continue as your child grows up, well into his teen years and all the way to adulthood. No one likes to get in trouble.

Intentionality also can come into play as a reason for not telling the truth as you see it. It may be perfectly clear that your child is responsible for a particular act that he is denying. But because the misdeed was not his intention, it is really hard for him to take responsibility. *"But I didn't mean to knock over David's building. I was only trying to help."* This child sees it differently than you do. It's not that he is bending reality; it is that he has a whole different point of view, one that is not based on reality from your perspective.

As the child gets older, into the five- and six- and even seven-year-old range, still other reasons for lying come into play. Not only does he now know the difference between fiction and reality, but he has also developed a conscience. He knows that certain things he does disappoint you, and he begins to experience feelings of guilt. He may bend reality in order to dodge your disapproval, as well as avoid getting in trouble. In addition, the older child may want to impress someone, so he tells a tale that he thinks will make him look good in another's eyes. He may stretch reality because he is not feeling so good about himself. In telling a tale, he thinks he will garner attention or praise from someone.

And finally, an older child might bend reality in order to get what he wants. Learning to delay gratification, along with learning to tolerate frustration and disappointment, are two of the hardest lessons young children must learn. *"I want it so badly that I will say whatever it takes to get it."*

So as you can see, the reasons for lying, otherwise known as bending reality, are complicated. Thus there is no one way to handle the stories that spin out of your darling's mouth.

Tips and Scripts for Dealing with "Bending Reality"

- **Do not overreact.** An overreaction on your part will make the act of lying into a much bigger deal than it actually is. Your reaction may actually bring the attention your child is needing, thereby encouraging the behavior in the future.

- **Do not punish your child for lying.** He might not even know that he has done something wrong. Your focus should remain on the reason for the bending of reality and on the misbehavior that the lie is trying to cover. Punishing for the lying will override and sabotage any other behavioral change you might want to create. In addition, it can cause resentment and fear in the child. Any consequences you impose for the lying should be age and developmentally appropriate.

- **Set your child up to tell the truth.** If you are quite sure that your child has committed a misdeed, don't ask him if he has. In a dispassionate way, tell him what you're pretty sure happened. No anger, just the facts, please: *"I know that you have not washed your hands. Please go wash them now."*

  When my own children were this age, upon asking them before a meal if they had washed their hands with soap (even though I knew they likely hadn't), they would look at me quizzically, then look at their hands, and then smell their hands. If there was even a hint of soap odor, the answer was yes. Knowing that they had not, it would have been much better for me simply to have said, *"Please go back and wash your hands, using soap this time."*

- **Never ask a question to which you already know the answer.** If you know who spilled the milk, don't call out, *"Who spilled the milk?"* I can promise you that no one will come leaping into the kitchen, exclaiming,*"I did! I did! Punish me!"* Better to say: *"I see that there is some spilled milk in here. I need someone to please come and help me clean it up."* Usually the culprit will be the one to volunteer, as it helps to relieve some of his guilt.

- **Don't shame your child.** Knowing that there is no malice in the child's lying, take care not to make him feel guilty or that he is a bad person. Shame is not a good child-rearing practice. Instead, deal with the behavior behind the reality bending.

- **Give information.** At a happier, calm time you can have a conversation with your child about telling the whole story. This is when you can explain how important it is to you that your child always tell you the whole, real story, and that that's how you learn to believe what he is saying: *"When something happens or when I ask you a question, it is really important to me that you tell me the whole, real story. That is called telling the truth. When you always tell me the whole story, I always believe you."* You can add, depending upon the child's age: *"When you tell me the whole, real story, I trust you. And I always want to be able to trust you."*

  Though it may be applicable, children under the age of six are too young to understand the message of the tale "The Boy Who Cried Wolf." Don't waste your breath.

- **Look for opportunities to teach the difference between fantasy and reality.** Young children will especially benefit from this lesson. While you are watching a TV program, you can say: *"That lion is make-believe. It's not real. Everyone knows that lions don't talk."* Point to examples of things that are really real versus make-believe in your child's daily life. There will be plenty of opportunities. Then watch the child start to notice and point them out to you.

- **Explain "white lies."** The world is filled with white lies, and as your five- and six-year-old child is learning the importance of telling the truth, he will need help to understand the concept of the white lie. This requires having empathy, which young children are still working on developing.

  White lies are lies, of course, but as a form of politeness and manners of a sort, they might be okay to tell sometimes. There is no malice or hurtfulness in a white lie. In fact, a white lie is told for the express purpose of protecting someone's feelings, out of consideration for another, and it may actually be an act of kindness.

  There are people who believe that it is never okay to tell a lie, even a white lie. But I would bet that even they tell white lies in the service of protecting someone's feelings. Here is how you can explain white lies to your child:

  > *"Once in a while, we might need to tell something called a 'white lie' so that another person's feelings don't get hurt. For example, if a friend asks you if you like her painting and you think it is really ugly, you are not going to say, 'Oh ick, that is really ugly,' because that would not be nice at all and it would make her feel bad. You might say, 'Yes, I like the color blue you used.' That is an example of telling a white lie. When your grandma gives you underwear for your birthday and you really wanted a skateboard, you would say, 'Thank you for the underwear, Grandma. I can use them,' even though you are so disappointed in the gift and wanted to scream out, 'Underwear is a terrible present!' White lies are when you say something that you might not really mean because you don't want to be hurtful."*

Tips and Scripts for Encouraging Truthfulness

- **Tell the truth even when it means saying something your child doesn't want to hear.** *"Yes, you do need to have a shot when we go to the doctor. And yes, I am sorry that it might hurt you. But pretty soon it will stop hurting."*

  The converse of this is the swimming teacher who promises he won't back up as the child struggles to swim toward him . . . and he backs up again and again. Not good. Telling your child the real story goes a long way in building his trust in you and in adults in general.

- **Keep your word and own it when you don't.** Of course you will always try to keep your promise; that's what a promise is all about. But when you have not been able to do as you had promised, step up and say so: *"I broke my promise. I did tell you that I would be home early, and we would play ball before dark, and I just couldn't make that happen. I am so sorry. Sometimes that happens, and I don't like it when it does. Promises are supposed to be for keeps."*

- **Praise the child's truthfulness.** When your child tells you the whole story, owns his misdeeds, and takes responsibility, go out of your way to praise his truth-telling. Behavior that is praised is likely to be repeated. While you will likely need to impose a logical consequence for the misdeed, it will be less severe as a result of the truth telling. Make that clear to your child: *"You told me the whole, real story, and I am really proud of you for doing that. You won't be having your story tonight, but you will tomorrow. The good part is that you are letting me know that I can trust you. That is so important."*

- **Notice and openly admire truth telling by others.** As your child is always watching and absorbing what you say, take pains to show admiration within your child's earshot for acts of honesty and truth telling. Whether it is something a sibling or relative does or something you see on the TV, comment favorably on it: *"That boy sure made the right choice when he told his daddy that he threw the baseball through the window."*

CHAPTER 7

．　　　　．　　　　．　　　❖　　　．　　　　．　　　　．

"How Did the Baby Get in Your Tummy?"

Learning about the Birds and the Bees

Today, couples are marrying later and starting families at an older age than ever before. For these parents, sex and baby making might have been mutually exclusive: *my husband (partner) and I have sex because we love each other. We went to the doctor (lawyer!) when we wanted to have a baby.* Even if you are a single parent by choice, if you adopted your child, if you are part of a gay or lesbian couple, or if you used a surrogate, your child still needs to know where babies come from and what having sex is. I haven't met a parent who doesn't want her child to learn about sex and making babies in the context of a loving relationship, regardless of how the child might have been conceived

We know that young people are becoming sexually active at earlier ages, which means that not only do your children need to know about sex, but they also need to learn about it from you sooner than you think. They need to have the facts in order to make the decisions that are right for them. So even though talking to your young child about sex may seem premature (and daunting), it is crucial. This chapter will help.

Each of us brings a different history to our role as parent and teacher of sex. Your own attitudes about sex and bodies have been developed over a long time, influenced by your experiences, your parents, even your grandparents, and by the culture in which you grew up. You carry your history in your personal and ever-present set of luggage. It is your template not only for how you feel about sex and sexuality but also for what you want your children to know and how you are going to teach it. For that reason alone, there is no single answer to any of the questions raised in this chapter.

I will tell you, however, that at some point soon you do need to address your own feelings about bodies, nudity, and sex. If you say one thing and feel or model another, your child will pick up on it. Children spot hypocrisy faster than you can imagine. Before you know it, your child will ask how old you were when you had your first "real" kiss or when you first had sex. Yikes! It's time to start thinking about it now.

In recalling how they learned about sex, most parents don't remember what they learned or thought when they were three, four, or five years old. Rather, they usually conjure up memories from when they were nine, ten, and thirteen years or older. When asked how they learned about sex, most parents tell me something along the lines of: *"I learned it from my friends"* or *"I learned it from the movies."* But the sex lessons begin way before that.

Sex Education

As the birds-and-the-bees conversations begin, there is a basic reality you must accept: just as you did, your children will learn about sex from the culture, and not only from you. Out in the world they see billboards, bus stop benches, magazine covers, and people who are provocatively dressed. But ours is a much more stimulating sexual culture than it used to be, and it is certainly very different from the one in which you were raised. Not only is sex all around for your children to behold, but they are also watching your reactions and hearing your comments about it too. It's all part of their lesson. And every experience is sending messages about bodies, sexuality, and relationships.

It is the parent's job to help the child digest this racy culture. You need to set standards for what you believe is appropriate, ones that demonstrate the values that you hope your child will take with her into adulthood. The world is certainly not going to convey this for you.

Tips for Helping Your Child Absorb
Your **Values in Our Culture of Sexuality**

. . . .

- **Have family meals.** You might be sick of hearing it, and you might think that your lifestyle simply doesn't allow you the opportunity to do so, but family meals do matter. Be it dinner or breakfast, eat and talk together. Share ideas, stories, and opinions. The more conversations you have, the more your child will learn about what is important to you and will take your values as her own.

- **Watch television and movies with your (older than three-year-old) child**. Talk about what you see as you are viewing it. You might not realize it now, but your child is absorbing the values behind your comments, in just the same way you absorbed those of your parents.

- **Comment on the billboards and bus stop benches you see.** Don't be afraid to give your own opinion. Even if you get the sigh or the eye roll as your child gets older, it is important for her to hear your opinion. Children need help in processing, digesting, and categorizing the vast amount of input they receive from the outside world.

- **Allow your child the time it takes to grow up.** Growing up is not supposed to happen overnight. In his book *The Hurried Child*, David Elkind describes well how our society is hurrying our children in unhealthy and unproductive ways.

- **Stand firm in your beliefs.** Do not be afraid to say *NO* to a movie you think your child is too young to see or that you think is inappropriate, or to impose restrictions on things that don't represent your values. This can be particularly difficult with your second child, who might be exposed to these things earlier than you first were. Don't fall victim to *"I want to go, too. It's not fair!"* or *"But Melanie's mommy lets her . . ."* Feel confident answering with, *"Yes, I know you are disappointed. The answer is still no. We will find something else to do"* or *"Yes, I know that about Melanie's mommy, and in our family . . ."*

- **Dress your child like a child**. Children should be children, and they do not wear provocative outfits. Just because you wear thong underwear (or very revealing clothing) doesn't mean your young daughter can or should.

- **Be aware of the message you are sending your child about what is important.** Is appearance getting more play than the way a child treats her friends or siblings?

- **Be the person you want your child to be.** To a great degree, your child is your apprentice as she grows up. She will develop your values by living with you, watching what is important to you, noticing how you dress, and how you behave as a person. It may not seem that way right now or even as she hits the teen years, but the adult version of your child can be surprisingly familiar.

Here's a question: in what room of your house do you think children learn about sexuality? Among the people in my parenting groups, the most common answer is the bathroom, followed by the bedroom. But I think the answer is the kitchen. Why? Because the kitchen is the center of family life. It is where children see the normal interactions of daily living. The kitchen is the center of home learning because here life is real and spontaneous. It is where parents chat, prepare dinner, and supervise the children playing.

Sexuality is more than the sex act; it is about bodies, self-image, attitudes, and relationships. It is about being genuinely at ease with someone; it is about being kind, tender, and respectful of another person.

Children need to learn about sex in a context; it is the context of relationships, feelings, and bodies. Many problems with relationships develop as a result of having viewed sex as a goal in and of itself and not as a form of intimacy with another human being.

When Mommy comes home from work, when Daddy arrives after some time away, do they greet each other with a big hug and a kiss, or even a loving slap on the tush? Or does one head right for the mail while the other throws out a cursory, *"Hi, hon, how was your day?"* Children need to see their parents being a couple, treating each other respectfully, lovingly kissing and hugging and laughing. Affection is the best context for the first lessons about sexuality. If Mom doesn't greet Dad with a hug or a kiss, but the greeting consists of *"Why are you home so late?"*, this too is a lesson about relationships.

Raising children to be thoughtful, kind, and compassionate teaches them more about how to be in adult relationships than will any lesson in anatomy. Teaching children to be respectful of others' feelings and bodies as well as their own will eventually generalize to their adult relationships. We model that respect day in and day out. It is our behavior and not just our words that teach the fundamental lessons about relationships.

No matter what the surrounding culture doles out, you play the biggest part in establishing most of the basics of your child's sexual life. You will build the foundation for her sexual knowledge. You will shape her moral views. There is even evidence that you will play a role in the age at which her sexual activity will begin as well as in the likelihood that she will take proper safety precautions when the time comes. As the parent, you will have an impact on your child's ability to make the tough decisions; yours will be the voice in her head when she has to withstand peer pressure. The point is that learning about sexuality *is* about *parenting*.

Setting the Stage for Sex Education

Sex education begins at birth. When your infant cries, you pick her up gently, whispering in her ear, calming her down. The lesson she learns is that the people who love you take care of you and respond to your needs. You carefully sponge warm water over her body when you bathe her, and your baby learns how good it feels to be touched and loved by another person.

Then it gets complicated because new messages are added to your love, messages about bodily functions that she can't help. When you scrunch up your nose as you change your baby's diaper and say, *"Oh icky, stinky diaper"* your baby is getting her first message about what you think about something her body does. Already the information is being learned and labeled.

You know the song "Head, Shoulders, Knees and Toes"? It names all the body parts, and none of those words ends in an *ie* or a *y*. Yet when it comes to naming the private body parts, we give them cutesie names, like "boobie," "tushie," and "cuchie." The song doesn't call them "headsies," "kneesies," and "toesies," does it? The message your child gets about those *other* parts is that there is something different about them. (Though "tushie" seems to be the one universally acceptable *-ie* name that is the exception.) But cutifying other private parts tells your child that there is something uncomfortable and maybe even unspeakable about those parts of his anatomy. It's a message. Use the real names for body parts with your child: penis, testicles, vulva, vagina, breast. Say them and your child will be as comfortable as you are, as well as have the proper words for communication. (Perhaps the reasons for your own comfort level—or lack thereof—in using accurate names for body parts is lurking in your own luggage.)

All babies are born with their sexual apparatus in place, and they have physical responses from the moment of birth. Male babies even have erections while they are still in utero. By ten months of age, babies can deliberately fondle themselves. A parent's response to this, as the baby is observing you, sends a message. Do you brush her hand away from her genitals? Do you say, *"No, No. Don't touch,"* or giggle and comment under your breath?

Young children, especially two- and three-year-olds, can be enthusiastically physical. In fact, three-year-olds are enthusiastic about lots of things. They are big huggers, kiss blowers, snugglers, and masturbators, and they love to be naked! Is that okay with you, or does it make you feel uncomfortable? Do you allow for naked time before bath or in the morning before she gets dressed? These are beginning lessons about bodies.

Public versus Private

When it comes to bodies, one of your biggest jobs as a parent and sex educator is teaching your child what is appropriate and under what circumstances. Just as you create rules for where it's okay to eat food, so you need to communicate rules for when your child can be naked and when and where she handles her private parts. When a child is three, you should introduce the concept of public versus private.

Tips and Scripts for Teaching Public Versus Private

- **Introduce the concept of public versus private.** *"Things that you do all by yourself are private. Things that you do when there are other people around are called public."*

- **Introducing the word *privacy*.** You can say: *"When I want to be alone, all by myself, that is called having my privacy."*

  When you are in the bathroom, and you want privacy, you can tell you child: *"I am in the bathroom now, and I would like some privacy; that's why I am closing the door. I will be out in a minute."*

  I offer no promises here, by the way, that this one will work. Children like to be with their parents *wherever* they are. I offer this script only as a lesson about privacy!

- **Teach that everyone is entitled to privacy.** Teach your child to knock on your bedroom, bathroom, or study door if it is closed, and then wait for your response. Likewise, you need to show respect for your child's privacy. If she is behind a closed door, you need to knock and ask to be admitted.

- **Explain about private parts.** Your child needs to be taught that certain parts of her body are private. Until you teach this lesson, the child doesn't have a clear notion of what her private parts are. You can say: *"Your private parts are the parts that are covered by a bathing suit or by my bra and panties or by Daddy's underpants. Everyone has private parts."*

- **Explain that some activities happen in private.** When your child is handling her genitals in the family room, she needs to learn that there is a place that activity happens, and it is a private place. Tell her: *"I know it feels good to touch your private parts. That is something that you can do in private, in your bedroom or in the bathroom."* (For information on masturbation, see below.)

Tips and Scripts for Talking to Your Child about Healthy Bodies

It is crucial that you give your child a positive sense of her own body and teach her to respect her body. Here's how:

- **Teach your child that her body is hers to take care of.** Tell her: *"There are lots of ways that we take care of our bodies. We eat food to keep us healthy and powerful; we exercise to keep our bodies fit; we keep ourselves clean, and we brush our teeth. In all these ways we keep our bodies healthy and safe. That is the way we respect our bodies."*

- **Teach your child that she is the boss of her body.** This is the beginning of teaching your children that it is *they* who are in control of their bodies: *"You are the boss of your own body. Only Mommy or Daddy (or the caregiver or Granny) or the doctor can touch you. You are the boss of who touches your body and what your body does."*

- **Model taking care of your own body.** Allow your child to see how you take care of your own body and narrate what you do: *"I take a shower or bath every day because that is one of the ways that I take good care of my own body. It is how I respect myself."*

Masturbation

Our culture is filled with notions, taboos, and many a comedy routine all about masturbation, but it is still accepted that adults masturbate. Isn't it funny how something that is considered "normal" for adults to do doesn't seem "normal" for children?

News bulletin: most children masturbate. It is a normal part of the child's growth and development. There is nothing harmful about it. It is not a precursor to your child becoming a sex maniac or a sexual deviant. She is simply getting to know her body and how it works. In the same way that she explores all the parts of her body, your child explores her genitals just because they are there. In her very first year of life, mid diaper change, the child figures out that it feels really good to touch herself. Little boys tug at their penises; little girls pull at their labia. And so it begins.

The young child has absolutely no awareness that her body exploration is a *loaded* activity. It is parental discomfort and embarrassment that make masturbation anything more than doing something that feels good. The message you give your child about masturbating, like everything else, depends upon your own feelings and history with it.

If you are not comfortable with masturbation and give your child that message, it will not necessarily stop the behavior. Once a child discovers the good feelings she gets from touching herself, the behavior cannot be extinguished—just ask the parent of a particularly avid masturbator! People, especially children, do what feels good. Whether they do it with guilt or shame is another issue. Your message of masturbation not being okay will only make your child feel guilty about doing something that she really likes to do.

A child's masturbation is a different story from the masturbation of a teen or adult, which involves some sexual fantasy. Your young child doesn't even know what sex is! We are not talking about bringing oneself to climax; we are talking about a young child handling her genitals, outside or inside her clothing.

Why Do Children Masturbate?

Children masturbate for many different reasons. As stated, it is a part of normal body exploration, and it just plain feels good.

Masturbation also meets other needs in the young child. It is one of the ways that a child relaxes and "chills out." Children, like adults, experience pressures and stresses throughout their day, and masturbating helps them to unwind. The child may get a dazed, faraway look on her face as she masturbates, relaxing and settling down. For the young child, it can have a soothing effect. When a child has been upset or when she is tired, she may masturbate, perhaps not even consciously, to relieve the tension that she feels.

A young child's masturbating usually peaks between the ages of two to five. Around the age of four or five, your child will become particularly sensitive to her peers and others who may comment or judge her. After that she learns what is socially acceptable to do and where to do it, and she understands public versus private. (Of course, the hormones and drives of puberty launch a resurgence of activity below the belt, but by that time you will have no idea what your child is up to in her bedroom or shower.)

Tips and Scripts for Dealing with Masturbation

- **Do not overreact.** Your *big* reaction will give masturbation a meaning for the young child that it ought not have. Your child needs to feel good and comfortable with her body. Don't nag, threaten, or punish the child, which will give the message that this normal activity is not acceptable. Your overreaction adds fear and stigma that could have a lifelong effect.

- **Ignore it.** If it is not excessive, not getting in the way of all the things the child can be doing during her day, ignore it. It's meeting a need, and soon the child will move on to a more interesting activity.

- **Especially at bedtime and naptime, ignore it.** These are the times when masturbation is completely "legal," so leave it alone.

- **Focus on the location and not the activity.** Without judgment, begin to teach your child that there is a time and a place for masturbation. Merely give her information, limits, and boundaries without commenting on the activity itself. As discussed, this is the lesson about public versus private activities.

- **Don't lose your cool over public masturbation.** Masturbating in public should be treated in the same way that you handle behaviors that are unacceptable in public (like nose picking, see chapter 5, page 99): *"Touching your private parts is something that you enjoy in private, when you are at home. It is not something that you do when other people are around."*

- **Be calm about masturbation at school.** It is not uncommon for a preschool-age child to sit in circle time, one hand in her pants, mindlessly touching herself. It is soothing and relaxing. It is important that you check with your child's teacher or school director so that you are clear about what (negative) messages your child might be getting there. Tell your child's teacher what your feelings are and how you deal with masturbating at home. Even in school, the teacher can quietly and privately remind the child that *"touching your private parts should be done in private, at home, when no one else is around."*

The teacher can also ignore it. Publicly calling attention to the behavior will only humiliate the child and draw attention to the forbidden aspect of masturbating.

- **Give information.** Girl children especially need to learn the safety message that they never put any foreign objects in their bodies: *"It is fine for you to use your hands to touch your private parts. But we never use anything else in our private parts. Other things may not be clean or safe and could hurt you."*

- **Try not to go overboard about cleanliness.** There are some people who feel it is unclean for a child, especially a female, to masturbate without first washing her hands. These people would also like their daughters to wash their hands when they are done. While each person has her own issues and ideas about cleanliness and health precautions, I suggest you not get carried away. Your child is already, presumably, learning to wash her hands after she uses the toilet. Eventually, the lesson will carry over to other bodily activities, like masturbation. Living with you, clean parent, she is liable to absorb your habits when it comes to hand washing. But be careful not to make her crazy!

While masturbation is completely normal, if you feel that it is interfering with your child's playtime and other regular daily activities, or if it seems to be excessive, it is a good idea to contact your pediatrician. Perhaps you are mistaking scratching for masturbating. Your child might have an infection or a physical problem that needs to be addressed.

Nudity and Modesty

You teach your children that they are the bosses of their bodies, but in order to be the boss, you need to know your body pretty well. Being naked is one of the ways the child gets to know her body and all the wonders it brings. (Young toddlers especially love being naked.) Having a healthy relationship with one's body begins with the child knowing what her body can do and feeling comfortable with it. It contributes to a child's self-image and to her self-esteem.

For parents of young children, nudity that occurs naturally in daily life, such as during bathtime or while getting dressed, is only as problematic as you feel it is. There comes a time, however, when parents begin to wonder: is it okay for my child to be naked in front of other people? Is my own nudity in front of my child problematic? On these topics, there is no completely right or wrong answer. They are merely factors to be considered as you and your partner grapple with the question of nudity in your home.

Tips and Scripts for Dealing with Nudity and Your Child

- **Explore your own attitudes.** Of all the things you may have discussed with your partner before you decided to have children, I'll bet nudity in the home wasn't one of them. The time has come. Jointly decide upon your family's ideas about when, where, and with whom it is and isn't okay to be naked.

- **Establish a time and place for nudity.** Young children love to be naked, but as your child gets older, she needs to be taught that there is a time and a place for being naked, as is the case with so many behaviors. You can say: *"I know how much you love to be naked. Before your bath (or after I take your diaper off) will be your naked time. You don't have to wear one single thing then. Now you need to put on your clothes."*

  Evening "Tushie Time" came right before baths every night in my household full of toddlers. It didn't get much cuter than three naked bodies jumping on the beds and rolling on the carpet! And then it was over.

- **Sibling nudity has its time and place.** Whether or not your children *want* to be naked with one another will depend upon their ages, but when they're young (one to six years) there is no reason for them not to be. Especially in the case of opposite gender siblings, seeing one another naked is a way they can learn about the differences between boys' and girls' bodies. My children had a friend named Rebecca, who had only a sister. She had no real exposure to boys and their bodies. Her mother used to call and beg for me to allow three-year-old Rebecca to come and play, knowing that she would have some good opportunities for penis viewing!

Rest assured, you will know when naked time among siblings is over. Either their naked play will have become overstimulating (see below), or it will become inappropriate, with unsolicited touching or even provocative actions. More often, when the older sibling reaches seven or so, she will seek her privacy and decide that she no longer likes to play "baby" games.

- **Set boundaries around peer nudity.** It is important that you teach your child to be mindful and respectful of other families' feelings about nudity, despite what you may allow.

  "When we are at home, just with our family, it is fine to be naked. But when friends and other people come over, our clothes stay on."
  or
  "Every family has different ideas about what is okay for their family, like about being naked. In our family it is okay to play in the nude, but that is just for our family. Steven's family might have different rules."

Is It Okay to Be Naked with My Child?

- **Mutual nudity with the baby, infant, and toddler.** Being naked with your young child is harmless, natural, and part of life, and seeing the way you care for your naked body teaches your child how to care for hers.
- **There comes a time for it to end.** Most experts agree on this. In deciding just when that time is, parents should consider their own comfort level, as well as how they think the child feels about it.
- **Be alert to signs of overstimulation.** It has already been established that even young children have sexual feelings; the apparatus is in place. So, at some point, seeing the opposite gender parent naked might be overstimulating for the child. This refers to the *child's* feeling awkward or uncomfortable, which might manifest in inappropriate, silly, or out-of-control behavior. (There are even fathers who have admitted that mutual nudity has created uncomfortable feelings in them, resulting in an unwelcome and embarrassing erection.)
- **When is it time to cover up?** Generally speaking, when a child is four years old the opposite gender parent needs to cover up in front of him. This is not a hard-and-fast rule, and it will be different for each family. Some experts say that when the opposite gender

child has grown to eye level with the parent's genitals, it is time to cover up. Coming face-to-face with an adult-size penis can be overwhelming for a little girl. Same-gender parent and child, however, need not worry, unless the child's behavior is inappropriate.

- **You will know when it is time to cover up.** The signs will be obvious. When your little boy begins staring at your breasts just a little longer than he used to, his head cocked to one side, eyes squinting quizzically, you will know it is time!
- **When it's time, you need to change your habits.** I am not talking about an hysterical reaction—Daddy running for a towel, screaming, *"Get out! Get out!"* Rather, when your opposite gender child walks into the bathroom after you have just climbed out of the shower, you can casually turn around, pick up your underwear or a towel, and remind your daughter that you would appreciate a little privacy: *"I would appreciate your giving me my privacy when I am in the bathroom."*
- **Watch your child's play.** If you see that frequent body talk and body play seem to have infiltrated your child's activities and conversations, it is probably a good idea to reexamine your family's nudity practices.
- **You make the call.** Some people tell me that nudity is completely natural in their family or that they grew up in homes where everyone was comfortable with family nudity through their adult years. That is not my experience. I will only say that it is difficult to know or anticipate how such nudity will affect the child. But you are the ones to make the nudity call, after you have considered what it might mean for your child.

Tips and Scripts for Bathing

- **When cobathing stops.** When your days of mutual nudity are over, so must end your nude cobathing with the child of the opposite gender. Now it's time for Daddy or Mommy to wear a bathing suit in the shower. (Dad and his son or Mom and her daughter can certainly continue to bathe together naked.)

In answer to your child's *"But whhyyy?"* remember that *"Whhyyyy"* is a protest. It is not necessarily that she cares so much; rather, it's that your wearing a bathing suit represents a change. You can, however, answer:

"When you were a baby, we bathed together. But now that you are getting to be a bigger boy, we practice the privacy rule. In order for us to bathe (shower) together, I wear my bathing suit."
or
"The time has come for me to keep my private body private. We don't have to stop showering together. But I will wear a bathing suit in the shower. I don't mind at all."

- **Sibling baths are fine . . . until they aren't.** Most siblings absolutely love their bathtime together. It can be a privilege, and if one or the other has a hard time keeping to your rules of no splashing or respecting one another's body, then the privilege will be removed. Tell them: *"When you respect each other's private bodies, you can continue to bathe together. If you cannot, the bath together is over."*

- **When siblings no longer bathe together.** Same gender siblings will likely continue to bathe together until one of them no longer wants to do so. But around the age of seven, it is no longer appropriate for opposite gender siblings to bathe together. Once again, you will know when it is time: one child will seem overly and continuously interested in the others' genitals, regardless of the gender, or the interest will overwhelm the bath. Even if you never see that heightened interest, by the time the child is seven, she needs to learn to practice privacy rules for herself and her siblings.

- **Bathing with peers—proceed with caution.** The time to end co-bathing with friends of the *opposite* gender will likely be when the children are younger than seven years old. Bathing with peers, even those of the same gender, can be overstimulating and exciting. Closely supervising these playdate extensions is the best idea; you will know when it is time to call it quits.

The Sex Questions

All parents want their children to come to them with the big questions, like those about sex. Setting up good communication habits can go a long way toward making that happen easily and comfortably. (If necessary, review "Tips and Scripts for Setting up a Communication," from chapter 1, page 4.)

Tips and Scripts for Answering Questions about Sex

- **Answer your child's questions.** That statement sounds obvious and perhaps ridiculous. But many parents avoid the loaded questions. Remember, unanswered questions lead to unasked questions. Your nonanswers give the child the clear message that she shouldn't be asking that particular question. Left alone with her active imagination, your child will certainly concoct her own answers, accurate or not.

- **Avoid responses that turn the child away.** Certain comments from you will give her the message that some questions are not okay to ask and might cause the child to seek answers elsewhere. You never want that to be the case, so don't say:

  "That's not an appropriate question."
  or
  "Go ask your mother."
  or
  "You're too young to know that information."
  or
  "I will explain that information later."
  or even
  "Why do you want to know; who told you about that?"

- **Consider which parent has the greater comfort level in answering particular questions.** Whether it is Mom or Dad who has "the talk" with the child will vary from family to family. However, it is common that one parent is a better talker or has a greater comfort level than the other. In many families it is assumed that Dad will talk with the boys and Mom will talk with the girls. That does not have to be the case, however. With young children it is often the parent with whom the child spends the most time who gets the questions, regardless of the gender.

  In order to avoid the child being given the message that one parent cannot answer the questions, you can say: *"Let's go and ask Mommy that question together. I know she wants to be a part of this conversation too."* Make sure you and your spouse have discussed this possibility (to say nothing of the answers) long before it happens.

- **Practice your script.** This may sound silly to you, but parents who are clear on their explanations and words and feel comfortable (to a degree) offering answers have the easiest time talking with their children. I continue to be amazed at how giddy some parents in my groups become at the mention of penises going in vaginas. Practice the exact words you want to use, saying them out loud so that they don't get stuck in your throat when the time comes. But remember, the most important answers you give your child are the unspoken ones. Your tone and demeanor send powerful messages.

- **When your child asks you a question, figure out what he is really asking.** There's a classic joke that exemplifies the common mistake of answering a question that wasn't asked: Jimmy says to his daddy, *"Where did I come from?"* Daddy begins to sweat, tugs at his collar, gulps hard, and begins. *"Well, Jimmy. Your mother and I love each other very much. First we kiss a lot. Then we take off our clothes. . . ."* And he tells the whole story. At the very end, Jimmy looks at his daddy quizzically and says, *"That's funny, Billy's daddy says he came from New Jersey."*

  For clarification, you might repeat the question your child has just asked: *"So, you are wondering how the baby gets out of the mommy's body?"* She will correct you if you are wrong.

- **Try to determine what your child already knows or has heard.** In so doing you will be able to pick up the story where it ended for the child or correct any mistaken ideas the child may have. You can say: *"Tell me what you already know about where babies come from so I will know what else to tell you"* or *"What is your idea about where babies come from? I want to tell you everything you need to know."*

- **Your child might ask the same question over and over.** She is just trying to make sense of the answers you have given her. Learning and processing take time.

- **No matter how clear your expectations, expect misunderstandings.** With this topic there is a good chance that there will be a mix-up. Don't be surprised.

- **For some children, the questions come sooner rather than later.** There is no precise age when children begin to ask the questions about where babies come from. If someone close to the child is pregnant, chances are there will be many questions. This child may begin asking when he is as young as two and a half or three.

• **What if you have no idea how to answer the question?** If you don't know how to answer a particular question, you can always say: *"I am so glad you asked me that question. I want to think about how I can answer in a way that you will understand. I will get right back to you."* (Then quickly grab this book, or call your best friend.)

• **And if they don't ask?** If your child is six years old and the sex question hasn't come up, you may want to bring it up yourself. At a casual moment, perhaps in the car (my favorite conversation venue), you can drop a gentle bomb:

> *"You have never asked me where babies come from, Melanie. Do you wonder about that?"*
>
> Wait for a response, and depending upon how receptive your child is, you can continue with: *"I wonder what is your idea about where they come from? What do you know about that already?"*
>
> If there was no response, you can say: *"I am definitely the one who can answer that question for you. Just let me know when you start wondering and we can talk about it."* And leave it at that. Chances are you will have stirred things up enough to bring a question to the surface. If not, I am a big fan of finding just the right book to help introduce the topic. See Related Books for Children at the end of this book or consult your local library or bookstore for some books that you would be comfortable reading with your child. I am fond of *How Babies Are Made* by Stephen Schepp and Andrew Andry.
>
> A client came to me because her nine-year-old daughter had never asked her where babies came from, and she was worried that something was wrong with the child. Since there were two younger siblings, I was, frankly, rather amazed. After some discussion, the mother explained that, truthfully, she didn't want her child to know about sex because she did not want her to *have sex* before she was married. She felt that by not talking about it, her daughter would neither know about nor be interested in it. Clearly, this child had received a message about what was and wasn't okay to discuss in her family.

To reiterate: Your children are sexual beings. They will find out about sex whether from you or from the stories from the playground. If your child hasn't brought up the topic, you might need to bring it up.

Not Your Parents' Explanations

- **"Where do babies come from?"** *"A baby grows inside a special place inside the mother's body called the uterus or womb. It is right next to her tummy. That is the big bump you see on a woman who is pregnant."*

  Some people are horrified by the idea of using the words *uterus* or *womb*. Children need to be taught that the only things that go into a tummy are food, drink, and medicine. Remember how you used to think you could grow a baby by eating a seed or an egg? They will too.

- **"What is pregnant?"** *"Pregnant means that a woman is growing a baby. Before a baby is born, it is called a fetus. It grows inside the woman's uterus for nine months until it becomes a baby. That is a really long time."*

- **"How long is nine months?"** Children under the age of seven have a hard time knowing how long this is. If you have just told your child the exciting news of your pregnancy, you might need to paint the picture of what this means: *"Nine months is a really long time. It is after your birthday and after Mommy's birthday, and after Christmas and after Valentine's Day and after Easter, etc. . . . and all the way to next summer."*

- **Hold off on giving your firstborn the news of your pregnancy.** If you are delivering the news of a pending brother or sister, I suggest that you put it off for as long as you can. Not only is nine months a long time for a young child to wait, but, unfortunately, some pregnancies are not viable. Too many clients have requested help for explaining to the young child where the baby went in the event of such an unhappy ending. So wait as long as you can before telling your young child the news. Caution family and friends not to discuss the good news anywhere within earshot of your firstborn. Wait until she shrieks out when you are in the grocery store, *"Mommy, you have a fat tummy!"* As you contain your embarrassment, you will know it is time to give your child the news.

  There are some cases where the child hasn't noticed that his otherwise twiglike Mommy now looks like a camel. In this case, six weeks in advance is a good amount of time for the firstborn to get used to the idea of his impending dethroning.

- **Explaining a terminated pregnancy.** In most cases, a pregnancy would be terminated before your children would know about it. In the unfortunate event that you need to explain what happened to the baby (fetus) who was growing inside your uterus and no longer is, adapt these words to meet your needs: *"Before a baby is born, while it is growing in the mother's uterus, it is called a fetus. It takes a long, long time for that fetus to grow into a baby. It has to grow all its parts and become a baby ready to be born. Sometimes there is a problem with the fetus and it doesn't grow the way it is supposed to. It doesn't become a baby."*

- **"But where does the baby come from?"** For some children the explanation of where the baby is growing will be enough . . . for the time being. From others you might get a plea for more information. Add: *"The baby starts from an ovum that is inside a grown woman's body. An ovum is a teeny tiny kind of an egg that is as big as a pencil dot* (and use a pencil to make a dot). *When a tiny seed called a sperm* (another pencil dot, with a tail) *from the grown man joins with the woman's ovum, it starts to grow into a baby."*

  Add more, if there is interest: *"When a uterus has a baby growing in it, it stretches and stretches as the baby gets bigger, big enough to be born. It's kind of like a balloon that can get bigger and bigger. That's why a pregnant woman looks like she has a big tummy. But it isn't her tummy; it is her stretched-out uterus."*

  It is important to differentiate between an ovum and a plain old egg, as your child will certainly picture a chicken's egg.

- **"How did the baby get into the woman's uterus?"** Soon (sometimes at age four, sometimes not until much later) you will get this question. This is when you might start to sweat, but remember that your child needs to know the facts: *"The man puts his seed, called sperm, inside the woman when they make love, something that grown-ups do as part of their special, private time together."*

  Depending upon your child's maturity and the extent of his curiosity and continuing questions, you can add: *"Making love is also called having sex. A grown-up man and a grown-up woman lie down very close together. They kiss and touch each other, and the man puts his penis in the woman's vagina. The sperm comes out of the man's penis and into the woman's vagina, where it joins with her ovum. Having sex or making love is something that grown-up people do."*

And you might want to add: *"Grown-ups have sex because they love each other very, very much and they want to share their bodies."*

It is important that the context for making babies is love between grown-up people. (Some of you may want to add that grown-ups have sex after they have finished college, have a job, and are self-supporting!) Remember how you thought your parents had sex twice, once to make you and once to make your little brother? Well, your child will think that too! Sex and lovemaking have an emotional context. It's part of a loving relationship, something that happens more than twice for baby making, something that grown-ups enjoy because it feels good to them.

- **When your child says, *"Oh that's yucky!"*** Sometimes children will respond with distaste. Younger children think it is yucky; older ones think it is just plain gross. You can say: *"Right now when you are little, it might sound yucky. But when you grow up and you have grown-up feelings, it won't seem yucky at all. It is something that grown-ups like."*

   Questions seem to grow over periods of days or weeks or even months. It takes time to process this information.

- ***"How does the baby get out?"*** is a question that your child may or may not ask. When it comes, you can answer: *"When the baby is big enough to be born, the muscles of the uterus begin to squeeze, and the baby starts to move out of the mother's body, out of her birth canal, her vagina. With the doctor helping, she pushes the baby out."*

- **For a cesarean section.** If your child was born by C-section, you may or may not choose to explain that method of childbirth. However, it is important that children know how babies usually are delivered, regardless of your having had a C-section. You may choose to say: *"Sometimes the woman is not able to push the baby out of her birth canal, her vagina. So the doctor makes an opening in her uterus and lifts the baby out. That is called having a C-section."*

These words are only suggestions. They are meant to "arm" you as you await the inevitable questions, for it is always better to have an idea about what you will say rather than drawing a total blank or saying you forgot! Hopefully, you will have plenty of time to practice your answers.

Tampons, Sanitary Napkins, and Menstruation

Young children ages two to six do not need to know anything about a woman's monthly cycle. But sometimes it isn't your choice. Occasionally children this age are inadvertently exposed to the trappings of your monthly period. (When was the last time you went to the bathroom all by yourself?)

Tips and Scripts for Dealing with Your Period and Its Trappings (If the Child Has Been Unintentionally Exposed to It)

- **Keep it private.** If at all possible, try to take care of your sanitary needs in private. Keep your napkins and tampons put away and out of sight.

- **Be calm about maintaining your privacy while you take care of yourself.** Frenzied behavior will add to your child's curiosity and pressing desire to be with you in the bathroom.

- **Answer your child's question about the sanitary napkin/tampon dispenser in a public restroom.** Long before your child will be ready to know about women's periods, she might notice and wonder about the dispensers in women's restrooms. You need not have a lengthy discussion about periods. Simply say: *"That box holds small cloth napkins, called pads or tampons, that women use to catch the special wetness that comes out of their bodies."* This same answer can be used if the child asks about the pads or tampons in your purse or bathroom, separate from having seen you use them.

    Having done your very best to shield yourself, sitting on the toilet and pulling your shirt way over your knees as you do your business, your child may still be exposed to your period. What the heck do you say?

- **Remember, blood spells trouble to the child.** To the young child, blood signals something bad. Blood means that someone is hurt. That is what makes this particular conversation tricky. You are introducing a very foreign concept to your blood-fearing, boo-boo-obsessed young child.

- ***"Mommy, is that blood? Why are you bleeding?"*** Your child will ask in amazement. Answering this question is so perplexing for parents that the tendency is to talk too much, too fast, and give too much information. Remember, always give just a little bit at a time. Less is more.

"Yes, I do have blood, but I don't have a cut or a boo-boo. I don't have a problem. The blood is supposed to be there."

Pause, wait, see what the child might ask. Possibly continue with: *"This blood is different from the blood that comes when you have a boo-boo. It is only a little bit of blood that is mixed with water I have inside my body. This mixture is what my body uses to wash itself out once a month. This happens to all grown-up women. It's called having my period, and it isn't a bad thing at all."*

Listen for a response, and possibly continue: *"I use this tampon (or sanitary napkin) to catch the blood so it doesn't get on my underwear."*

Depending upon the age of the child and your guess about how she is processing the information, you might want to say: *"Do have any questions you want to ask me?"*

If the child continues to ask questions, you can repeat these answers. The exact words now are less important than the overall communication: you are there to answer her questions.

When your child begins to wonder about the birds and the bees and related topics, there are so many considerations. In addition to wondering what to say, how much to say, and when to say it, some parents worry that their child will become the town crier to the rest of the kids on the block. That may happen. You can say, *"These things that I have told you are just for you and our family."* Think about how much information you learned from your friends. But I stand on the importance of answering your child's questions honestly and factually. While you may have to endure your neighbor's ire, it is important that you put your child's needs and your relationship with her first.

CHAPTER 8

❖

"Why Did Mommy's Hair Fall Out?"

Talking about Serious Illness

When a serious illness befalls a family, everyone, including the extended family, as well as close friends, will be affected. For the parent who is not ill there are fears, anxiety, and additional responsibilities, all of which create stress and tension in the home. For the well child, it means living in an environment that is different. There are unexpected changes and, sometimes, upheaval. Not only is the child's daily routine disrupted, but the people who normally facilitate his life may also be different. Friends drive car pools, relatives bring meals and provide care. It can also mean *separation* for the child: a parent might be hospitalized or need to spend enormous amounts of time away from home and the child. No one escapes the ripple effects of a serious illness when it hits home or close to it.

There may be no topic more difficult or painful to discuss with a child. Knowing the words to use, figuring out an explanation that your particular child can grasp, is daunting at the very least. Most parents feel uncomfortable, intimidated, ill equipped, and terrified when it comes to talking with their child about serious illness. Even if you are prepared to explain what is happening with Grandpa, your own feelings, fears, and anxiety put an added spin on your words.

Parents often postpone or even avoid having the conversation. Feeling inadequate or awkward, they subscribe to the "ostrich philosophy": just stick your head in the ground and pretend your children don't know what is going on. But your children already know that something is happening. Hard as you may try to dodge the subject, not talk about it in front of your children, and put on a happy face, it's just not possible. How could it not affect you if your sister is having heart surgery, if your father is having radiation, if your best friend has breast cancer? You are filled with feelings, and these are going to leak out, if not in your words, then in your tone and your touch, your jaw grinding, your knitted brows, and your lack of patience and tolerance. You have a heavy heart, and your children sense it. Children of all ages, even infants, are highly sensitive, observant, and absorbent. They pick up on the emotional climate in which they live. They know right away that something is not right.

Not telling your child about serious illness leaves him alone with what is not being said—and with his active imagination. A child's imagination is one of the ways that he deciphers and makes sense of the world he is coming to know. It is clear to him that something is going on, but he doesn't know what it is, so he'll just make up something—and it might be worse than the reality. Not talking about the illness that has already been sensed by the child and that has directly affected him may lead him to believe that this unknown thing is just too terrible to talk about.

Further, not talking to the child isolates him with his feelings and can lead him to conclude that he is not worthy of knowing what is going on. Somehow he is different from those who are whispering about what they know. Is he not valued in the same way, not important enough to be given that information?

Left alone in his ignorance, with answers he has created with his imagination, with his routine changed, with his family's attention divided and diluted, it is possible that the child will look inward and blame himself for whatever is going on, thinking it happened because of his bad behavior or bad thoughts about the person who became ill: *"I was whining too much and so something bad happened to my father"* or *"I shouldn't have grabbed the toys from the baby, and now he is in the hospital."*

As a member of the family, your child deserves and needs to be told when serious illness strikes. He needs to hear what is happening in his family, the family with whom he feels most secure and safe, whom he most trusts. Each child in his own way will absorb the words you share, based on his age, development, and temperament. Don't underestimate a child's ability to deal with the truth. Sad realities are easier to digest than not knowing what is going on. Given the opportunity to process the story, to experience and share their feelings, children demonstrate strength and courage; they are amazingly resilient. Your child will reflect your confidence in him and his ability to adapt, as long as he knows you are right there with him, being honest, keeping him in the loop, and making sure he too is cared for. The child must be told, but before you do, consider the following tips. They will help prepare you for those conversations.

Tips and Scripts for Sharing the News of Serious Illness

- **Take care of yourself.** In order to be the parent your child requires, it is a good idea to get the help or support you need. It is the "oxygen mask" theory: when you're on a plane and the oxygen masks drop, you're supposed to cover your own face first. You need to be able to breathe in order to help your child do so. In this case, that may mean talking to a friend, a member of the clergy, another parent in a similar situation, or a mental health professional.

- **Know your story.** Before you begin to talk with your child about the illness, you need to do your research and know the important parts of your script. Searching for the right words and tripping over your explanations will not demonstrate the confidence your child needs you to have. "Telling the story" to yourself first can reduce your own anxiety. At the same time, trust that you will do your best. Your child will hear what your heart is saying just as much as your exact words. He will hear your confidence and feel comforted by your presence. Trust in your instincts and your ability as a parent.

- **Be hopeful.** As frightened as you might be, it is always helpful to be hopeful. The child gauges his response and feelings according to you. He absorbs your expressions of emotion, including fear and hopelessness. While being realistic, it always feels better to have hope. You could say: *"We are so hopeful that the doctor will be able to help Grandma be better really soon."*

- **Who should tell the child.** A parent—the person whom the child most trusts and loves—should tell the child the news. He should not hear it through whispers, school gossip, overheard phone conversations, or unwitting relatives or caregivers. When it is a parent who is ill, both the well and the ill parent should have the conversation with the child, if at all possible. Perhaps the ill parent will not have the strength (physical or emotional) for the conversation, but just his presence will have meaning and provide comfort for the child. It will let him know that there are no secrets and that everyone knows the same story.

- **Time the conversation.** Only you know when you and your child seem to have your best conversations. It may be during bathtime, while in the car, or at a meal. It is not a good idea, however, to start this conversation when the child is going to be alone with his thoughts. Before bedtime or a nap or in the morning before school are not the right times for this conversation. You need to remain available for the questions that will inevitably bubble up.

- **Children of different ages may need to hear different stories.** With your older child you are able to use a lexicon suited to his age. With a younger child, you will not only use different words but you will also say less. While it is fine for your thirteen-year-old to hear what you are telling your five-year-old, the converse is not always a good idea. Older children have a different capacity for comprehending the details of the illness, anticipating the future, and inferring the meaning of the illness.

- **Keep it simple.** Though you should use the "real" words to describe conditions, do not use complicated, technical terms that cannot be understood. You do not want to overload the child, but at the same time you don't want to downplay the seriousness of the situation.

  Children are egocentric. They view the world as it affects them. *Who will take care of me? Am I okay? Am I going to become ill? Is Mommy or Daddy now going to be ill?* Their view of the illness is as it affects their own lives. With this reality in mind, try to tell the child only the bare details of the illness and what is going to happen in the immediate future. He needs to know the plan and what it means for him, so he is not surprised. Your child needs to know that Grandpa won't be coming to "story time" at school because he is ill, but he doesn't need to know that Grandpa is going to be in the hospital for a long, long time or even that Grandpa may not live.

- **Talk, then *listen*.** Tell your child the story and then stop. It takes a child time to process whatever he has heard. But his response is a window into what he is thinking. The questions that he first asks or his initial comments are clues to the way in which he is processing the information he has been given.

- **Test the child's understanding.** After you have told your child the news of the illness, you may want to gauge his understanding of what you have just said. You can do so by saying:

"Tell me the story we have just told you."
or
"What is your idea about what we have just told you?"
or
"What do you think (how do you feel) about what we just told you?"

- **Help the child to play out the story.** Having the child play out the story with dolls or stuffed animals can also tell you a great deal about how the story has been heard.

- **Know when to stop talking.** Pay attention to your child while you are talking to him and notice when you start to lose him. Children can easily be flooded by too many words at once, and they will let you know by becoming fidgety, by changing the subject, or by having obviously lost interest. Understanding is a process that takes time. Respect the child's point of saturation and stop. I promise you that this is only the beginning of the conversation. You will have plenty of opportunity for revisits as the child's understanding unfolds and he asks the same questions over and over again.

- **Answer his questions as they arise.** Remember, children take in information a bit at a time. There is a degree of "scaffolding" that occurs as they absorb and learn, piece by piece, building their understanding. The child may ask nothing at all at first, but will come back to you hours later with a question. Follow your child's lead, and only answer the question he has asked. You will be surprised at how easily a child can be satisfied.

- **It's okay *not* to know the answer.** No doubt, at some point your child will ask you a question to which you will not know the answer. That's the very thing that makes all people anxious, including your child. Knowing that you will tell the child what you *do* know makes your *not knowing* perfectly fine. Say:

  "That's a question we just don't know the answer to. I will be sure to tell you as soon as I know."
  or
  "I don't know the answer to that question. But I am going to find out the answer and tell you as soon as I know."

Then be absolutely sure to get back to the child with an answer, even if it is two days later. This adds to his trust in you and promotes his feeling comfortable asking questions.

- **It's okay to be sad.** Parents worry that they may cry when talking to their children, knowing that children take their cues from their parents. Seeing that a parent feels sad is not a bad thing. In fact, a parent crying sometimes gives the child permission to be sad and to share his feelings with you. Tell him: *"I feel really sad when I think about Aunt Mary. It makes me cry. I want her to be better. Crying is one of the ways that I get my sad feelings out, and that makes me feel better."*

  Seeing a parent become hysterical or out of control, however, is frightening to the child. While you best know your typical reactions, emotions can be unwieldy and surprising. Consider having another adult with you to step in as necessary when you talk to your child

Tips and Scripts for What to Say

What follows are some suggestions for words to say to children for a variety of illnesses and situations. Some of these scripts have been adapted from *When a Parent Is Sick: Helping Explain Serious Illness to Children* by Joan Hamilton, R.N. While they are aimed at the two- to six-year-old, your explanations will have to be crafted for your particular child, given his age, development, temperament, and needs, as well as for the actual illness.

- **Beware of the word *sick*.** Children think of being sick as having a tummy ache or cold. They comprehend the word as it relates to them and their experience. When a child gets sick, it is usually not a big deal. He feels crummy, he misses school, and then he gets better. It is also difficult for the young child to understand degrees of sickness. At his young age, the world is black or white: you are sick or you are well. It is hard for him to understand that someone who is *really, really sick* is different from the kind of sick that could happen to him. It is for these reasons that I suggest using different language to describe what is going on: *"Grandma has a problem with her heart. It is not working the way it is supposed to. She is in the hospital where the doctors are trying to fix the problem."* Take careful note here of the use of the word *problem* in lieu of the word *sick*.

- **For hospitalization:** *"Grandma has a problem in her body; she is having a hard time breathing. The doctors are trying to figure out what the problem is, so she is staying in the hospital. That is where they can watch her and examine her and find out how to make the problem go away. She will probably stay in the hospital for three nighttime sleeps, and then she will go back home."*

- **For surgery:** *"There is something in my body that needs to come out. (It's called an appendix, and it isn't working anymore.) I will have an operation to take it out. It is called an operation when the doctor has to take something out of your body or fix something that will stay in there."*

  If the child asks, *"How does he get inside your body?"* you can say, *"The doctor uses special instruments to make an opening right where the problem is. He fixes the problem and then closes the opening, making stitches to keep it closed. After a while when the opening grows back together, the doctor will take the stitches out. It will leave a pink mark called a scar."*

- **Some other examples:**

  "Daddy has a problem in his knee. It is not working the way it is supposed to. I am going to the hospital, where the doctor is going to do an operation to fix the problem. When I come home I am not supposed to walk. My knee will be sore, and it will take time for it to get better. I will need to rest and be calm and not even walk for a while. At home, you and Mommy will help me to get better. You can visit and quietly play with me while I am in my bed in my room and make me the food I like to eat."
  or
  "Grandpa has a problem in his stomach. He is going to the hospital where the doctor is going to do an operation to fix the problem. He will need to stay in the hospital for three or four nighttime sleeps. We will visit him there."
  or
  "Uncle Mark has a problem with his heart. It is not working the way it is supposed to, and the doctors are going to do an operation to fix the problem. Uncle Mark will stay in the hospital for four or five nighttime sleeps. Aunt Janice will sleep at her home with Cousin Peter. They will visit Uncle Mark in the hospital. Uncle Mark will need to rest and be calm when he comes home to help his heart get better."

- **For a lumpectomy:** *"There is a lump in Mommy's body that isn't supposed to be there. The doctors need to take it out. I will have a sore place on my chest that* *will be covered with a bandage. When I come home, I will have to keep my body calm and quiet so my body will get better."*

- **For a mastectomy:** *"Aunt Sharon has something inside her body that is not supposed to be there. It is called cancer. It is in her breast. The doctors need to do an operation to remove Aunt Sharon's breast and take the cancer away. Aunt Sharon will have a big bandage to cover the owie where her breast was. She will need to keep her body very calm, and she will rest so that her body can get better."*

- **For cancer treatment:** *"The doctors know a lot about how to take care of people who have cancer. They know the treatments to give to make it go away, but it is going to take some time."*

- **For chemotherapy:** *"Mommy is getting some really strong medicine that will help me get better. The medicine is called chemotherapy, and it will get rid of the cancer that's in my body."*

  "The medicine is very powerful. While it gets rid of the cancer, it makes me feel very tired and weak. It even makes me feel sick in my tummy, and sometimes I need to throw up. But the medicine is doing its job. Mommy needs to rest and let the medicine work. After a few days, I will feel stronger and better.

  "Sometimes really strong medicine can do yucky stuff to other parts of my body. It makes me feel so tired, and it makes me feel not hungry at all. But when I am done taking the medicine, I will feel much better."
  or
  "The medicine the doctors are giving me doesn't go in my mouth. They give it to me through a long tube that they put in my body. It doesn't hurt me at all, but it takes a long time to put all the medicine inside of me. I need to sit in a chair and wait a while as the medicine goes in and does its job. I like to read a book (or listen to music) while I am sitting in the chair."

- **For radiation:** *"The doctors are using a special kind of treatment to make my cancer go away, called radiation. It is a different kind of medicine because it doesn't go into my mouth or go into my body through a tube. It goes into my body like an X-ray machine and gets rid of the cancer. These purple marks on my skin show the machine just where to put the radiation that will make the cancer go away."*

- **For hair loss:** As prepared as you would like your child to be, it is not a good idea to tell him too far in advance about the hair loss that will likely occur. A good time to have this conversation is as close as possible to the start of the shedding, knowing that it happens quickly. You can say: *"The chemotherapy is so strong and powerful that while it is doing its job of getting rid of the cancer, it makes my hair fall out. Strong medicine makes my hair and the cancer go away. The cancer won't come back, but my hair sure will. I know that I look really different without my hair, but I am still your same mommy who loves you so much. Do you want to look at a picture of me before my hair fell out? That way you can remember that I am still Mommy. My hair will grow back when I am all done getting my chemotherapy."*

  When there is sudden hair loss from cancer treatment, most children are very curious. Some can be frightened by the change, however. As the child becomes accustomed to seeing you without hair or wearing your head covering, he will become more comfortable and will likely share his curiosity about your new look. As difficult as the hair loss may be for you, this may be a time when you will need to put your vanity aside and allow your child to explore your bald head. He may want to touch it; he may say things that are not particularly kind. Hair loss represents huge change for the child. Questions should be answered honestly and directly: *"I don't like the way I look without my hair, either. But I know that when my hair falls out, it means the medicine is working hard to get rid of the cancer in my body. My hair will grow back."*

  The child might fear that his hair will fall out, and he will need to be reassured: *"Your hair is not going to fall out. You do not have cancer, and you have not taken the very strong medicine. Your hair is just fine."*

- **Reassure the child:** After your explanation of the illness, you may need to add: *"Uncle William's body has a problem, but my body and Daddy's body and your body are just fine. We do not have problems with our bodies."*

- **"Is Grandma going to die?"** This may be the most difficult of all questions. Not only do you often not really know the answer, but the thought alone makes one so sad. Children need to be told the truth, as much as you can tell it: *"The doctors are doing everything they can to fix the problem in Grandma's heart. She will die someday, but we hope that won't be for a long time. We hope that the doctors can make her better this time."*

Tips and Scripts for When a Serious Illness Occurs

- **No surprises.** Children are better able to handle most changes that come their way when they know what is happening. For example, if Daddy isn't going to be able to walk and will use crutches after his knee surgery, let the child know in advance. Being open and honest with your child about what is to come protects the trust he has in you.

- **Clue in the adults in your child's life.** It is important that the adults who come into contact with your child (relatives, caregivers, teachers, neighbors) know the language and explanation your child has been given about the illness, so they will be able to reiterate it and support the child when he is not in your presence.

- **Share the plan.** As soon as you know the plan for anything that will affect the child, let him know: *"Here is the plan. Today I am going to visit Grandpa in the hospital and Mrs. Flynn is going to bring you home from school. She will give you lunch, and I will be home after you wake up from your nap."*

- **Expect your child to act out . . . and be grateful if he doesn't.** It shouldn't surprise you that when a child is frightened or anxious about a family member's illness or when this kind of disruption comes to a child's life, he acts out. You are the person on whom he relies, and the best way to get your attention is to misbehave. While you may think that you should ease up on your limits and boundaries during these times, it is not actually in your child's best interest. Your child is making sure you are still there for him. Your rules are still your rules, so stick to them.

- **Allow for and prepare for hospital visits.** Most children benefit from visiting a family member (especially a nuclear family member) who is hospitalized. Often the person who is ill benefits too. The exceptions are:

    if the person is gravely ill and will not be able to respond to the child;

    if the ill person is not recognizable at all;

    if the ill person is attached to so many tubes and machines that the experience will be scary for the child;

if the surrounding hospital scenes will be too much for the
child to see.

It is always your choice as to whether or not you will bring the child
to the hospital. Some children find the hospital visit a little scary and
even overwhelming. In this case, it is understandable that you might
decide not to take a child or, if you do, that your child would be clingy
and needy. Be prepared to leave if you sense the child or the patient is
not able to handle the visit.

Prepare the child for the visit by telling him what he will see: *"You
will see that Grandma is lying in a big bed. She is very tired and it is hard for her
to talk. But she will be so happy to see you. She has a tube in her nose that helps
her to breathe by putting air in her body. The tube doesn't hurt her at all. We are
only going to stay for a little while because it makes Grandma so tired to talk and
pay attention."*

- **Stick to the child's routine.** As much as possible, keep the child's life
as regular as possible. Stick to his routines and rules. In so doing, you'll
be helping him to feel safe and secure in the knowledge that things do
stay the same, even when someone is ill.

- **Do not make promises you cannot keep.** When serious illness hits a
family, your child is liable to become more needy just when you are
needed by everyone else. In trying to meet everyone's needs, promises
are made to the child: *"I will be the one to pick you up from school today. I
promise."* You need to be realistic about what you truly think you *can* and
will manage. If you think that there is even the slightest possibility that
you will be unable to come through, then don't promise. You can say: *"I
am really going to try to pick you up from school today, but I may not be able to. If
I am not there, then Aunt Sally will pick you up. But I sure will try."*

- **Invite discussion.** Take advantage of opportunities to talk about the ill
person. At the dinner table, perhaps offer, *"I visited Uncle Brian in the hospital today, and he was so happy to see me. He is very tired and weak. The doctors
hope he can go home in a few days."* Keeping the communication open in-
vites the child to ask whatever questions he may have.

- **Invite the child's participation.** When possible, allow your child to
participate in the caring acts we do for people who are ill. Let him join
in making the meal for the family of the ill person or encourage him to

make a picture to decorate the hospital room. Let him know that you are driving your neighbor's car pool or feeding her pets to help her out. Modeling the ways in which we take care of people who are in need teaches the child loving acts of kindness and support.

- **Seek help, if needed.** Sometimes a child needs some extra support in the face of a family member's serious illness. If despite your best efforts a child's negative behavior persists, if he appears to be depressed and withdrawn, or if he develops fears and anxieties that seem out of proportion or are persistent, seek the help of a mental health professional.

When Your Child Has a Serious Illness

Young children know what it means to be sick, but serious illness is a whole different story, especially when it involves a procedure, surgery, or a hospital stay.

Tips and Scripts For Helping a Child with His Personal Illness

- **Get a handle on your fear and anxiety.** Your child looks to you to know how to react. The less worry you show, the less scared he will be. Your own anxiety about the illness and about sharing the news with your child will be lessened by practicing what you are going to tell him. Be sure to clue in your friends and extended family, even telling them exactly the story you have told your child.

- **Your young child will want to know just three things:** (1) What is going to happen? (2) Will you be with him all the time (separation)? and (3) Will it hurt?

- **Be honest ... to an extent.** Your child needs to know what is really going to happen, but he doesn't need to know all the details. Keep your explanations simple and short.

  "There is a lump inside your body that is not supposed to be there. The doctor needs to take it out."
  or
  "There is a problem in a part of your body called the kidney. The doctor is going to open up your body and fix it. That is called having an operation.

He will do that operation in the hospital. He will give you medicine that will make you sleep, and you will not feel it. I will be with you the whole time."

- **The less uncertainty, the better.** Using language that is appropriate to the child's age and development, tell him as much as you can about what is going to happen, step by step. Call your doctor or the hospital's child life specialist and ask for specifics about the procedure. Whether it is having blood drawn or tonsils removed, your child will be much less anxious if he knows just what to expect. You might say:

  "Very early in the morning, even before the sun is up, we will drive to the hospital together. First, you will be given a paper bracelet to wear that says your name. The nurse will give you special hospital pj's to wear, and there will be a bed just for you. The nurse will take your temperature and your blood pressure, and I will be with you the whole time. You will be given something to drink that will make you feel sleepy, and you'll fall asleep. When you wake up, I will be right there, and your tonsils will be gone."
  or
  "The doctor needs to close up the cut on your forehead with some stitches. You will have a shot that will hurt for a quick minute. I will be right there with you. When he is done, you will have a bandage on your head to cover the stitches."

- **Time your explanation.** As there is no need to create anxiety too soon, if possible, wait to tell your child the news until the day before or the morning of the procedure. If there will be lab work before the operation, present it as a separate procedure and not part of the surgery. Often the lab work is the worst part, as the child is awake and sees what is happening: *"Just like the doctor examines your body on the outside, he needs to know what is going on in the inside too. We are going to an office called a lab where a nurse is going to take a little bit of blood from your arm for the doctor to look at. I will be with you the whole time."*

- **Is it going to hurt?** *"Yes, the prick from the needle will hurt, but only for a minute. Then it will be done and the hurting part will be all over."*

- **Prepare the child for how she might feel afterward:** *"When the operation is over, you will have a sore throat. You might not even feel like talking or playing. You'll want to eat soft foods that won't hurt your throat, like ice cream and smoothies. Yum!"*

  Remember, the child will not be familiar with who he is postprocedure.

He might be tired or weak or have to take medicine that makes him sleepy or gives him a tummy ache. Knowing what to expect makes it less scary: *"You might feel tired and just want to sleep. I will stay with you while you rest. Soon you will feel better, and stronger, and just like your old self."*

- **Document the experience.** It will take your child a long time, even many months, to process his illness or procedure. Take photographs of every step of the experience, and make a simple book telling the whole story. In the absence of photographs, you can draw stick figures. With each reading and sharing of the book, he will digest the story. Shirt cardboard and staples, pictures and glue do the trick. Sample text might read:

  > *"Here is a picture of the hospital where I had my tonsils out."*
  > *"I got a special bracelet with my name on it."* (Keep the bracelet and put it in the book.)
  > *"The nurse took my temperature."*
  > *"Here I am in my special hospital pj's."*
  > *"When I woke up I was really sad and I cried a lot. My throat hurt and I wanted to go home."*

- **Play doctor.** Children work out their experiences, fears, and anxieties through play. Create a "Doctor Setup," complete with stethoscope, Band-Aids, creams with cotton balls, eyedroppers with colored water medicine, a syringe without the needle, and a rubber dolly patient. Now, who is the doctor?

- **With very serious illness, even terminal illness, the same principles apply.** As terrifying as it may be for you, your young child need not know what the illness may mean for the future. You must tune in to the young child's perspective, which spans only today and tomorrow. He doesn't think about or need to know what lurks down the road. Your job is to remain positive and hopeful.

When a Sibling Has a Serious Illness

When a sibling has a serious illness, or is having a surgical procedure, the healthy child can be affected. Understandably, the lion's share of the parent's attention is on the child who is ill, and the healthy child becomes second fiddle.

The climate in the household changes as the focus turns toward the well-being of the ill sibling. Schedules and routines are adjusted. Life is different. The healthy sibling's life is affected by his sibling's condition, and he needs special consideration and attention too.

The effect on the healthy child of an ill sibling depends upon many factors, including his age, development, and temperament. The one thing that is certain is that he will be affected in some way. It is well within the range of normal for the healthy sibling to experience a variety of feelings, be needy in new ways, and display undesirable behaviors.

Tips and Scripts for Dealing with the Healthy Sibling in the Face of a Seriously Ill Child

- **Be honest and direct in telling the sibling what is happening to his brother.** Keep the child in the loop about his brother's illness, about what is happening, and about the plan for his (the healthy child's) care.

- **Reassure the child that he is not at fault.** It would not be surprising for the healthy child to believe that somehow he is to blame for his sibling's illness. Reassure him: *"We don't know why Jeremy has the problem in his body, but you need to know that it is not your fault. You have nothing to do with his needing the operation."*

- **Expect negative behaviors.** The child's negative or regressive behaviors may be his way of dealing with his fears and anxiety about his sibling not being well. When illness befalls a sibling, it hits very close to home. These behaviors, as stated above, are also attention-seeking in the face of your not being as available as you were before the illness. While the behaviors remain unacceptable, they can be understood as reminders that your other child needs your attention too.

- **Expect jealousy.** While most children accept and understand the attention and gifts that the sibling who is not well receives, feelings of jealousy and resentment may arise. Acknowledging how hard it is to see his sibling receive gifts and so much attention helps the healthy child to know that he is understood.

- **Expect clinginess.** When a parent needs to cut back the amount of time and attention she gives a child, clinginess and renewed separation anxiety are well within normal. Invite your child to spend some "alone time" with you when at all possible: *"Do you want to play with your trains in here with me while I make dinner?"* Just being close may be the fix your child needs.

In the face of a difficult separation, it is always a good idea to share the plan with your child, reassuring him of when you will next be together and how he will be cared for: *"It is so hard to say good-bye right now. I know it. I am sad too. Susie Smith will pick you up after school, and I will definitely be home before dinnertime. What shall we do together when I get home?"*

- **Share your feelings.** Though you are unable to change the reality, sharing feelings can take away some of the sting. Share your feelings of sadness about the ill sibling or about missing the child who is at the hospital. Also share your feelings about being tired of going to the hospital and being sorry that you aren't able to spend as much time with the healthy sibling as you would like. Doing so gives your child permission to share his feelings. For example: *"I wish I didn't have to spend so much time at the hospital. But right now Devon needs me to be with him. I would really like to be able to take you to karate class and I am so disappointed that I can't."*

- **Allow the healthy sibling to be angry.** The healthy sibling will likely have sad and angry feelings. He needs to express them all without fear of making you angry at him. While it may go against your grain, it really is okay for your child to be angry at his brother for having a problem with his body. After all, that brother is taking up so much time and getting so much attention. The healthy child doesn't know that it is not the brother's fault, but rather the illness that is to blame. You can even voice the feelings you imagine your child is having: *"Darn that asthma. I am so mad that Robbie has it and is in the hospital."*

- **Explain what will happen with his routine.** Let your child know that while some things in his routine will stay the same (going to school, taking a bath after dinner), some things will have to change. Let him know that you will try to do as much as you can to keep things the same and to take care of him, but that you may need some help. He needs to know that you too are disappointed that there might be some things that you are unable to do, but that soon, when his sibling is better, everything will be back to the way it was.

- **Allow the healthy sibling to make choices and decisions.** When there needs to be a change in the child's regular routine, the healthy sibling may feel more in control if he is allowed to have a choice in the nature of the change: *"I sure wish I could drive you to soccer practice. I just can't do it. Would you like Aunt Jane or Aunt Barbara to drive you to soccer practice today?"* Allowing the child the choice helps him to feel that you are looking out for him too.

- **Don't overload the healthy sibling with responsibilities.** The healthy child should not feel overly burdened by his sibling's problem. If he volunteers to take on added responsibilities, go for it. He is helping himself to feel less isolated and more a part of the solution. But refrain from piling on the added responsibilities. I can promise you that he already has a fair amount of big feelings to deal with—anxiety, anger, resentment, jealousy—so you need not add to these by putting more on his shoulders than he should have to bear.

- **Spend time with the healthy sibling.** As difficult as it may be to find enough hours in the day, your healthy sibling needs your time and attention more than ever, and it shouldn't be while you're doing your errands or chores. Rather, he needs your full attention, doing something *he* wants to do. Twenty minutes might do the trick, if it is pure, uninterrupted attention.

- **Remind the healthy child of just how much you love him.** While this tip may seem obvious, it is worth emphasizing. Children need to hear over and over that they are loved more than anything in the whole wide world: *"I wish I could spend more time with you right now. I just can't. But that doesn't mean I don't love you. I love you so much; I love you to the moon and back! I love you when I am with you and I love you when I am not with you."*

- **Allow the healthy sibling to participate in his brother's care.** Find ways that the child can help his brother feel better or happy. This might include making a decoration for his hospital room wall, looking at a storybook together, playing a round of Candyland, or baking some of his favorite muffins. Involving the child helps him to feel less isolated, to feel needed, and to be part of the sibling's cure.

. . . ❖ . . .

CHAPTER 9

"Why Is My Goldfish Floating in the Toilet?"

Learning about Death

Death is a mystery even to our world's most brilliant thinkers. Philosophers spend their lives trying to figure it out; people in the clergy ponder such concepts as the spirit, the soul, heaven, and the afterlife. No one *really* gets it, so how can we expect our young children to understand death?

As I have said elsewhere, you bring to your job as parent a set of luggage in which you have hauled around everything that has happened in your life thus far, including your mom's and dad's attitudes toward death, what a grandparent once said about dying, and what happened when the family dog died when you were three. The way in which you address and answer your children's questions about death, as with all their questions, has everything to do with what you are carrying in your luggage.

Before you can begin to have a discussion with your child about death, you first need to examine your own feelings and experiences with the topic. Once you have done so, talking about death with your child will be easier. I have to remind you, however, that your true feelings will always leak out. Keep this in mind as you respond to your child, as children spot inconsistencies and hypocrisy just as fast as you sniffed out your own parents' hypocrisy. No surprise there.

Parents have a great deal of influence over how a child interprets death. When you flush Goldie down the toilet or kick aside the dead bird in the road with hardly a word, the child is taught that death is a topic to be avoided or brushed away. When the child witnesses strangely hushed voices and powerful outpourings of grief, a different message is delivered: *"Look at what happens to people when there is a death. It's so scary."* Both the avoidance and the excessive drama sabotage a child's ability to learn about death in a safe and nurturing environment that takes into account his development, his experience, and his feelings. What was a neutral concept to be learned about becomes a loaded topic.

In the United States, parents tend to avoid the subject of death, thinking they are protecting the child from the emotional pain that comes when a loved one, an acquaintance, or even a pet dies. In their attempts to shelter their kids from sadness and the reality of death, parents teach that it is something to fear, and they inadvertently build barriers to open and productive communication and necessary, cumulative learning.

In Japan, death is viewed quite differently, and the rituals of the after-death experience present quite a contrast to the way we handle death in the United States. Jim, a client of mine, had just returned from his grandmother's funeral in Japan, to which he had taken his five-year-old son. My parenting group listened with jaws dropped as Jim described the details of this family affair. As was the custom, children of all ages joined the adults at the funeral service, witnessed the body being placed in the crematorium and, after waiting for the cremation to be over, addressed the bones of the deceased grandmother. Young children, teens, and adults all embraced the process. In contrast, in the United States, we say that *"the doggie went to play in the country"* or that Grandmother *"passed away."*

One culture's way isn't necessarily better than another's; each gives the child a different message. Children will come to understand what they are given the opportunity to get to know. They look to the adults in their lives for cues about how to feel and how to respond.

As parents, you play the starring role in creating the foundation for your child's understanding of death. The good news is that you can start building this foundation long before it will become necessary for you to answer your child's questions about death.

Recently (unfortunately, this happens too often), I answered the phone to a parent sobbing, *"Betsy, we just found out that my husband's father has stage four pancreatic cancer. They've given him two months. What should I tell my five-year-old?"* I held back from saying, *"And why did you wait until now to begin the death lesson?"* Had she begun the death lesson long ago, she wouldn't feel so helpless now. This chapter will help you to begin that conversation.

The Context of the Life Cycle

According to Jean Piaget, the great child psychologist, biologist, and philosopher, a child learns by being exposed to new concepts over and over, through varied and repeated experiences. She needs to "accommodate" and "assimilate" the information and then gather more related information. Death is no exception. Now, I am not suggesting you hang out at the local funeral parlor or that you go on a snail-killing rampage, but I am saying that each child needs to build her own framework for understanding what death means, that children start developing this framework when they are very young—at two years of age and even younger.

Tips and Scripts for Introducing the Life Cycle

- **Use the real words.** With each use of the words *dead, death, die, died, dying*, your child adds understanding and expands his cognitive framework labeled "death."

- **Death needs to be taught in a context.** Teach your children that death is part of the life cycle.

- **"What is a life cycle?"** Tell your child: *"Everything that is alive has a life cycle: first it is little; then it grows up; then it begins to get old; then it is all done living and it dies. Dying is what happens at the very, very end of a life cycle. Whether it is a plant or an animal or an insect or a person, it has a life cycle."*

- **Take walks and point out plants and other bounty from Mother Nature that are in various stages of the life cycle.** Show the roses that are in full bloom and the ones that are finished and dying. You can say: *"First the roses were baby buds, and then they opened and became blossomed flowers. Then they got old and kind of droopy, and pretty soon they died and fell off the bush. Now they are dead."*

  In the fall, notice the leaves that have *died* and fallen off the trees. Talk about the *dead* bird you notice on the lawn—without *"Eeewwwww"* sound effects. Instead of immediately throwing away the dead fly or moth found on the windowsill, let your child see it. Say: *"Look! The fly is all done living; it is dead."* After a rainfall, wait before sweeping all those dead worms off the sidewalk and into the grass.

Life Spans

Even though it may not appear to you that they are doing so, young children actually seek an order to things. It helps them to make sense of their world, and it gives their lives a measure of predictability, which is tremendously reassuring. Life spans are a consistent part of the world and provide the child with a framework for beginning to understand death.

Every creature on this planet has a life span, from 15 to 30 days for a fly, to 152 years for a giant tortoise. Learning that all living things have a life span helps a child to know that parents and other important people in her life usually live for a long time, through all the years it will take her to grow and become a grown-up herself.

Tips and Scripts for Explaining a Life Span

- **What is a life span?** *"The life span is the amount of time that something is supposed to live."*

- **Display baby pictures.** Look at your child's baby pictures and videos with your child and talk about the changes and growth that have occurred. Share your own baby pictures and point out your own growing-up process.

- **Create a growth chart.** Have a growth chart for each of your children, whether it is pencil marks and dates inside a closet door or a commercially made hanging chart. Twice or three times a year, mark your child's height and talk about her growth.

- **Point out old people.** Notice an obviously wrinkled face. You might say: *"Like all natural things, bodies change as they get older. People get wrinkles on their skin, and their hair starts to turn gray. Even Buddy Dog's fur is starting to turn gray as he gets older."*

- **Expect your child to notice signs of age as she begins to understand the process.** Don't be shocked, judgmental, or embarrassed by your child's candor in blurting out her observations to people in her life. A parent reported to me that her son had marched right up to her father and announced, *"Grandpa, you are getting old and you're going to die soon."* It is easy (gulp) to do damage control by sharing with Grandpa that his grandson is learning about life spans and means no disrespect. He is simply sharing with pride his newfound understanding.

- **Seek out life spans in action.** Look for opportunities to see a life span from the beginning in animals, such as newborn puppies that have lost their puppy fur. One of the best times to see baby animals is at the zoo in the spring. Then go back in the summer and see how those animals have grown. Also point out the elderly dog's slowed-down gait; see the sleepy old cat that doesn't run around much anymore. Talk about all of this in the context of the life span.

- **Demonstrate a reverence for life.** Since children are learning about death in the context of life, the life cycle, and life span, it's a good idea to demonstrate a reverence for life at the same time. This is not the time to bring out the Raid ant spray, and it's a good idea to put spider squashing, snail stomping, and fly swatting on hold. Instead of flushing Goldie down the toilet when Johnny is asleep, give the goldfish a proper funeral with Johnny's help. Place her in a little box (a small, cotton-lined jewelry box is the perfect choice), and bury her in the ground. Talk about what you liked about Goldie and what you will remember about her.

- **Tell the truth: *"The dog died."*** Allow your child to know that the dog died. Don't hide the reality by saying that she *"went to live in the country."* Tell your child the real story: *"Remember that it got to be so hard for Buddy to walk? I took him to the vet, and the vet said that parts of Buddy's body weren't working any more. This morning Buddy Dog died. His body stopped working and he died."* (There will be more on this script later in this chapter.)

- **Wait to replace the pet that died.** Don't rob your child of the opportunity to feel sad, to miss the pet, and to master her feelings by rushing out and buying a replacement pet.

ABOUT FLUSHING

It is not uncommon for very young children to be both fascinated with and frightened by flushing things down the toilet. Think about the mystery of the toilet from the child's point of view. Something is in that water, we flush it away, and it disappears. Wow! It is exciting, puzzling, and terrifying. Many children first learn about death when they are right in the middle of acquiring toilet skills or have only recently achieved mastery in this area, so the toilet has special meaning for them. Flushing beloved Goldie into oblivion, to the same place where Daddy's poop and Mommy's pee pee and all the yucky toilet paper goes, can be very confusing to the young child. A trip down the toilet drain to mark the end of Goldie's life doesn't instill a reverence for life or any understanding about death. In fact, it confuses and complicates the issue.

The Aging Process

In many areas of the United States, children don't get to see what *old* looks like because it's less common for most elderly people to live with their extended families—nor do they interact with old people on a regular basis. That's not only because the really old people aren't a part of most children's daily world, but also because *old* doesn't even look *old* anymore. Hair is dyed; faces are lifted; bodies are toned; senior citizens are healthier and more fit than ever before.

Here is what our children see: first you are young; then you are a grown-up; then you die. Where is the *getting old* part? It must be confusing for them.

Children don't commonly get to see faces mapped with wrinkles, gray hair, tired, bent-over bodies, walkers, and canes. I am not encouraging you to take a field trip to a rest home, but I am pointing to the reality that there are not many opportunities to see the results of the aging process at work.

On my children's fifth birthday, Jessie received the fifth pearl on her Add-a-Pearl necklace. This ritual was a carryover from days gone by, when women wore their finally completed, full pearl necklace, which was many years in the making. Later that same day, my family went to a party at a relative's house. There we met a magnificent, stately old woman. She had brilliant white-gray hair pulled back in a bun and a face of lines reflecting her years. Upon meeting her, my son Ben said, *"You must be very old."* Without missing a beat, she replied, *"I am, but how did you know?"* Five-year-old Ben proudly declared, *"Because your pearls are so long!"* The opera-length pearls told the tale for Ben, who paid no mind to the other obvious but (to him) unfamiliar signs of aging.

How Children Understand Death at Different Ages

As is the case with all aspects of children's maturation, children will understand explanations about death differently, depending on their age and development. In addition, children who have experienced the death of a pet or, unfortunately, of a family member or other close adult will certainly have a different capacity for processing the information.

Children under Three

It is believed that young children under the age of six have at best only an incomplete understanding of death; there is a certain predictability to that understanding. Children under the age of three, for example, see death as meaning simply that someone or something isn't there anymore. They will continue to ask for the person or pet and wonder when he will return.

Children under Five

Children older than three and a half begin to understand what it means for someone to die, but they also expect the person to return. You are likely to see death appearing in a four-year-old's imaginative play; they think of death as living in another place. *"What will Grandpa eat?"* and *"How will Grandma breathe if she is buried?"* are the kinds of questions asked by this age group.

Five-Year-Old Children

Five-year-old children are in the stage of cognitive development where they are very concrete thinkers. They are interested, even obsessed, with the minute and tangible aspects of death: *"What does a dead person look like? What happens to the body when it is buried? Where does the flesh go?"* Many five-year-olds actually want to *see* a dead person. This interest may seem morbid to some, but that is not at all the case. It is completely in keeping with what is typical for a child who is passionately engaged in understanding life in a concrete way. In the only way she knows how, this child is trying to understand death.

My client Annie, mother of five-year-old Max, recently sent me an e-mail announcing her father's death. Annie's father had been diagnosed with cancer a year ago, and she had taken my "death seminar" to learn how to help Max with the death she knew was coming. I had advised her to take Max to visit Poppy, even as he got closer and closer to death. Annie's fear was that Max would be scared by the person Poppy was becoming. Max hardly noticed. He greeted Poppy with the same gusto, climbing into his lap when he could and babbling on about all his news. Annie was so relieved. Finally, upon telling him that Poppy had died, here is what five-year-old Max wanted to know: *"Where was he going to be buried? Where will his soul go?"* And, most important of all, *"What was Poppy going to wear?"* Perfect five-year-old questions.

Six-Year-Old Children

As children approach the age of six, the reality that death is final, that the person or animal will not come back to life, comes into focus. After this time, as children approach the age when they are capable of more abstract thinking (though not much before the age of nine), they begin to understand that death is something that happens to everyone. It is the end of the life cycle for all living creatures.

Tips and Scripts for Answering Questions about Death

- **Keep it simple and offer small bites.** Explain, describe, and clarify, over and over, until your child stops listening. It takes time to hear and process words and ideas. Keep your explanations simple, direct, and factual. It is better to give numerous short explanations over a period of time than one overly long, overly detailed one. As is the case with answers to most of the tough questions, keep your answers short and wait for your child's response. Give just a bit of information at a time so that the child can take it in. You may not hear any comments or questions for two or three days, but they will come. You will know your child is sated when the questions stop coming.

- **Be patient.** Your child is liable to ask you the same question over and over. She is just trying to make sense of the information you have given. With each explanation, she "gets it" a little better. So be sure you are consistent with your answers or she will become confused.

- **Expect blunt questions.** Over the course of the discussion, your child will probably ask some pretty blunt questions. They may throw you for a loop. You may even wonder how the heck your child knows to ask the questions. But these questions are good. Your lines of communication are wide open—your child is coming to *you*. That is just what you want. Further, this shows your child trusts that you will give her the real answers. Remember, your child's questions usually match her cognitive development at the time, so give answers that will encourage the same healthy kinds and degree of questions in the future.

- **Try to understand what your child is really asking.** If you aren't sure about the question or don't understand it, you can first ask her: *"What is your idea about that?"* or *"What do you think?"* Her answers will give you a clue as to the real nature of the question.

- **Avoid euphemisms.** When talking about death, avoid expressions like *"He passed away"* or *"He lost his father"* or *"He went on a long journey."* Expressions such as these will only confuse your very literal child. On being told that a grown-up *"had lost someone,"* a child will respond along the lines of *"when will we find him?"*

- **Avoid the word *sick*.** In describing why or how a person has died, steer clear of this word. The child thinks of being sick as having a cold or a tummy ache, something that keeps her home from school. This is quite different from the type of sickness that can be fatal. (The answer to *"Well, what do I say instead?"* is coming soon.)

- **Do not associate sleep with death.** Sometimes a parent will answer a child's question, *"What does a dead person look like?"* by saying, *"It looks like the person is sleeping."* This association could pave the road to sleep issues—and I know you definitely don't want any of those! You can respond: *"The all-done person is totally still. Nothing moves at all because none of the parts work anymore."*

- **It is okay to admit that you don't have all the answers.** Sometimes children ask some real doozies, and you will be truly stumped. In such cases, you can brainstorm about whom you might ask together, or you can promise to find the answer and get back to her. Then be sure you do.

Tips and Scripts for Talking about Death

- **For the one- to two-and-a-half-year-old:** *"Grandpa has died. When someone dies, we can't see him anymore. It makes us feel sad that we won't see him ever again."*

- **For the three- to six-year-old**: *"Dead means a person or animal is not alive anymore, he is all done living; the body has stopped working and won't work anymore. The body won't do any of the things it used to do: it won't talk, it won't walk, it won't move or see or hear. None of the parts work anymore. The person will not eat or drink or go the bathroom."*

- **For the four-year-old and older,** you might want to add: *"The person who has died won't feel any of the feelings he used to feel. He won't feel sad or happy or angry or scared. He won't feel anything at all."*

- **And for all young children,** add: *"Usually people only die when they have grown very, very, very old. You and I will live a long, long time and do so many things together."*

- **Be prepared for the next question, which you will surely get.** Upon hearing this definition, the first thing most children say is, *"Are you doing to die?"* or *"Is Daddy going to die?"* or *"I don't want to die."* While a parent might see this comment as selfish, it is merely a reflection of the child's predictable and normal egocentricity. Young children think about themselves first, what matters most to them, and what makes them feel safe. In this light, it makes complete sense that the child would immediately worry about herself and her parents, who are her lifelines. So you answer: *"Yes. Everything that is alive will die someday. But you and Daddy and I are not going to die for a long, long, long, long time."*

- **Death is about separation.** Remember, for the child, learning about death is all about separation from those who are most important to her. She immediately worries about being separated from her mommy and her daddy. Reassure her by saying: *"I plan on being alive and being your mommy for as long as you need me, a really long time."*

- **Some children will need more.** Tell the tale of just how very long you will be alive. Take the time to paint the picture in great detail. Prepare yourself, as it will take a while to say all of this. Take a good, deep breath, and begin:

> *"I am going to be your mommy for a long, long, long time. I am going to be your mommy when you are in nursery school. And I am going to be your mommy when you finish the four-year-old class and go to kindergarten, and I will be your mommy when you have your first sleepover. I will be your mommy when you play soccer in the summer, and I will be your mommy when you are in first grade and in second grade and in third grade. I will be your mommy when you are in Girl Scouts and when you go to ballet and to piano lessons. I will be your mommy when you go to camp, and I will be your mommy when you start playing baseball. I will still be your mommy when you go to sleepaway camp and when you are all finished with elementary school. I will still be your mommy when you are in middle school, and I will be your mommy when you have your bat mitzvah* (your confirmation, your first communion, your quinceañera). *I will be your mommy when I teach you how to drive a car and when you go on a date. I will be your mommy when you graduate from high school and when you go to college. . . ."*

Are you getting the idea? And it continues. . . .

> *"I will be your mommy when you finish with college and get a job, and I will be your mommy when you move into your own house. I will be your mommy when you get married, and I will be at that wedding. I will be your mommy (daddy) who walks you down the aisle. Then I will be your mommy when you decide to start a family and when you have a baby. And then I will be your mommy when you are a mommy, and I will be your baby's grandmother. I will babysit for your baby and drive your child to school, but I will still be your mommy. So, I am going to be your mommy for a long, long, long, long time."*

Now breathe.

"Where *Is* Grandpa?" Dealing with Questions about What Happens after Death

The child who is nearing age five will inevitably ask where Grandpa is sometime after hearing that he has died. Each parent's personal beliefs, religion, and culture will affect the way he chooses to answer this question. What I am offering here are the words to explain the traditional way most Americans deal with the after-death process.

- **The finality of death.** Regardless of your spiritual beliefs, it is important for children to be exposed to the finality of death, even though they may not be fully capable of understanding that reality from a developmental perspective. The lesson that a creature that has died will never come back to life again or have consciousness or feelings is a challenging one to explain. It is particularly difficult because it has both concrete and abstract aspects: *"The empty body that is all done living is placed in a special container called a casket. It is usually made of wood. That casket is placed in the ground, and it becomes part of the earth. The place where caskets are buried is called a cemetery."*
- ***"What happens to the body in the ground?"*** The older the child is, the more likely that he will ask this next question. You can respond: *"A body is made of lots of different parts, hard parts and soft parts. Can you feel your soft parts? (Pinch his cheeks, calves, etc.) And can you feel the hard parts? (Feel the bones and the teeth.) After a long time, the soft parts disintegrate and go away. The hard parts, the bones and teeth, last forever. The only parts of a body that has died that remain are the bones, which are called the skeleton, and the teeth."*

   Do not worry that your child will not comprehend the meaning of the word *disintegrate*. The focus will likely be on the whole story and not on just that one word. If there are further questions, you can use words like *dissolve* and *melt away*.

   Depending upon his age, your child may make some connection to dinosaur bones and other skeletons with which he is familiar. Be prepared for the first Halloween after he has learned this information. *"You mean* that *is what a skeleton is?"* the child will say as reality dawns.

The Soul or the Spirit

Expecting a young child to be able to grasp something as abstract as the concept of a soul is daunting at the very least. This idea needs to be introduced using a concrete image that the child can hold on to. In addition, your personal, religious, and cultural beliefs will influence your explanation. My suggestions below are based simply on taking the perspective of the child in helping her to understand the concept of a soul or spirit.

Tips and Scripts for Talking about the Soul or Spirit

- **Explain that the empty body is empty.** The child needs to understand that the person who lived in that body is no longer there. The body is empty. To convey the idea of the empty body, the analogy of an empty seashell can be helpful, as the child can create an image in her mind: *"It is kind of like a Hermit crab that has left its shell. The crab is gone, but the shell remains. When the crab is gone, the shell is no longer a hermit crab. It is just an empty shell."*

- **There are two parts to every person:** *"Many people believe that there are two parts to people . . . the body, the part that you can see and touch, and the soul or spirit, the part that you cannot see or touch. When somebody dies, the body becomes empty. That's because the soul is no longer in the body."*

- **Explaining the soul.** I don't think there is any explanation as difficult as one for the soul. Here are some scripts to consider:

  "Every person has a soul. It is something that you cannot actually see, like you can see the body."
  or
  "The soul is the part of the person that is there when the body isn't there. When Mommy takes you to school, you kiss me good-bye, I walk out the door, and I leave. You can't see me anymore, but you can think about me. You can remember me and how my hug feels. You can picture my face. You even miss me while you're at school and I have left. You think about me, and you feel safe and good and cozy. That is Mommy's soul. Mommy's soul

is the part of me that is there when Mommy's body isn't there. My soul stays with you while you are at school."

or

"A person's soul is all the parts of a person that you know and remember about him. It's his voice, his laugh, the things he likes to eat, the jokes he makes, the sports he is good at, all the things he knows how and likes to do. It is everything that you think and know and remember and love about another person."

or

"When you talk to someone on the phone, you can't see her, but you know she is there. Grandma calls you; you hear her voice and you talk. Where is Grandma? She is not there in the room with you, but you know what she looks like and sounds like. You know she likes to eat spaghetti, and you know she loves to hear your stories, and you know you love her. Then you hang up the phone, and Grandma is gone, but you are still thinking about her. When you think about her, part of her is there with you. That is Grandma's soul."

or

"When people are far away, or when they are in another room or down-stairs, you are able to think and imagine them somewhere else. The idea of them you have in your head is their soul."

And add:

"If people didn't have souls, we wouldn't be able to think about them or picture them or miss them when they were gone. Every person has a soul and a body."

The idea that something exists that we cannot see, like a soul, is exciting, puzzling, and sometimes scary for a child. A rabbi with whom I once worked introduced me to a concrete way for teaching about the spirit.

- **A science experiment to help make a very abstract concept con-crete for the child**

1. Find a clear plastic or glass cup.
2. Fill it three-quarters of the way with warm water. Ask your child to taste it and confirm that it is indeed water.
3. Fill a small cup with granulated sugar. Ask your child to taste it and confirm that it is indeed sugar.
4. Mix several tablespoons of the sugar in the water, stirring until it is dissolved.

5. Ask the child where the sugar went. Hopefully, she will say that it has disappeared, it is gone.
6. Ask her to taste the sugar-water. She will say it is sweet.
7. Ask her why it is sweet. Hopefully she will say because there is sugar in it.
8. You will reply: *"So, the sugar is there even though you can't see it? It's like a person's soul. It is there, but you just can't see it."*

Heaven

Children who are concrete thinkers will have a hard time understanding the concept of heaven, especially because it means that people will be separated from one another. The idea that somehow people exist in different places but no longer together is a frightening thought for a young child. Different people hold different beliefs about heaven, and since I am not a member of the clergy, I don't want to step on anyone's toes by suggesting what to convey to your child about this concept.

Cremation

There is not much to be said about cremation in a book directed at parents of children ages two to six. Suffice it to say that children this age should not be exposed to cremation at all. (If you live in Japan or if cremation has always been a cultural ritual for your whole family, then it is a different story.) Understanding that a dead body gets burned up and that the ashes are buried or scattered or even kept in a container is beyond the grasp of young children. Don't go there.

Untimely Death

We have explained death as a natural part of the aging process. But unfortunately, sometimes a person dies before he is old. This is an untimely death, as is the case when a mother miscarries.

Death is death, regardless of the age of the deceased. All of the same explanations about death hold true, but these situations are especially painful because no one expects a person to die before his time.

- **Be honest:** *"Sarah had a problem with her body. The doctors tried very hard to fix it, but they could not, and Sarah died. Her body could not work the way it needed to, and so she died."* And then you add: *"Usually this does not happen. Usually people live until they are very, very old."*

- **Reassure the child about your well-being:** *"My body is just fine. Daddy's body is just fine. Your body is just fine. Your sister's body is just fine. We have no problems with our bodies."*

- **Fetal Death.** In the unfortunate event that the mother miscarries and the firstborn child has been counting the days until the birth of her sibling, the child must be told. It is one of life's lessons. *"When a baby starts to grow, it is a fetus. It takes a long time for a fetus to become a baby. It has to grow and grow, a little bit at a time, until it is a baby, ready to be born. The doctor found out that our fetus was not growing the way it was supposed to, and it could not become a baby."*

  As always, wait for the response, and respond to *that* comment or question: *"That's right. Now we are not going to have a baby, like we hoped we would. The fetus did not and will not grow into a baby."*

Accidental Death

Sadly enough, once in a while a parent has to explain to a child that there's been an accidental death, such as from a car accident or even a natural disaster. What makes the conversation more difficult is that, in addition to discussing death, you are introducing ideas that are scary and often anxiety provoking. In deciding what you are going to say, first consider if you *need* to say anything and, if so, how much should be said beyond the basic facts. Often parents look back and realize that they gave TMI—too much information.

Tips and Scripts for Explaining an Accidental Death
....

- **The key word to emphasize is** *accident*: *"An accident is something that is not supposed to happen. Accidents don't usually happen, that's why they're called accidents.*

  "There are little accidents and big accidents. A little accident would be when a glass of milk gets knocked over and spills. A big accident would be when a body gets so badly broken that it cannot be fixed and the person dies."

- **An accidental death is a death that is not supposed to happen. It happened before the end of the person's life span.** *"Max was driving in the car and he had a very bad accident. His body got badly hurt, and the doctor could not fix him. So Max died. His body could not work anymore."*

- **Offer reassurance.** After hearing about an accident, whether or not it results in a death, a child will need reassuring. Even though you know that you cannot predict the future, it is not worth the child's wakeful nights and other demonstrations of anxiety, which could result without that reassurance. Tell him: *"I am a very careful driver; Daddy is a very careful driver. We are not going to get in an accident."*

Should My Child Go to the Funeral?

There was a time when it was thought that children should not attend a funeral even for a relative. Now we are not so quick to take this stance. While there is no set age for when a child is "ready" to go to a funeral, there are some questions you ought to ask yourself to help you make that decision:

- Will I be able to mourn the way I need to if my child is there? (This question is probably the most important of all.)
- Will my child be a distraction to me, to family members, or to others?
- Does anyone in my family feel strongly about my child's *not* being there? (Whether she can attend is your choice; but if someone else *doesn't* want her there, you may have no choice.)
- Am I bringing the child to meet my needs at her expense?
- Does the child want to go?

- Will leaving the child at home be worse than taking her?
- Are all the other cousins attending, so she would be the only one left at home?
- Is there someone to whom I can assign the child, who will be able to take the child away from the service if necessary or answer her questions, and is this someone she'd be willing to be with and, therefore, not make a fuss about not being with you?

If you decide that the child will attend the service, take the time to explain to the child exactly what will happen. Surprises at funerals are not good things.

Tips and Scripts for Preparing Your Child for a Funeral

- **A child two (and perhaps three) years old and younger will get nothing out of attending a funeral.** It is not reasonable to expect a child this age to "behave" at a funeral. She will be a distraction to those who are there to mourn and pay respects. In addition, she is too young to understand the meaning of the event in any way, regardless of your explanation.

- **Explain what will happen at the funeral service:** *"A lot of people will meet together to talk about Grandpa, to tell stories about him, to say what they loved about him. The minister* (the rabbi, the cantor, the priest) *will be there to lead us in prayers and songs to help us say good-bye to Grandpa."*

- **Give clear warning that there will be crying.** Children are not accustomed to seeing grown-ups cry, especially the way some do at a funeral. It can be scary and disturbing to a child. You can say: *"Grown-ups often cry at funerals. Sometimes they cry very loudly because they feel so sad that someone has died."*

- **Give the child permission to cry if you think that is a possibility:** *"You may or may not feel like crying. Sometimes just seeing other people cry makes you cry. Either way, it's okay."*

- **The burial.** Child development experts have differing opinions about whether a young child should witness a burial. It is quite powerful, as you have probably experienced, to see a casket lowered into the ground or sealed into a crypt. If you choose to include your child in this part of the service, be sure to explain exactly what the child will see: *"After the talking part, everyone will go to the place where the casket will be put in the ground. People will say some more prayers and watch as the casket is lowered into the ground."*

How much you decide to describe will depend upon how much your child is going to witness. If there is no graveside service, there is no need to describe the burial process. However, you will need to answer the questions your child asks. Remember, short, simple, and factual responses are key. Pause periodically to hear the child's reaction or additional questions.

Tips and Scripts about Mourning

- **Grieving is okay.** Do not be afraid to show your grief in front of your children. Children learn how to grieve from watching their parents and others. There is certainly nothing wrong or bad about your child seeing your sadness. If fact, it is an important lesson about feelings. Even grown-ups can be really sad and cry, and pretty soon they feel better. You might say: *"I am feeling so sad right now. I am thinking about Grandpa and missing him, and that makes me need to cry. Crying helps me to wash away my sad feelings. Pretty soon I will feel better, but right now I need to cry and feel sad."*

- **Teach your child to commemorate the person who has died.** In the spirit of teaching your child how we remember people who have died, how we keep their souls alive within us in our thoughts, you might talk about ways in which you commemorate the person who has died.

  1. Plant a tree or a flowering bush in memory of the person. *"This is Grandma's rosebush. When it blooms, I will always think of her."*
  2. Candles are used to commemorate many events and occasions. Light a candle to remind you of Grandma's spirit.
  3. Each year on her birthday or on the anniversary of her death, light a candle to remind you of Grandma's spirit and discuss with your children how we never forget a person. Bodies die, but souls live on within us forever.
  4. Display photographs of the person and talk about her. Talk is good medicine for all people.

5. Create a collage of pictures and memorabilia about the person who has died and display it prominently.

6. Write down your feelings about the person who has died and share them with your child. Invite her to dictate her feelings to you or draw a picture, but don't force it.

- **Children mourn differently from adults.** A child may be deeply saddened by the loss of a family member, friend, or pet, but she may not show her feelings in traditional ways. While adults tend to be enveloped by their sadness for a period of time, children grieve intermittently, often moving in and out of sadness. They can be temporarily distracted; they can even appear to have forgotten about their sadness. The only thing we know for sure is that we really can't say how an individual child will process a death. It is your job to open the lines of communication and allow every opportunity for the child to express her feelings (or not).

Condolences

The last part of learning about death is the lesson about offering condolences. Children can learn to be empathetic at a very early age, though no one is sure if this behavior comes from feeling genuine empathy, from having seen such empathy modeled by a parent, or from not being clear on who is sad: *"Oh dear. Someone is crying. Should I be crying? Am I sad? I'd better comfort you. That will bring me comfort."* Regardless, you need to teach your child about condolences.

Tips and Scripts for Offering Condolences

- **Create a concrete show of condolence.** If your child is aware of the death and knows someone who is affected by it, help her to make a card or draw a picture to give to the family, explaining: *"Telling someone you are sorry that he feels sad sometimes helps him to feel better. People like to know that other people care about them."*

  Help your child to bake cookies or make a meal to bring to the mourning family. This shows your child how you can take care of people who are mourning: *"When people are feeling sad, they don't always feel like doing regular things, like going to the grocery store and cooking. We are going to help Mrs. Green by cooking a dinner for her and bringing it to her house. I think it will make her feel good."*

- **Model for your child how you do favors for a person who is mourning.** Explain how you do so by offering to drive a car pool or run an errand or invite the person's children to your home so she can have a break.

❖

CHAPTER 10

"Mommy and Daddy Have Something to Tell You."

Talking with Your Children about Divorce

Divorce presents a tremendous change in the life of the child. In fact, it may be the epitome of change, as so much of what the child has known will be different. It can shake the very foundation on which the child's whole life sits. That's pretty big stuff, and parents know it. This particular change represents a huge loss in the life of the child too. It is not only a loss of what is familiar, comfortable, and predictable, but it is also literally the loss of one parent on a day-to-day basis. Life as he has known it will never be the same. It won't necessarily be bad, but it will be different.

Not telling your child about a pending divorce is not a choice. Children are very absorbent little creatures. They pick up on everything, spoken and unspoken. They are acutely tuned into the emotional climate of their homes. While you may think that your child has been unaware that you and your spouse haven't been getting along, or that you have actually hated each other for ages, this is usually not the case. Nathan hears the tone in your voice when you respond to your spouse through gritted teeth. He sees the eye rolls, hears the sighs and the "tsks." The sounds of the fights that go on behind closed doors reach him. The avoided kisses, the careless greetings do not go unnoticed. The air is thick with tension.

A divorcing client shared with me that her two-and-a-half-year-old child, who had witnessed no out-and-out fighting (or so she thought), took a framed photograph of Mommy and another one of Daddy and said, "Give Daddy a kiss, Mommy." Do you think that child didn't know that her parents weren't getting along?

In some families, no attempt is made to hide the deteriorating relationship.

The disagreements and the fighting are active and in full view. Sometimes it has gone beyond the verbal and extends to physical fighting. In either case, you are kidding yourself if you think your child doesn't know that something isn't right in the family.

Child development experts agree that while children are seldom happy that their parents are splitting up, they may not be surprised. Children as young as six months old can sense tension and that something is different in their world. Some children even feel a sense of relief when the parents actually separate, because the discord they have sensed is out in the open. At last the fighting will stop, and the tension will be reduced.

As with other aspects of parenting, the care with which you handle your divorce can make a tremendous difference in the life of your child, not only now but also in the future. Many divorcing parents come to me claiming that they absolutely want to do what is in the best interest of the child; the child's well-being comes first. When they follow through on that commitment, these children have had the least difficult adjustments—not perfect, not easy, but the best that could be hoped for. After the bumps of the transition period, everyone adapts to their new lives and the child does fairly well, following the cues of his parents, and develops some comfort in having two families. Unfortunately, this is not often the case. Anger, hurt, guilt, disappointment, and greed rear their heads, and the best-laid plans are thrown out the window.

Regardless of the "best" timing, the "right" words, the "respectful" agreements, and the "perfect" coparenting plan, your child will react. He is a feeling organism, attached to both of his parents. The way in which your child reacts, processes the news, and adjusts to his changed life will depend upon his age, his temperament, his development, and each of you. While no one can offer an exact script that will guarantee a pain-free divorce for your child, there are things you can do to lessen the blow.

Breaking the News

Telling your child that you are separating or getting a divorce may be one of the most difficult tasks you will ever have to face. The size of the lump in your throat grows every time you imagine the pending conversation. Yet the lumpectomy will begin as soon as that first conversation is over. In fact, you will feel a tremendous sense of relief. The way in which you tell your child, the care that you give not only to the words you speak but also to your tone, to the time of day and to what happens thereafter, sets the stage for and will affect the way your child processes the news of this gigantic change in his life.

Tips for the Setup for Delivering the News of a Pending Divorce

- **Wait until you are sure.** If you are *thinking* about separating or getting a divorce, wait until you are sure before telling your child. While it is important to tell him early on, the news should come when it is happening and not a month away. Children think in black and white. They don't do well with *mights* and *maybes*. It is either happening or it isn't. There is no need to create anxiety where it doesn't need to exist . . . yet.

- **Tell the news together.** The news of a divorce or separation itself will eclipse the presenters. Which parent tells the child the news seems to be more important to the parents than to the child. In the best of circumstances, both parents should deliver the news together to all of their children. However, if yours is a family where one parent has played a much more active role, it is important that you, the trusted parent, give the news.

  Telling the news together removes the possibility of the child hearing different stories from each parent. Hearing a single version is a good thing. In addition, your joint presentation gives the child his first taste of your coparenting. The child hears about the pending change as a mutual decision. He sees how Mommy and Daddy agree and work together. How great it will be if this model is maintained.

- **Choose your time.** The news itself will have a greater impact than the time and location of the conversation, but have it far away from bedtime or a separation and not right before school or gym class, for example. It is a good idea to have a plan that enables you to be together after you have had the conversation. For this reason a weekend or a day off from school are usually the best days. Plan an activity that will be a distraction after your discussion. Go to a movie, play miniature golf, go on a bike ride . . . be busy. Ideally for the child's benefit, both parents will participate in the activity, depending upon the tone of your relationship at that time. Your child needs to see right away that life will continue, and both parents will be in it. While it may seem a mixed message, it is not;

though you won't be married and living together anymore, you'll both be parenting the child.

The Explanation for Divorce

Like all children, your child is egocentric. When he hears the news of the divorce, his first concern is for himself. *"Am I going to be okay?"* is the question that will be underlying every other question. He will want to know: *"What does this mean for me?"*

Whatever explanation you give, it must include the following spoken elements and assurances:

I am still your mommy, and Daddy is still your daddy.
I will always be your mommy who loves you, and Daddy will always be your daddy who loves you, always and forever.
Our family is going to be different.
We have a plan.
We will both take care of you.
It is not your fault.

- **Be honest.** In an attempt to shield your child from the pain of the truth (and because it is hard to face it yourself) and perhaps to buy some time for yourself, it is tempting to make up a story about where Daddy is: *"Daddy is away on business for a while. It's just you and me together in the house."* This is not a good idea, unless it is true. If Daddy has gone to a hotel or to Uncle Eddie's house to sleep, your child needs to know.

- **Keep it simple.** Words are clutter for children. They need simple, short explanations. Do not assume that your child knows what *divorce* means. Your child does not need to know minute details or reasons. He just needs to know what is up. Here are a few phrases that are simple and to the point:

  "Mommy and Daddy have decided that we are not going to live together in the same house. That means that we will each still take care of you, but not in the same house."
  or

"Daddy and Mommy are not going to be married anymore. We are going to be divorced."

or

"Divorce is when two people who are married stop being married."

or

"Our family is going to be different. You are a family with Daddy, and you are a family with Mommy."

- **Love is confusing.** Be careful about bringing *love* into the explanation. For young children it is difficult to grasp the fine differences between the *love* parents have (had) for each other and the *love* a parent always has for a child. Rather than saying *"Mommy and I don't love each other anymore,"* it might be better to say: *"Mommy and I have different feelings for each other. When you are a grown-up sometimes feelings can change."*

   Every explanation needs to be punctuated with the following phrase: *"I will never stop being your mommy, and Daddy will never stop being your daddy. We will both always love you forever and ever. That will never change."*

- **The *Why* question.** As previously discussed, when a young child asks, *"But whhhyyyy?"* he is not usually looking for an explanation. *Why?* is a protest. *Why?* is his way of telling you he doesn't like what is happening. But parents fall into the trap of trying to explain. Don't do it! Children do not need to know the sordid details of your breakup, that Mommy was cheating, that Daddy had a gambling issue, or whatever. It will be tempting to fall into the explanation trap, especially if there is some blame to be tossed around. Don't go there! Children will be overwhelmed by the details. But what you can do is describe in words what the child has observed. Depending upon the age of the child (three years old and older), you can simply say, *"You have heard loud voices, and you have seen Mommy crying. Mommy and I don't agree on many things anymore. We don't like to do the same things. We do not want to be married anymore."*

   To this explanation you may add the following, depending on your beliefs: *"Usually when grown-ups fall deeply in love, want to be together forever, and decide to get married, they stay married for their whole lives. But sometimes, not usually, they decide that they don't want to be together forever, and they get a divorce. They end their marriage."*

There are people who will take issue with this last statement, especially in light of the statistics about how many marriages these days do end in divorce. But I believe, for our children's sense of security and in the interest of perpetuating the institution of marriage, you need to promote marriage as something that usually lasts a lifetime and should not be taken lightly. It is, of course, your choice.

The child may hound you for details and explanations, but it is your job to stick to your guns and tell him exactly as much as he *needs* to hear. The resolve and strength in your delivery will give the child the message that you are still in charge, you will take care of him, and he is safe.

The Explanation for Separation

The explanation for separation, a temporary state, is even more challenging for the child to understand than is divorce. His way of seeing the world in absolutes makes it difficult for him to grasp the uncertainty and the nuances of separation.

"Mommy and Daddy are not going to live together in the same house for a while."
or
"Daddy and Mommy need some thinking time. We are not getting along, and we have different ideas. We need some time apart, so we can think about whether we want to live together in the same house. We are having a separation."

As with a divorce, the child needs to be assured that: *"I am still your mommy and Daddy is still your daddy. That will never change. You will spend some time with Daddy and some time with Mommy."*

It is common that the child will ask when the separation will be over or other questions to which you genuinely do not know the answer. To these you can say: *"This is the plan for now. Daddy is living at Uncle Richie's house, and I am living here. We will let you know when it is time for a new plan."*

It is also okay to respond to those murky questions by saying: *"We don't know the answer to that question now. We will tell you when we know."*

It is important not to discourage the child from asking questions. You would rather he ask you than anyone else, after all.

Moving Out

Sooner or later one of you is going to move out. As difficult as it will be for the one who is moving, it will be equally hard for the child. Regardless of who is leaving, the move represents a reality that your child now has to understand: *I have two different parents who live in two different homes.* It is the start of his beginning to be a part of two separate families, one with Daddy and one with Mommy. Life as he has known it will not be the same. The move underscores that reality. Up until now, it was all supposition. Now it is real.

Tips and Scripts for Moving Out

The house the child has known is going to feel very different without Daddy and his things in it. While it will be the same home, it will feel different to the child.

It would be so easy to just get on with it. Find a place; get a moving van; move your stuff; get out and be done with it . . . then tell your child. But if you are considering your child, that may not be such a good idea. Daddy getting a new house, whether it is a room in Uncle Richie's house, an apartment, or a mansion, is a big deal to the child. Sooner or later, it will be his new home too. It is a change that will require some adjustment. Here are some tips to make the moving-out process more palatable:

- **When your child is not around, decide what goes and what stays.** The discussion about who gets Aunt Sophie's porcelain pitcher, your wedding silver, and even the dog, needs to happen out of your child's earshot.

- **The more he can see, the better it will be for the child.** Since the young child is an interactive, concrete learner, he will benefit from being involved in the move. Instead of sending the child away for the day, allow him to be involved in the move. Invite him to help Daddy pack some of his things in boxes. Let him help load up the car.

- **Provide a nest for the child at the new house.** While unquestionably the parent is the most important part of the new house, the child needs to have space there too. Even if the child will be sharing your bedroom (which would not be my first choice), he needs his own bed, his own drawers, a special place for his special toys, and a space that's just his own. You cannot expect the child to feel at home if it appears that there is no room for him. Remember, a child sees his toys and his stuff as extensions of himself. Let him choose certain of his toys, clothes, and treasures to keep at the new house. Know that it will take time for him to feel comfortable there. The transition between Mommy's house and Daddy's house will be smoothest if there isn't a whole lot of stuff that has to be taken back and forth. Make sure both houses are well stocked.

- **Invite the child to help make a home out of the house.** Enlist the help of the child in decorating Daddy's new house. Take him with you to the linen store, the kitchen store, and involve him in the process. Let him pick out his sheets and tub toys. Let him draw a picture to decorate a wall in the new house. Children who are involved feel a sense of ownership.

- **Take the child on a visit to the "new house."** As soon as you know where you will be living, bring the child to see the new digs. Have a pizza picnic on the living room floor and decide together that you need to buy a table and chairs. Begin to define your life together in your new home without anyone else.

- **Parents don't disappear.** As much as you might dislike your soon-to-be-ex, your child doesn't. When your child comes to your house, it is crucial that he know from the start that his other parent does not disappear. Allow him to have at your house the things that remind him that his other parent still exists, such as photographs and a gift from the former in-laws.

More Tips and Scripts for Weathering the Divorce

- **Listen, Listen, Listen!** No parent wants to cause his child pain or sadness, yet this is exactly what he knows he is doing in getting a divorce. In a parent's eagerness to "make it all better," he sometimes forgets to let his child do the talking. In fact, some parents find it difficult just to listen without interrupting or responding. It is as if your words will make the child's pain go away, and so you talk constantly to try to fix it. That isn't going to happen.

It takes children time to process the news of the divorce or separation. Each will do it in his own way and in his own time. It is the job of both parents to provide plenty of opportunities for the child to talk, to ask questions, and to complain, while you, the parents, simply listen.

- **Allow your child to feel his feelings.** Your child will experience many different feelings as he adjusts to the change in his life. Expressing these is part of what helps him to adapt. Resist the urge to tell your child how much better his life will be; he can't imagine that to be true. Allow your child to be sad or angry. When he is sad, for example, telling the child to *"Be strong!"* gives him the message that it isn't okay to have his feelings. Worse, it plugs up one of the ways that he has to let off steam by crying or showing his sadness. When negative feelings are shared, they don't feel quite so bad. That is the first step in feeling better.

- **Do not place blame.** As tempting as it may be, do not place blame of any kind on the other parent, ever. While it might meet your need for retribution, it only puts the child in the terrible position of having to take sides. It is certainly not a good idea for the child to think there is a good parent or a bad parent. He wants and needs to love you both. That is what is good for children.

Your divorce may, in reality, put you in difficult straits. Your status as a single parent may mean that you are now the sole bread winner and have much less money. It may mean that you have no relief in the twenty-four-hour-a-day job of parenting. There are so many changes that might affect your spirit and would be visible to your child. But not only does your child love his *"no-good, depriving, selfish"* daddy, but he needs to feel safe with both of you. Blaming your ex for your current circumstances is a double-edged sword. *"I will always take care of you and we will be just fine"* is the message. Steer clear of *"We can't have that because Daddy doesn't give us enough money, and if we buy that, we won't have enough money for food."*

I can just hear you asking, *"But what if that is the reality?"* Then you respond in the same way that you say no to anything you don't want to buy: *"That is not something that I choose to spend our money on. What we do in our house is different from at Daddy's."*

- **No "bad-mouthing" the other parent in front of the child, or when you think he can't hear you, or when you think he won't get what you're saying.** Your child loves and feels loyal to both of you; don't make him choose between you. Remember to mind your side comments, your phone comments, your whispered comments. The walls have big ears.

- **Whenever possible, present yourselves as a "we."** In the conversations that you will have with your child during and following the initial news brief, make every attempt to refer to your parenting decisions and ideas using "we." *"We have decided." "Your mommy and I think it would be a good idea to. . . ."* In this way, your child will see you as united in your jobs as parents, both of whom take care of him and keep him safe.

- **Let your child know it is not his fault.** At some point during the breakup and beyond, it would not be uncommon for a child to think he is responsible for the divorce or separation. This is especially true for young children who have a hard time distinguishing between fantasy and reality. You two may have disagreed on how to handle certain of his behaviors or may have displayed anger over something he did, so the child sees himself as the cause. It is, therefore, important that you be very direct in telling your child: *"The divorce is just between Mommy and Daddy. It has nothing to do with children and parents. It is not about you or your behavior or your feelings."* In clearly stating that the divorce has nothing to do with him, the message is also given that reconciliation will also not be his decision or have anything to do with him.

- **Have a plan.** Children always feel better when they know there is a plan and they know what it is. This is not always possible, but it is always preferable. Early on it would be good to be able to say:

  "Daddy is going to live in an apartment close by, and Mommy is going to live in this house."
  or
  "You are going to spend some time with Mommy in this house and some time with Daddy in his house. Now you are going to have two houses."

As your own plan comes into focus, let your child in on what is happening.

- **Prepare for a lot of talk.** Remember, a child's understanding is a process that unfolds over time. It comes with repeated conversations and questions, often the same ones over and over, as he tries to wrap his arms around what has happened to his family. Invite and welcome your child's questions and answer them with gratitude that he has brought them to you. Divorce is really difficult to understand.

- **Be available to your child.** Since you cannot produce what your child wants most—to have his family whole again—be sure to give him the next best thing: *you*. When you are with your child, *be* with your child. Just having your child in your custody doesn't count. Your child needs your undivided attention. He doesn't want to share you with the phone, the computer, or the television. You cannot make things all better, but you can go a long way toward helping your child feel better by being available to receive his comments and complaints, and hearing his wishes, worries, and woes.

- **When to get help.** Your child's adjustment to the changes brought on by divorce depends not only on your parenting and the custody plan, but also on his temperament and his development. Since the adjustment path is not usually a smooth one, you can anticipate a variety of behaviors in response to the divorce: clinginess, regressions to previously mastered behaviors like night wakings or toilet accidents, nightmares, introversion, whininess, aggressive behaviors, naughtiness, and defiance . . . to name just a few. Any or all of these would be normal in the face of your child needing your attention and feeling out of control. Eventually, with time and experience, as the child sees that life goes on and his life has fallen into a new pattern, these behaviors should begin to decline. If, however, any of these behaviors continues beyond a reasonable amount of time (beyond eight weeks), it would be a good idea to seek the help of a mental health professional.

Tips and Scripts for Coparenting

You and your (soon to be) ex are about to enter a whole new realm, life as coparents. It is the start of a relationship that you and he will have for the rest of your child's life. Your child will be watching and absorbing the way you two now relate, the way you treat each other, the comments you make, the dirty looks you give. Be aware and be on the alert. As stated above, it is never in your child's best interest to allow your negative feelings about your ex to leak out. He loves and needs you both. Do not put him in a position of having to split his loyalty.

- **Avoid arguments in front of your child.** While most parents know this admonition to be crucial, they often get sucked into the fighting zone. Do whatever you can to save your "heated discussions" for when your child is not anywhere to be seen and when you are absolutely certain he is not within earshot: Create a signal for each other that this discussion must stop; one of you leave the room; do whatever it takes to avoid a fight. It is particularly never okay for a child to hear his parents fighting about *him*. Remember, you have been telling him that your divorce wasn't his fault.

- **Allow for and accept that your child loves his other parent.** As much as you may not, your child still loves his other parent. This is a good thing. When he is with you, allow him to miss his other parent, to talk about her, to think about her, and to call her. When the child expresses that he misses his Mommy, you can say: *"I know that you miss your mommy. She misses you too. Would you like to talk to her on the phone?"*

- **Continue to refer to your ex as "Mommy" or "Daddy."** Calling your ex "your father" in conversation is a clear message to your child. Despite your feelings, he is still *Daddy* to your child, and he needs to feel secure about that.

- **Don't ever put your child in the middle.** If you have a message, any message at all, for your ex, give it to her yourself by phone, by text message, or by e-mail . . . but not through your child. Ever. Also, do not put your child through "Twenty Questions" when he comes home from being with Mommy. Your child should never feel that he needs to report in or "tattle" on the other parent. Doing so only puts him in the middle.

- **Her house is her house; his house is his house.** As hard as this reality may be, what happens at your ex's house during her custody time *is her business* and vice versa. You may not like it or approve of it, but there is not much you can do about it when your child is within earshot. In front of your child, being critical of the way your ex parents is a bad idea. Again, it forces the child to take sides. If it isn't a problem for the child, it isn't something to which he should be privy. The child can easily feel guilty for having participated in or caused something of which you do not approve.

You may decide that you and your ex need to consult with an objective mental health professional who can help you to find a common or acceptable ground for you both. The bottom line is that what is most important is your own relationship with your child when you and he are together. That is truly the only thing over which you have complete control.

- **Beware of manipulation.** Very quickly your child will learn what is or isn't okay with Daddy at his house and with Mommy at hers. He is smart and will figure out just what your hot buttons are, so beware! The child will do whatever works to get his needs met, and sometimes that means pouring on the sappy stuff. It is well within the range of normal for the child to say he misses or wants his mommy in response to a reprimand or the simple turning down of a request. *"I miss my Mommy"* in this case just means, *"I don't like what you said."* You can say: *"I know that you miss your mommy. You still need to turn off the TV right now."*

Coparenting More Than One Child

When divorcing parents share two or more children of different ages, there are added complications.

- **Different ages may require different explanations.** Parents will need to craft their explanations keeping in mind each child's age and development, and remembering that siblings share information. So consistency and honesty are crucial.
- **Siblings have their own relationship that will be affected by the divorce and the climate in the household.** While sibling relationships can be volatile and reflect the issues and moods of the family environment, divorce can yield a newfound closeness among siblings. Often the children band together, giving one another the security and stability they seek and need.

- **Make time for each child with each parent, alone.** In most custody arrangements, the children are seen as a unit, together going back and forth to each parent's home. The child's much-needed individual time with Daddy or Mommy gets eliminated. Guard against this by making a plan for alone time with each child. Even if it is just once a month, each child needs and deserves to have his coveted time alone with each parent.

Tips and Scripts for Dealing with Relatives and Friends

Divorce and separation can have far-reaching effects outside of the nuclear family. However, the immediacy and immensity of the divorce for you and your children often clouds the reality that others will be affected also. They will welcome your lead in attitude, explanations, and behavior. It's important to coach them in how you and your ex are handling this momentous change with your children.

- **Talk to the relatives.** Your own parents may be aware of the pain you are suffering during your divorce, but they may not have a clue about what to say to your children. Your children need consistent messages. So that they can back your story, take the time to explain to your families what you have told your children, giving the exact words: *"Bob and I both told Jeremy that we would not be living together anymore, that we are getting a divorce. When he asked why, we simply said that we do not agree on things and have different feelings."*

- **Do not take sides ... within earshot of the children (including the cousins).** Your family will be fiercely loyal to you, and that may be expressed in their dislike for your ex. You must implore your family not to show their feelings about your ex in any way in front or within earshot of your (or their) highly observant and absorbent child.

- **The cousins need to be told.** The children in your extended family are liable to be affected by your divorce. Not only will they be aware of your ex's absence at family events, but they also may fear that the same fate will happen to their parents. Share with your adult relatives the words you used in talking to your children. The relatives can tell their kids: *"Aunt Jody and Uncle Fred are not going to be married anymore. They are* *getting a divorce. (Pause. . . . Wait for comments. . . .) Uncle Fred is moving into a new house, and Aunt Jody is staying in the house where they live now. (Pause. . . . Wait for comments. . . .) Cousin Rena and Cousin Jake will have a room at each house, and they will spend time with both Uncle Fred and Aunt Jody. They both still love their children very much and will still be their mommy and daddy forever and ever."*

They may need to add: *"Aunt Jody and Uncle Fred are getting a divorce. We are not. Your mommy and daddy are staying married."*

These parents may find themselves having to reassure their children over and over that no divorce is coming for them. This will be especially true when the parents have a normal disagreement. It wouldn't be surprising, then, for the children to ask if they are getting a divorce. To this the adults should answer: *"Sometimes we disagree or have a small fight, but that does not mean we are getting a divorce."*

- **Your close friends' children need to be told.** While it is not your job to be the bearer of bad news all over town, the friends with whom your children regularly come into contact will likely notice that your ex is not around so much, or be aware that her friend is staying at her daddy's house, or will hear the news directly from your child. These children need to be told. I believe your adult friends will be grateful to know the words you used in explaining your divorce so that they can talk with their children. You can offer them this script: *"Nicky's daddy is not living at Nicky's house anymore. His parents are not going to be married anymore; they are getting a divorce. Nicky will spend some time with his daddy at his new house and some time with his mommy at his old house."*

❖

CHAPTER 11

"Is the Fire Going to Come to Our House?"

Answering Questions about Natural Disasters,

Terrorism, and War

Finding the words to use with your children to deal with the hard stuff of everyday life is difficult; such a task can be daunting, if not overwhelming, when a parent is trying to explain terrorism, war, or other disasters.

The moment you became a parent, everything changed. Not only was a new kind of fear added to every waking moment of your life—the fear that something would happen to your most precious possession, your child—but your priorities changed. Nothing is more important than your child's well-being. Nothing is as powerful as your connection to that child. Each year at school orientation when I, as director, explained the school's disaster preparedness plan, it was common to look out at the audience and see parents struggling to hold back tears. Just the thought of not being with your child or not being able to get to your child during a disaster is highly charged for every parent. And that's the way your child feels. We ponder with such great deliberation just the right words to use in explaining the war or the tsunami. In reality, what your child most needs to hear is that you and she will not be separated, that you will be safe together.

The material in this chapter is not intended for those who have been directly affected by natural disasters, terrorism, or war. It's not geared to those with a family member who has been deployed or those who have lost someone in a war or other disaster. Rather it is meant for the rest of us who live in a society where exposure to these events has become unavoidable.

Our increasingly complex world is filled with issues and events that are highly disturbing to all people. These situations are extremely difficult, even impossible, for children to comprehend; they are just as hard for grown-ups to explain. As adults, you have a context and experience with which to understand the tragedies that happen. Even so, these events may shatter your sense of safety, threaten your ability to protect your children, sabotage your sense of control, and honestly, just take your breath away. You are terrified because you *know* what they mean.

When terrorism strikes, when airports add checkpoints and security is heightened, when there is a war or a natural disaster in a far-off land, when a hurricane strikes, when a plane crashes, the aftershocks of these events can reach your children but, let's hope, not directly. Regardless, they can touch your children because they affect you, your daily existence and sense of well-being.

Whether or not you feel it is appropriate to discuss such events with your children or expose them to the media coverage will be your call. But what all families share is the reality that today's media allows us all, including our children, to be exposed in the most graphic ways to things that in the past would never have entered your children's worlds. Today's technologically advanced media brings immediate and vivid images into our kitchens and living rooms, as if they were happening next door, leaving us all to feel a clear, imminent, and really present danger.

When disasters, acts of terrorism, wars abroad, or the implementation of precautions against terrorism happen, we open the media floodgates to gather as much information as possible. A contagious anxiety permeates our daily lives. You turn on the television, check the Internet, blast the car radio, grab printed material, all to feed your need to know. You talk to your partner and to friends on the phone. You feel like this barrage of news and discussion is necessary, but at the same time, you are overwhelmed by it. All the while, you forget that there are four-year-old eyes and ears taking it all in. And that four-year-old knows that something is up. She hears the stories, sees the images, hears her older siblings' questions, and she is confused and frightened. Most importantly, she looks at you, the trusted parent, sees worry written all over your face, and thinks: *"There must be something to worry about. Just look at my daddy. Something is bad, and maybe I should be scared."*

Truth be told, it is almost impossible to completely shelter your young children from the news. But that doesn't mean you shouldn't try. When you have children of different ages, monitoring your young child's news intake is compounded by what your older children have heard and learned in their less sheltered lives away from home and wandering the world through the media.

In the eyes of the child, the parent's number one job is to keep her safe. She trusts you to do your job all the time. And she looks to you to interpret the parts of her world that she doesn't understand. Children of all ages take their cues about how to feel and respond to any given situation from their parents and the trusted adults in their lives. In fact, children respond more to a parent's or adult's reaction to big news than to the news itself. The parent is the barometer of the child's sense of her own safety.

As parents, you can make choices about the information to which you want your young children to be exposed. Some parents will attempt to control all access and every bit of information. Others will be less concerned, less vigilant, or less able to restrict the information flow. Regardless of where you fall on this continuum, we know that all children have a profound need to feel cared for by the trusted adults in their lives. When you help them manage the information and resulting feelings that they have, they feel safe. When, without your guidance, they absorb scary and threatening information from snippets heard on the radio, scenes glimpsed on the television, front-page photos and magazine covers, and red alerts from their peers, they do not feel safe. The results can be far-reaching.

Whether you are explaining an act of terrorism, a war, a security precaution, or a natural disaster, the child's ability to understand and process what is going on will depend upon her age, development, temperament, and experience. The child's reaction and ability to understand what has happened are not in an adult context. In other words, she hasn't lived long enough to know that people recover, eventually things will be okay, and life goes on. In addition, young children easily confuse the facts with their own fears. They lack not only the ability to sort out reality from fiction, but also the experience and development that gives them perspective. The graphic nature of news makes it seem as if the event is happening right now, just across the street. Young children are very egocentric and concrete thinkers. They understand the ins and outs of everyday life as it affects them, and that is their major concern. *Am I okay?* Their first reaction, whether immediate or delayed, will likely be fear.

As each child is different, each child will have a different response. You know your child best. But experts agree that children under the age of seven do not need to know this information. They can, and how we wish they would, blissfully skip through their daily lives without knowing the horrors of this world.

The Most Important Message: *I Will Keep You Safe*

The single most important message for you to communicate calmly and confidently to your young child when it comes to disasters, war, terrorism, and widespread safety precautions is: *"You are safe. I know how to keep you and our whole family safe. That is my job. There are lots of grown-ups who work to keep us safe. We are all safe now, and we will continue to be safe."*

Remember the scene in *The Wizard of Oz* when Dorothy is unable to get back home from Oz, when she thinks that all is lost and only the wizard can help her? She asks, *"Will I ever see Auntie Em again?"* None of the other horrors—including flying monkeys and the witches—freaked her out as much as her fear that she wouldn't get back home to be with her Auntie Em. The bond between parent and child is so strong and powerful that your need to be together and take care of your child supersedes all else.

Tips and Scripts for Talking with Your Children about Disasters

- **Take care of your own feelings first.** Remember the oxygen mask theory. (See chapter 8, page 151.) Your reactions and your way of being with your child are based on your own fear and anxiety, not necessarily on logic or reality. So first take care of yourself. If you don't deal with your own anxiety and stress, you will not be available to meet your child's needs with confidence and to use clear thinking. Talk to your spouse, your partner, your friends, your doctor, a counselor . . . far out of your children's earshot. Find a safe place for yourself where you can let out your fear and worry. In getting it out, you will have made the room needed to contain your child's feelings, if need be. And your fear will not leak out for your child to absorb.

- **Don't whisper!** There are many times when we don't want our children to hear what we are saying. Parents spell, speak a different language, talk in code or "pig Latin," and whisper. Do you think your child doesn't know that you are saying something you don't want her to hear? The moment you whisper, your child's ears perk right up. Now she is listening, and now she knows that there is something going on that she isn't supposed to know about. Red alert!

- **It's okay *not* to talk about it.** If your child is not directly affected by the event, it is possible that she has escaped without unwanted exposure. In this very fortunate case, it is actually preferable not to discuss it. There is no reason to raise the subject with a child who is seven years old or younger. How lucky she is to be unburdened by these events and the resulting worries. The young child needs to know that the world is a safe place. Hearing about disasters and terrorism only eats away at her feelings of safety.

- **Protect your children (under the age of seven) from the media.** Young children should not be intentionally exposed to the news, period. Don't listen to news radio when you're driving the car pool, and don't read the newspaper at the breakfast table. You might be buried in an article on page twenty-three, but your child is staring at the front-page photo of the forest fire in Canada, the gun battle in Baghdad. Turn off the little television in the kitchen that is background to your meal preparation. While you think your child isn't watching and listening, she is absorbing the news, and she certainly is observing your reactions.

  In addition, the repetitive nature of the news makes events seem even bigger. The young child may think that the same event has happened over and over, which not only confuses her but also raises her anxiety and overall feeling of stress.

  Television and radio news also fill the air with vocabulary and expressions that your child is unaccustomed to hearing. For example, during the Clinton impeachment hearings, the words *oral sex* were heard over and over by children who ordinarily would not have been introduced to those words for many years. After repeated hearings, what child wouldn't begin to wonder, *just what is oral sex?* The foreign names and places that accompany stories not only have no meaning to young children but actually can confuse them. The words that describe terror and disasters—car bombs, killing, ammunition, explosives, brutality, destruction—are really scary and will create fear where none may have existed.

  Finally, repeated exposure to the violence and death that accompany so many of these news stories can desensitize the child to such horrors. Hearing day after day about how many people have been killed in the streets of Baghdad numbs you to the reality. No big deal.

- **Mind your affect.** Children absorb your affect, that is, your tone and nonverbal communications, more than they hear your words. When you speak with your child about these terrifying issues, it is crucial that your affect be calm and confident. Your tone shouldn't confirm her fear about her own safety and well-being. The message your tone must communicate is that you, the parent, are in control and will take care of business.

- **Don't avoid questions.** Thinking about events over which you have no control is often difficult. You might just like to ignore the whole situation. But if your child has been exposed to a scary event, hopefully she will come to you with her questions. *Not* answering her questions, avoiding the discussion, will be damaging. Lack of discussion leaves your child alone with her fears and anxieties. In addition, the child will be left feeling that the subject is taboo. Her likely conclusions: maybe she really shouldn't come to you with her questions and concerns.

- **Find out what the child knows.** If your child comes to you with a question, your first job is to figure out what she already knows. You can say: *"I am so glad that you are asking me because I want to talk with you about that. Tell me, where did you hear about a tidal wave?"*

  Hopefully, because of the way in which you calmly welcomed her question, your child will say, *"Michelle told me that a huge wave covered the whole city and everyone drowned."* Now you can continue your discussion based on what she knows and what you think she is really asking. But take note, most parents tend to talk too much and to give too much information. Usually, the young child is not asking for actual details; she is asking if she is safe.

- **Listen for the question beneath the question.** Often when a young child asks a question, something else is brewing underneath those words. Children do not always have the ability to access their real concerns, nor do they have the language to articulate them. It is your job to figure out what her real question is and to clarify what she is feeling. Sometimes you may have to probe a little deeper: *"Are you wondering if the tsunami is near our house?"*

  And sometimes you will just take a stab at what you think the child is really asking: *"I think you are worried that a tsunami is going to happen to us and we will not be safe."*

  Then you speak to that underlying question or worry: *"The tidal wave in the ocean happened far, far away in a whole different side of the world. We are just fine here in California; we are all safe."*

- **Don't downplay your child's feelings.** Resist the urge to say *"Don't worry"* or *"Don't be sad"* to your child. We all know that saying *"Don't worry"* doesn't really work. You still worry! So will your child. Your child's feelings are real, even if you think they are unfounded or needless. Your child needs to have her feelings validated and to be reassured. You don't need to fix her feelings; you need to respect them. She needs you to hear her, to receive and be a container for her feelings. She needs to know that she can always tell you how she is feeling and you will listen. You might say: *"I know that you are really worried about the fire you have heard about. That fire is happening far, far away from here, far from where we are."*

  At the same time, it is important not to downplay the seriousness of the situation. It usually *is* serious, very serious. Saying, *"Don't cry. Everything will be okay"* is not only another way of denying the child her feelings, but it is also somewhat crazy-making. The child knows something big is up, but you are telling her it isn't so. The child needs to learn to pay attention to her feelings, to recognize, name, and get those feelings out. That is one of the ways that people deal with feelings. In your admonition not to cry or be worried, the child becomes confused about trusting her own feelings. It is most effective to be honest and to acknowledge and reassure the child at the same time. You might say: *"Yes, it is a terrible fire. I know that makes you feel really scared. Fires are scary. But we are safe here. The fire is not close to us and nothing is going to happen to us."*

- **Share your own feelings to the appropriate degree.** Sharing your feelings can validate your child's feelings and let her know that she is not alone with them. You must also show and communicate that you are in control of your emotions and not overwhelmed by them. Sharing your feelings must be done carefully and without compounding your child's anxiety. You can say: *"You are so sad that those people's houses were wrecked by the tidal wave. I am really sad about that too. It was a terrible accident."*

- **Remind your child that you are the parent who is in charge and who knows how to make things happen.** It is tremendously reassuring for the child to know that as the person who keeps the family safe, you know how to make things happen. It is an adult's job. You know how to solve problems, and you know whom to call when you need help. *You* may not know how to fix things, but you know what it takes to get things fixed and how to go about making that happen: *"Moms and dads and grown-ups know what to do when there is a problem or* *when there is trouble. We can figure things out, and we do the things that help us to be safe."*

The reality is that you may lose your home to a disaster or you may have a disaster in your home on a less serious (but nonetheless scary) scale—broken pipes, loss of electricity—but you know what to do. You never lose your resources or your ability to make things get better. That is a comforting message for your child.

- **Talk with your child about all the adults who work to take care of people.** Not only are there grown-ups whose job is to keep us safe, but there are people who take care of us when we need help: doctors, firefighters, plumbers, electricians, city workers of all kinds.

- **Be brief and try to use simple language and concepts that your child can understand.** When speaking with your four-year-old, you will use different language than you would with your twelve-year-old. The young child needs simple explanations with very few words. She should not be overloaded with information.

- **Be honest and give accurate information . . . but only as needed and only the bare essentials, a bit at a time.** Your child may ask you a question, wanting to verify what she has heard. Just answer the question, nothing more. *"Yes, some people were killed when the building collapsed."* See below for additional suggested answers.

- **Use the event to reiterate how we are supposed to solve problems.** Your child may have heard that *"bad people"* did *"terrible things"* (like killing and hurting people). If your children are exposed to some of the violence of current events, you have an opportunity to emphasize how problems get solved: *"When you are angry, you use your angry words, and you try to work out your problems. Hurting people is never okay."*

    You might want to add: *"Everyone gets angry sometimes; we get our feelings out in safe ways. We use words and not hurting to solve our problems."*

- **Never intentionally expose your children to violent scenes as a way to educate them on problem solving.** The fear you will have engendered will eclipse any misguided lesson.

- **Be prepared for several conversations.** Children often ask the same question over and over again. That repetition may be the child's attempt to wrap her arms around your answer, or it may represent a need for reassurance. In addition, the concept of events continuing over time is difficult for the young child to understand. She thinks, *"The fighting happened yesterday, and so maybe it's all done today. People were hurt yesterday, but today everyone is fine."* Being able to understand that some things go on and on, some are one-time-only events, and some things fall somewhere in the middle, requires developmental readiness. Older children will get it; younger ones will not.

As your child processes the information she has learned or as she hears additional information, she will have new thoughts and questions. Answering questions and addressing concerns and fears doesn't happen in one conversation. Your discussions about these things that worry your child and test her ability to comprehend will be ongoing. Your availability to listen and your willingness to speak to your child's concerns must also continue until the questions stop coming.

- **Why children ask "*Why?*"** As discussed, very often when children ask "*Why?*" they aren't really looking for an answer; they are telling you they don't like what is happening. But adults make the mistake of attempting to answer the *Why?* question. You stumble around to find an answer, or you give long-winded explanations that go right over the child's head, and it doesn't work anyway. She just needs to protest. When a child asks *Why?* you may need to skirt that question and answer the concern she is likely expressing: *"Nothing bad is going to happen to you or to anyone in this family or to anyone we know. We are all safe."*

- ***What if?* questions.** *What if?* questions are not unlike *Why?* questions. Usually the child is looking for reassurance that you will keep her safe no matter what. There are those children who will keep after you, *"But what if the plane does crash? What if the fire does come to our house? What if there is a tsunami and the wave comes and we get flooded? What if and what if and what if? . . ."* If you have a child like this, you know it! These kinds of questions can be answered with straightforward and clearly delivered information: *"There will be no flood at our house. We are completely safe here, and I will keep it that way."*

- **Is lying okay?** This question is a tricky one, because no one really believes that lying is okay. At the same time, hearing the whole truth may be a source of tremendous anxiety and worry for your young child. I am not telling you to lie; I am telling you that it is your job to be exceedingly reassuring to your child.

When you are going on a trip without your child and are about to get on an airplane, and your child asks, *"Is the plane going to crash?"* you wouldn't say, *"Well, it might crash, but I sure hope it doesn't."* Your answer to your child who is worried about being separated from you is a confident and emphatic, *"NO! It is not going to crash. I am flying to New York, and then I am flying right back home to you."* If that plane crashes and, God forbid, you die, your child will need emotional support and therapy for a whole lot more than the fact that you led her to believe it wouldn't crash. Make sure you add: *"We are all safe here. You are safe and Mommy is safe and your sister is safe and Grandpa and Grandma are safe. Nothing is going to happen to us."* Not only do you cross your fingers that this will be so, but you do everything you can to make sure it is the case.

- **It is okay not to know the answer to a question.** While your child expects you, the omniscient parent, to know the answers to all her questions, it is not always possible. You may need a moment to gather your thoughts, come up with a suitable answer, or call an experienced friend for help. You can say: *"I am so glad that you asked me that question, and I am going to answer you. I want to think about how to explain the answer in a way that you will understand. Give me a few minutes."* Then be absolutely sure to get back to your child with the answer, even if it appears that she has moved on to other things.

Tips and Scripts for Some of *Those* Questions

Children younger than seven usually do not want nor do they *need* the answers to the questions they are asking. I cannot stress this strongly enough. However, should your child under seven ask one of these questions, you should always respond to it and let her guide the discussion. Offer only a little information, pause, and wait for a response. Do not flood her with information, and take time at the end to check her understanding of what you have said. Regardless of your values or feelings about war or terrorism, your child's primary need is to feel safe. That need ought not to be sacrificed in the service of teaching your political beliefs to your children. And remember, never have the conversation before bedtime.

Right before bed is not a good time to talk about your child's safety. Just imagine the dreams she will have . . . and the number of night wakings to which you will be subjected. Bedtime is a good time to remind your child of how much you love her and what an important part of the family she is. Save the talks about scary stuff for the earlier hours of the day when you can respond to any anxiety that might arise.

- **What is a terrorist?** *"A terrorist is someone who tries to scare or frighten and sometimes hurt other people.* Terror *is another word for* frighten. *Most people are good. There are not many terrorists."*

- **Why are terrorists trying to scare people?** *"I don't know the exact reason terrorists want to scare people, but I do know that terrorists are very angry about something and don't use safe ways to let their feelings out. I can tell you that I will keep you safe. There are lots of grown-ups who work to keep you safe."*

- **Why did he (the terrorist) do that?** *"That was a really bad thing that he did. There are some people who are really angry, and they let their feelings out in very bad ways. Sometimes there are bad people who do bad things. But most people are good."*

- **What is a war?** *"War is a fight between countries; it is very different from a fight between two people. It is a fight when soldiers use weapons. War happens when countries have different ideas and believe different things, and they cannot agree."*

- **Why does a war happen?** It is not likely that a child under seven would ask this question, and it is a particularly difficult question to answer. Your child has always been taught to use her words to express her feelings and thoughts and not physically hurt anybody. Should she ask this question, you can say:

> *"War can happen when the leaders of the countries have talked and talked and talked and really tried to solve their disagreements and it didn't work."*
> or
> *"War happens when people stop trying to solve their disagreements peacefully and stop listening to one another. They start to fight. No one wants to have a war."*
> or
> *"War doesn't happen often. People do as much as they can* not *to have a war. It's not the way we believe countries should solve their problems."*

- **Are we going to be bombed?** *"There is not a war in our country. It is very far, far away. There are no bombs in our country."*

- **Consider the question carefully.** Questions such as: *"Why did the people die?" "Why did the plane crash?" "Why did the buildings fall down?"* require careful consideration. Remember to consider the hidden meaning of *Why?* questions before you answer them, knowing that your child may really be asking something else, such as whether she is going to be separated from you or whether you might even die, or it just might be a protest. Keep your answers short and simple, always speaking to the child's safety.

  Why did the people die? *"Some of the people's bodies got hurt so badly that they could not live anymore."*
  Why did the plane crash? *"The plane crashed because something was wrong with its engine and it couldn't fly."*
  Why did the building fall down?
  "The airplane hit the building and the building broke. It could not stay standing."
  or
  "The ground shook so hard when the earthquake came that the building fell down."

  Expect that your child will ask the same question over and over again, even when you least expect it, as she tries to process the answer. Stay patient and calm and welcome her willingness to bring her questions to you, the trusted parent.

- **Dealing with security precautions.** When security is heightened, everyone gets nervous. Schedules change to accommodate the extra time given to security checks, parents get edgy, and the news is awash with the topic. Your child will certainly observe the changes and absorb your affect during these times. You will need to be prepared for the *"What's going on?"* questions that you will inevitably get. In your answers to these questions focus on the safety aspect of what is going on.

  Why are they looking in our suitcases? *"Looking in our suitcases is one of the ways that airport people make sure we are safe on the airplanes. They want to make sure there is nothing in our suitcase that could hurt the airplane."*

Why is the policeman looking in our car? *"Looking in all of the cars that come to the airport is one of the ways they make sure that everything is safe at the airport. That is one of the ways that the police protect us."*

Most children will be satisfied with these answers and by the fact that you have responded. The unusually inquisitive child (and you know if you have one) might continue with, *"What do you mean? What could hurt the airplane?"* This child likely has something in mind, and knowing that specific details can feed her anxiety, you can answer: *"What is your idea about that?"* Hear her response and confirm, *"Maybe. And airport police would take that (bomb) away."*

- **When you have an emotional reaction.** There may be times when you will hear news to which you will have an emotional reaction. Of course, if it is possible, save your big reactions for the time when your children are not around. Seeing you sad, upset, or even unnerved can be frightening for the child. *"Am I okay? Is there something I need to worry about?"* the child will think. She might ask:

  Why are you crying? *"I am feeling sad that some people who are far away were hurt (killed) where the fighting is happening."*
  or
  "I feel so sad and so sorry that some peoples' houses got wrecked in the storm, even though our house is just fine."

- **Take pains not to direct your feelings (anger) at a particular person or people.** Children cannot understand the broader issues of terrorism and war, nor why you feel the way you do. While most people have clear political views and opinions about the rightness or wrongness of the current events of the world, it does not help the child if you assign blame. Presumably, your children are being raised to respect different points of view and to be tolerant and considerate of all human beings. Not only do prejudice and discrimination not speak to these goals, but they are beyond the young child's comprehension. Children are better served when taught ways to solve a problem (such as gathering used clothing or donating toys) rather than to perpetuate the problem.

Tips and Scripts for Supporting Your Children in Times of Crisis

- **Talk with your children.** Ideally, you have created an environment in your home that is open and welcoming of communication of all kinds. If chatting and talking about good things and worries is part of your regular day, then your child will be more likely to come to you with her questions and concerns. During heavy times, redouble your efforts to talk with your child about anything and everything. This will make her feel connected and grounded, and it increases her sense of security and well-being.

- **Use your *talk times*.** Most parents have more opportunities to chat with their children than they realize. My personal favorite time is in the car. *Car talks* are the best. Not only is your child captive, but there is also a clear beginning and end to the discussion. It doesn't seem to you or to your child that it will go on forever. Of course, there is *tuck time*, which is the perfect time to have light conversation about your day.

  Perhaps you remember when you were a child and your dad delivered another one of his famous long-winded lectures. You hated those, right? And often you just tuned out your father. Your child is no different. She will do the same. When your child thinks she is in for a lecture, that just might be her signal to shut down. A lecture is not a talk time. Talk times are natural, warm, spontaneous, and mutual dialogues.

- **Listen to your children.** Given the pace of life these days, it is easy not to pay full attention to your children's questions and running commentary. But these are the times when you need to do a better job of listening. If your child comes to you, pay attention. She may be letting you know that she needs you or she may just be wanting to connect with you, checking in so she can go on with her day.

- **During the time of crisis, spend extra time with your children.** This is the time to circle the wagons. Children feel safe and secure in the context of family, and so do parents. Add more family time to your regular schedule. Cancel your evening plans, that adults-only trip, and stick around the home. Allow for extra time when you are tucking your child in, or linger at the dinner table (if your two-year-old doesn't sabotage that effort).

- **Give physical comfort.** During stressful times, many children will seek more physical closeness (hugs, holding hands, sitting on laps). You know your child best, her signals and her needs. Remember that your love and support are the most important factors in building her sense of security.

- **Expect some difficult or uncharacteristic behavior.** This includes the child being more volatile, using strong language, or testing some previously untested limits. She is just making sure you are still manning the ship.

- **Maintain your household rules and routines.** Continue to set and maintain your regular limits and to impose your regular consequences. They will underscore the fact that nothing has changed for your child and that she is safe. Someone is in charge. You might even need to impose some new limits on scary or hurtful play. Keep your child's schedule and routine the same. Go to the park and to soccer practice, eat dinner at 6:00 P.M., maintain regular bedtimes, and don't allow your child to sleep in your bed if that's not your regular family practice. It is the familiarity and predictability of her daily life that helps your child to feel in control, secure, and safe.

- **Make every attempt to maintain a calm atmosphere in your home.** Remember that calm breeds calm. The opposite holds true too.

- **Provide plenty of opportunities for your child to play and to do art projects.** Both of these are great outlets for all kinds of feelings. Have available props of all kinds (toy fire trucks and ambulances, doctor kits, etc.). Play is strong medicine.

- **Be aware that the need for additional nighttime comforts may arise.** Don't be alarmed if your child suddenly needs a nightlight or wants to have the previously closed door kept open.

- **Postpone introducing new experiences or challenges.** During this time, it is a good idea to avoid that new class and to rely on the tried and true. Feeling successful and not challenged is one of the things that enables your child to feel confident and secure.

- **Communicate with your child's school and other after-school activity centers.** Find out what has been said and what will be discussed about the event at school so that you can be prepared if she comes home with questions. In addition, be sure to share with your child's school or activity teachers any specific fears or concerns that your child has displayed.

- **Have an emergency plan.** Every family should have emergency plans for a variety of situations, such as fire or earthquake. Share this information with your child, letting her know that, once again, you will keep her safe and that you are looking out for her at all times.

- **Reassure your child about all the people who work to keep us safe.** Remind your child about how much safety there is in our everyday lives as well as during times of crisis. Help your child to know about all the ways in which people are kept safe in our country. Focus on all the helpers there are in our city—firefighters and police officers; traffic officers and patrol people; teachers, security guards, and crossing guards; the army, the navy, the air force, the marines . . . all these people's jobs are to keep everyone safe.

- **Teach your child about the regular safety precautions we take in our daily lives.** There are so many things that we all do every day, *just in case*, that we don't even think about anymore. I grew up in a time when wearing a seat belt wasn't mandatory. Now, you wouldn't even consider being in a moving car without wearing one. Remind your child:

  We wash our hands after we use the toilet.
  We use toilet seat covers in public restrooms.
  We wash our hands before we eat.
  We wear seat belts in moving vehicles.
  We put children in car seats.
  We stop at stop signs, even if there are no other cars around.
  We hold hands and look both ways before we cross the street.
  We lock our doors.

- **Arrange something practical that you and your child can do to help people in need.** When children know that others have suffered losses, it is healing to offer help. When they feel that they are making a contribution, their rebound is likely to happen more quickly. Whether it is finding toys to share with children who have lost theirs, collecting food for those who are needy, or baking cookies for the firefighters who are working hard to protect us, you are teaching your child not only to help others but also the healing benefits of being proactive.

- **Remind your child about all the good things that happen in our lives.** It is helpful and reassuring to bring up the good stuff in the child's life as a way of reminding her that the bad stuff is the exception, not the rule. There are birthdays, holidays such as Thanksgiving and Christmas/Hanukkah, special celebrations, family vacations, dinners out, visits to the park, baseball games, sleepovers, and playdates. The list can go on and on.

- **Let your child be a child.** Although you may be vigilantly following the current event, your child is not. She does not want to think about things that don't affect her regular life, that happen far away from her. Allow her to go about her business, doing the things she normally does. If you do not see her react to any of the day's tragedies, thank your lucky stars. Know that you have done a good job of appropriately sheltering your child or offering the reassurance and security that she needs.

Signs That Your Child Might Be Having Trouble

Some young children who are particularly verbal and articulate will clearly let you know that they are worried and are having trouble in the face of a terrible current event. Other children might not be so obvious in their discomfort. Each and all of these reactions are within the range of normal. When children regress in their behavior, they are often reverting to a time when they were younger, more closely cared for by you, and felt safer. You will need to be alert to signs that trouble is brewing. The child may display:

- Extreme withdrawal or reluctance to participate in normal activities
- A particular and unusual sensitivity
- Uncharacteristic whininess or susceptibility to tears
- Unusual wakefulness at night
- More than the usual number of nightmares

- Unusual clinginess to parents or caregivers, difficulty letting you out of his sight
- Difficulty at separation times
- Regressions in a variety of areas (toileting skills, loss of motor skills, etc.)
- A desire once again to have security objects that were given up long ago, such as bottles, pacifiers, blankies
- An atypical refusal to go to school
- Uncharacteristic sadness, crying, fussiness, or neediness
- New fears about otherwise familiar things
- Aggressive behaviors and unusual displays of anger
- Symptoms of illness such as tummy aches or headaches

Any of these behaviors could be expected for a short period of time as a reaction to exposure to a trauma of any kind. However, if any of these persists for more than six weeks, it would be a good idea to seek the help of a mental health professional.

Related Books for Children

. ❖ .

While there are countless wonderful books for children, not all books are good for all children. Age, development, and individual circumstances must be considered in choosing your child's books. It is crucial to read a book all the way through before reading it to your child. Once unleashed, worries, nightmares, and other uninvited inhabitants are hard to get rid of! You may need to tweak a story to make it just right for your child. Use the book to start the dialogue with your child and discuss her particular story.

For Discipline and Temper Tantrums

Alexander and the Terrible, Horrible, No Good, Very Bad Day by Judith Viorst (Aladdin Paperbacks).

David Gets in Trouble by David Shannon (The Blue Sky Press).

Harriet, You'll Drive Me Wild by Mem Fox (Voyager Books).

I Am Not Sleepy and I Will Not Go to Bed by Lauren Child (Candlewick Press).

Mean Soup by Betsy Everitt (Harcourt Brace Books).

No, David! by David Shannon (The Blue Sky Press).

The Temper Tantrum Book by Edna Mitchell Presto (Puffin Books).

Two Bad Babies by Jeffie Ross Gordon (Boyds Mills Press).

When Sophie Gets Angry—Really Really Angry . . . by Molly Bang (The Blue Sky Press).

Where the Wild Things Are by Maurice Sendak (Harper and Row).

For Sibling Issues (including those resulting from the recent birth of a sibling)

I Used to Be the Baby by Robert Ballard (Greenwillow Books).

I Wish I Were a Baby by Eve Tharlet (North-South Books).

I Wish My Brother Was a Dog by Carol Diggory Shields (Puffin Books).

I'm a Big Brother by Joanna Cole (HarperCollins).

I'm a Big Sister by Joanna Cole (HarperCollins).

Julius, The Baby of the World by Kevin Henkes (Greenwillow Books).

Little Bear's Little Boat by Eve Bunting (Clarion Books).

On Mother's Lap by Ann Herbert Scott (Clarion Books).

The New Baby by Fred Rogers (G. P. Putnam's Sons).

Peter's Chair by Ezra Jack Keats (Harper and Row).

For Food Issues and the Picky Eater

Bread and Jam for Frances by Russell Hoban (HarperCollins).

Eat Up, Gemma by Sarah Hayes (Lothrup, Lee and Shepard).

Gregory the Terrible Eater by Mitchell Sharmat (Scholastic).

I Will Never Not Ever Eat a Tomato by Lauren Child (Candlewick).

The Seven Silly Eaters by Mary Ann Hoberman (Browndeer).

For the Shy Child

Buster, the Very Shy Dog by Lisze Bechtold (Houghton Mifflin Company).

Halibut Jackson by David Lucas (Alfred A. Knopf).

For Lying

The Show-and-Tell Lion by Barbara Abercrombie (Margaret K. McElderry Books).

For the Birds and the Bees

How Are Babies Made? by Alastair Wheatley (EDC Publishing/Usborne).

How Babies Are Made by Andrew Andry and Stephen Schepp (Time Life Books).

The Birth of Sunset's Kittens by Carla Stevens (Young Scott Books).

For Learning about Death

Annie and the Old One by Miska Miles (Little, Brown and Company).

The Fall of Freddy the Leaf by Leo Buscaglia (Slack, Inc.).

Lifetimes: The Wonderful Way to Explain Death to Children by Bryan Mellonie and Robert Ingpen (Bantam Books).

Nana Upstairs and Nana Downstairs by Tomie DePaola (Penguin Books).

So Much to Think About by Fred Rogers (Penguin Books).

The Tenth Good Thing about Barney by Judith Viorst (Atheneum).

When Dinosaurs Die by Laurene Krasny Brown and Marc Brown (Little, Brown and Company).

For Divorce

Charlie Anderson by Barbara Abercrombie (Aladdin Paperbacks).

Dinosaurs Divorce by Laurene Krasny Brown and Marc Brown (Little, Brown and Company).

Fred Stays with Me by Nancy Coffelt (Little, Brown and Company).

Two Homes by Claire Masurel (Candlewick Press).

Selected Sources

. ❖ .

Throughout my professional life I have read countless books and articles that have guided me in my work with parents and children. Listed below are some sources that have been particularly valuable, influential, and helpful in writing this book.

Books and Articles

Ames, Louise Bates, and Frances L. Ilg. *Your Two Year Old*. New York: Delta, 1976.

———. *Your Three Year Old*. New York: Delta, 1976.

———. *Your Four Year Old*. New York: Delta, 1976.

———. *Your Five Year Old*. New York: Delta, 1976.

———. *Your Six Year Old*. New York: Delta, 1976.

Brennen, Mark L. *When "No" Gets You Nowhere*. New York: Prima Publishing, 1997.

Briggs, Dorothy Corkville. *Your Child's Self-Esteem*. New York: Dolphin Books, 1975.

Calderone, Dr. Mary S., and Dr. James W. Ramey. *Talking with Your Child about Sex*. New York: Random House, 1982.

Davis, Laura, and Janis Keyser. *Becoming the Parent You Want to Be*. New York: Broadway Books, 1997.

Elkind, David. *The Hurried Child*. Reading, MA: Addison-Wesley Publishing, 1981.

Faber, Adele, and Elaine Mazlish. *Siblings without Rivalry*. New York: W. W. Norton and Company, 1987.

Fraiberg, Selma H. *The Magic Years*. New York: Charles Scribner's Sons, 1959.

Gardner, Howard. *Multiple Intelligences*. New York: Basic Books, 1993.

Ginsberg, Herbert, and Sylvia Opper. *Piaget's Theory of Intellectual Development*. Englewood Cliffs, NJ: Prentice Hall, Inc., 1969.

Goleman, Daniel. *Emotional Intelligence*. New York: Bantam Books, 1995.

Hamilton, Joan. *When a Parent Is Sick: Helping Explain Serious Illness to Children*. Halifax, Nova Scotia: Pottersfield Press, 1999.

Hallowell, Edward M. *The Childhood Roots of Adult Happiness*. New York: Ballantine Books, 2002.

Katz, Lilian G. "Are We Confusing Self-Esteem and Narcissism?" *Young Children*, November 1993.

Kindlon, Daniel. *Too Much of a Good Thing*. New York: Miramax Books, 2001.

Kohn, Alfie. "Five Reasons to Stop Saying 'Good Job!' " *Young Children*, September 2001.

Levine, Mel. *A Mind at a Time*. New York: Simon & Schuster, 2002.

Martin, William. *The Parents' Tao Te Ching*. New York: Marlowe and Company, 1999.

Mogel, Wendy. *The Blessing of a Skinned Knee: Using Jewish Teachings to Raise Self-Reliant Children*. New York: Scribner, 2001.

Richardson, Justin and Mark A. Schuster. *Everything You Never Wanted Your Kids to Know about Sex (But Were Afraid They'd Ask)*. New York: Crown Publishers, 1963.

Turecki, Stanley. *Normal Children Have Problems, Too*. New York: Bantam Books, 1994.

Wolf, Anthony E. *Mom, Jason's Breathing on Me*. New York: Ballantine Books, 2003.

Web Sites

www.aboutoutkids.org New York University Child Study Center.

www.aacap.org American Academy of Child and Adolescent Psychiatry. Of particular use is the link, "Facts for Families."

www.cancerbackup.org Web site whose mission is to provide information and support to cancer patients and their families. Particularly useful are their articles about talking to children about cancer.

www.med.nyu/edu/patients/support/straighttalk New York University Cancer Institute for Public and Patients.

www.naeyc.org National Association for the Education of Young Children.

www.naspcenter.org National Mental Health and Education Center.

www.ncptsd.va.gov National Center for Post-Traumatic Stress Disorder, Department of Veteran Affairs. ("Terrorist Attacks and Children" by Jessica Hamblen Ph.D.)

www.parentcenter.babycenter.com Online resource for parents of children two to eight.

www.parenting-ed.org The Center for Effective Parenting. Arkansas State Parent Information and Resource Center.

www.pbs.org Public Broadcasting System. See also www.pbskids.org and www.pbsparents.org: The link to *Mr. Rogers' Neighborhood* and advice from Fred Rogers are especially pertinent and useful.

www.plwc.org People Living with Cancer. A resource for cancer information from the American Society of Clinical Oncology.

www.zerotothree.org Zero to Three is an organization that addresses the needs and development of infants, toddlers, and families.

Index

❖